"All the World Is Here!"

THE BLACK PRESENCE
AT WHITE CITY

Christopher Robert Reed

Indiana
University
Press
BLOOMINGTON & INDIANAPOLIS

This book is a publication of

Indiana University Press
601 North Morton Street
Bloomington, IN 47404-3797 USA

http://www.indiana.edu/~iupress
Telephone orders 800-842-6796
Fax orders 812-855-7931
E-mail orders iuporder@indiana.edu

MANUFACTURED IN THE UNITED STATES OF AMERICA

Library of Congress Cataloging-in-Publication Data

Reed, Christopher Robert.
All the world is here! : the Black presence at White City / Christopher Robert Reed.
p.   cm. — (Blacks in the diaspora)
Includes bibliographical refereences and index.
ISBN 0-253-33566-3 (cloth : alk. paper)
1. Afro-Americans — Illinois — Chicago Exhibitions — History — 19th century. 2. Africans —
Illinois — Chicago Exhibitions — History — 19th century. 3. Afro-Americans — Illinois —
Chicago — Social conditions — 19th century. 4. World's Columbian Exposition (1893 :
Chicago, Ill.) — Social aspects. 5. Chicago (Ill.) — Race relations. 6. African diaspora.
7. Afro-Americans — Social conditions — To 1964. 8. United States — Race relations.
9. Afro-Americans — Relations with Africans. I. Title. II. Series.
IN PROCESS
977.3'1100496073 — dc21   99-29925
1   2   3   4   5   04   03   02   01   00   99

CONTENTS

PREFACE

I undertook to write this study in an effort to discover the answer to an important historical question. Somewhere between the explanation offered by the contemporary pamphlet *The Reason Why the Colored American Is Not in the World's Columbian Exposition,* and the enthusiasm of the popular refrain heard at the fair, "All the World Is Here!," there was a set of answers to be extracted about the extent to which sundry persons of African descent, both diasporan and continental, participated in the activities of the World's Columbian Exposition of 1893. Using America's second world's fair as a prism, this study attempts to discover *some* of the meanings of the many and disparate expectations, both those fulfilled and those unmet, of New and Old World Africans during the last decade of the nineteenth century. I examine the experience of New World Africans in North America and the Caribbean, with special focus on Hayti, while the literary, photographic, and existential importance of Old World African life is addressed through a study of the Fon people of Dahomey.

There is an abundance of contemporary literature on the World's Columbian Exposition of 1893, popularly known as the Chicago World's Fair, but to the extent that it addresses the issue of race, the literature, interestingly, focuses on externally imposed limits to diasporan and continental African initiative. Little was written about the transcendence of black human agency in the face of external constraints. Major biographies of Frederick Douglass by Benjamin Quarles (1948) and William S. McFeely (1991) underscored this omission, as did articles by August Meier and Elliott Rudwick, Frank A. Cassell, and Thomas J. Schlereth describing the participation of African Americans at the fair.[1] When an optimistic account by fair participant James Weldon Johnson did not jibe with his biographer's interpretation, the biographer chastised his subject posthumously.[2] Recent inquiries into black feminist/womanist thinking and activities have viewed the fair as a fulcrum for black feminist development but have nevertheless reproduced several conventional beliefs about African American inaction.[3]

The notion that African American thought and behavior lacked coherence—except in cases of overt, systemic challenges to pervasive American racism—also appeared in many peripheral references in works on the fair dealing with much broader themes. Some of these works managed, more-over, to revive disparaging perceptions about the presence at the fair of the Fon people of Dahomey. This was the case with Burg's *Chicago's White City of 1893*, Badger's *The Great American Fair: The World's Columbian Exposition and American Culture*, Rydell's *All the World's a Fair: Visions of Empire at American International Expositions, 1876-1916*, and Gilbert's *Perfect Cities: Chicago's Utopias of 1893*.[4] Hinsley's "The World as Marketplace: Commodification of the Exotic at the World's Columbian Exposition, Chicago, 1893," argued that the event brought about contact with foreign peoples but that it was "mediated by the terms of the marketplace, [and] produced an early form of touristic consumption."[5] Hinsley invalidated the scientific approach proposed by anthropology and instead proposed an exploitive relationship from a distance.

Examining this conceptual path, I found myself having to evaluate a paradigm emphasizing conflict, or protest, that had captivated a generation of scholars. Adapting the sociological model of conflict in vogue in the 1950s and 1960s that challenged the functionalism of Talcott Parsons and others, this framework appeared during a period of intense scholarly examination of dysfunctional societies, institutions, and groups. It appealed to persons who embraced the dynamic of conflict, or protest, as an essential component of progress in a racially static society committed, under most circumstances, to inequality. As popular and appropriate for a race-conscious society as this model was, it necessarily precluded a great deal of the African American thought, behavior, and organizational effort that was manifested before and during 1893, and throughout the remainder of the decade.

A fortuitous assignment at a NEH summer seminar at the University of Kansas several years ago first led me to question the widely accepted model that measured African American achievement more or less exclusively in terms of its level of protest or conflict—a model that had unfortunately assumed the status of gospel by that time. On a personal level, my perception of the world's fair of 1893 had been shaped for more than three decades primarily by a chapter written by Arna Bontemps and Jack C. Conroy in *They Seek a City* (1945) entitled "They Met at the Fair," and by Ida B. Wells's recollections in Alfreda Duster, ed., *Crusade for Justice: The Autobiography of Ida B. Wells* (1966).[6] "They Met at the Fair" focused on the struggle against racial exclusion and on the lives and rising careers of poet Paul Lawrence Dunbar, journalist Ida B. Wells, and newspaper publisher Robert S. Abbott. The autobiography of Ida B. Wells articulated Wells's views on the exclusion of African Americans from the fair. Both gave an impression of basically proscribed activities and prohibited thinking that supported the validity of dealing with the fair and all of its intricacies from within the context of the protest tradition.

By the winter of 1993-1994, however, I was convinced that some major component in the human experience was being overlooked. The extent to which any group devises, improvises, implements, and succeeds or fails in any particular endeavor must be considered in order to fully understand the meaning of that group's collective life. As with the literature on the Chicago World's Fair, the conventional view of slavery during the 1960s extolled the virtues of organized revolt while overlooking the importance of sustained, day-to-day resistance, whether by individuals or by small groups such as families and plantation populations. Measuring black progress through the prism of what was forbidden by whites, of what allegedly could not be accomplished because of impediments imposed by a white world, failed miserably as a comprehensive tool for understanding given the level of human agency evinced by Africans since their arrival in the New World. Furthermore, reliance on a binary approach that envisioned the New World African historical experience as either inclusionary or exclusionary, assimilationist or accommodationist, or even integrationist or nationalist, could not endure scholarly scrutiny.

Working with one major, contemporary document in particular illustrated the nature of the complications to be overcome as well as the complexities of the historical circumstances to be understood. For over a century, *The Reason Why the Colored American Is Not in the World's Columbian Exposition* has been considered the definitive statement on the status of all African American thinking and action at the Chicago World's Fair. As an exceptional statement of the hopes, the fears, the achievements, the disappointments, and, significantly, the current grievances of many African Americans, it was and remains compelling. However, this assessment of race status and race relations in times past would prove misleading both in its context and its particulars. Most important, what the title of this pamphlet implied—an absence— and the course of events that it described—a successful effort by whites at racial proscription—profoundly influenced twentieth century historians and writers and precipitated the creation of a set of paradigmatic problems that beset this study from its beginning and provides the grist for debate into the future.

Polished and detailed, the pamphlet represented a new level of rejection of American racism. As it denounced the nation's failed attempts to keep its promises, it concomitantly expounded on data highlighting African American achievement. However, because it was conceived of and written as the fair was opening, up to late August, its use as an evaluative instrument with broad temporal value is limited. Significantly, it missed the broad character of the event as it unfolded over the summer and concluded at the end of October. As Ida B. Wells admitted, her absence in the spring of 1893 while lecturing abroad delayed both the collection of money and "the collection of facts."[7]

Over a wide expanse of time, including the operation of the fair in the spring and summer of 1893, during the immediate years that followed, and for generations so far removed in time that the exposition has become an abstraction to be interpreted as one's ideology sees fit, *The Reason Why the Colored American Is Not in the World's Columbian Exposition* has become the ultimate source of information on African Americans at the world's fair. It has been allowed, unfortunately, to subordinate extant, documented African American participation that rightly amounted to a triumph for the times. Much to its credit, though, even as a class-conscious document, it included a denunciation of the economic exploitation of southern blacks along with its recognition of snubs discernible primarily to a rising elite, and it resonated with a sense of power and determination.

Given the rigidity of American race relations up to the time of the modern Civil Rights Movement of the 1960s, the pamphlet assumed a unique role in the next century by reason of its very *existence*; in the eyes of some, it supposedly was the only physical exhibit of any substance that African Americans produced at the fair.[8] The document thus assumed a life of its own. As a printed record for posterity it, importantly, had Frederick Douglass's blessing, but, unknown to many, also that of white liberal Albion W. Tourgée, who gave his endorsement to African American racial militancy. Also less known today is the opposition the pamphlet generated among blacks and the nature of their antagonism. Contemporarily, Douglass acknowledged and addressed this problem: "We know we shall be censured for the publication of this volume. The time for its publication will be thought to be ill chosen."[9]

Documenting their race's travails and triumphs through three channels of time, the past, the present, and the future, the four publicists who contributed to *The Reason Why the Colored American Is Not in the World's Columbian Exposition* forcefully told of their race's predicaments, status, laments, and dreams. Ida B. Wells explained their purpose: "The pamphlet is intended as a calm, dignified statement of the Afro-American's side of the story, from the beginning to the present; a recital of the obstacles which have hampered him; a sketch of what he has done in the twenty-five years with all his persecution, and a statement of the fruitless efforts he made for representation at the world's fair."[10] In Chapter I, "Introduction," Frederick Douglass, because of his experiences in the antebellum and emancipation periods and the nearness to his life's end, appropriately spoke of a past that both his white friends and foes wished to bury. He tackled the roots of racism. Slavery was the moral blight that white America could never deny. In the planning for the fair, white leadership ignored the Negro because he and she represented a living and breathing symbol of whites' past transgressions against humanity. Accordingly, "When it is asked why we are excluded from the World's Columbian Exposition, the answer is slavery." Douglass continued: "The Americans are a great and magnanimous people and this great exposition adds greatly to their honor and renown, but in the pride of their success they have cause for repentance as well as complaisance, and for shame as well as for glory, and hence we set forth this volume to be read to all men."[11]

Ida B. Wells, in Chapter IV, "Lynch Law," highlighted this national horror and exposed a national present that embraced the manipulation of lynchings by whites into an instrument of instant terror, perpetual labor control, and lingering fear among black women and families as well as black males.

Likewise, Ferdinand L. Barnett in Chapter VI, "The Reason Why," submitted a legal brief of sorts that indicted America for its racism as he showed a present that contradicted the principles of fair play and decency for which the nation purportedly stood. After having cited seven points primarily involving exclusion from employment, directorial representation, exhibitions, and other related areas, Barnett felt compelled to conclude that "theoretically open to all Americans, the Exposition practically is, literally and figuratively, a 'White City,' in the building of which the Colored American was allowed no helping hand, and in its glorious success he has no share."[12] Reflecting this account, information or misinformation emanating from the pamphlet became widespread. Four years later, in the widely read *Progress of a Race; or, The Remarkable Advancement of the Afro-American*, the following appeared: "Think of it! The great World's fair, or exposition, in Chicago out of more than ten thousand employees, gave no recognition to the colored race beyond taking charge of the toilet rooms."[13]

In Chapter V, "The Progress of the Afro-American since Emancipation," I. Garland Penn detailed the achievements of African Americans as he wrote of the future by revealing the present, substantiating that the potential of blacks would be realized despite the obstacles. Penn saw progress everywhere in the arenas in which white America least expected it. In the professions, in which more than four hundred physicians and nearly seventy dentists served, in the arts, where Henry O. Tanner and Edmonia Lewis painted and sculpted, and in the accumulation of wealth in the hundreds of millions, advancement shone paramount. Douglass had seen this future also and had written metaphorically: "A ship rotting at anchor meets with no resistance, but when she sets sail on the sea, she has to buffet opposing bellows. The enemies of the Negro see that he is making progress and they naturally wish to stop him and keep him in just what they consider his proper place."[14]

Lastly, the pamphlet appeared to its writers and supporters as a substitute African American Declaration of Independence and answered for the lack of administrative representation at the highest levels of governance at the fair along with the absence of a visual representation of African American achievement through a Negro exhibition. Just as Jefferson had constructed his case against the British Crown and nation, *The Reason Why the Colored American Is Not in the World's Columbian Exposition* stood as a compendium of all things that blacks had done right, as manifested by their accomplishments since emancipation; it exposed things done wrong by whites against African Americans, as evidenced through America's legal and extralegal atrocities involving convict leasing and lynchings. It also explained what they perceived as their systemic exclusion at the fair for the understanding of the liberal, Western white world.

If the basis of African American experience could only be understood in its relationship to what the white world permitted or prohibited, what would become of the desires, expectations, and dreams that were constructed free of the fetters of American racism? Indeed, what would become of efforts that produced successful results for one segment of a heterogeneous black population but not for another? W. E. B. Du Bois posed a solution, but one restricted to accepting an external definition of self and purpose. He wrote:

> The Negro is a sort of seventh son, born with a veil, and gifted with second-sight in this American world, — a world which yields him *no true self-consciousness, but only lets him see himself through the revelation of the other world.* It is a peculiar sensation, this double-consciousness, this sense of always looking at one's self through the eyes of others, of measuring one's soul by the tape of a world that looks on in amused contempt and pity [emphasis added].[15]

As Du Bois assessed the African American condition, it required a solution demanding continuous resistance, or confrontation, or challenge. As a reformist, he never considered revolution. Within the context of his thinking, though, circumstances demanded some kind of response, and it could manifest itself through nonviolent protest, such as that conducted with the pen or the researcher's theory and findings. Du Bois concluded that any objective examination of the problem historically clearly showed "the history of the American Negro is the history of this strife."[16] Consistent with this mode of thought, strife, or strenuous endeavor, best translated into a posture of protest.

Over time, the racially militant *Chicago Defender* resurrected the element of protest from the basic arguments in *The Reason Why the Colored American Is Not in the World's Columbian Exposition* on the eve of the city's hosting its second international exposition in 1933. The charge of past racial exclusion appeared quite credible to a generation of African Americans accustomed to countless disappointments along the color line. Pointedly, the *Defender* heralded its "recently discovered facts" of how blacks were excluded from the fair's operations and activities, and how they were kept "beyond the pale." The author of the article, however, was Albert G. Barnett, who predictably relied on the interpretations and conclusions of his parents.[17]

In contrast, accessible data showed a level of participation that belied total exclusion both before and during the fair. Dr. M. A. Majors, a vice president on the committee planning Colored American Day, recollected in 1929 the fair's "black spots" which brought "wonder and amaze[ment]." Majors's essay, which appeared in an abbreviated, popular history on Black Chicago, showed that not one voice but many disparate voices spoke before, during, and after the fair.[18]

The compelling nature of this mixed base of contemporary data necessitated the formulation of a comprehensive framework to determine the extent to which the temper of times during the 1890s encouraged a multifaceted, rather than a narrow, course of action and thinking. Embracing the framework both of protest and of consensus, holism became the most usable conceptualization from which to evaluate the meaning of the African American as well as the continental African presence at the fair. Looking at how continental Africans functioned as members of their own societies before placing them into a context of how they were externally perceived by uninformed, unfamiliar, and sometimes overtly racist American writers and journalists permitted transcending the most commonly held racist notions. Further, as a holistic approach dictated an introspective, more inclusive treatment of historical data,[19] any adaptation to changing conditions and other forms of accomplishment took on more illuminating dimensions.

Validation of this choice came quickly. Extant multidimensional black participation revealed an initiating tendency along with one that was reactive. Along with protest advocacy, there was adaptive, often ameliorative behavior, such as that exhibited in connection with the celebration of Colored American Day or the effort to extol the academic achievements of African American students in higher education at Wilberforce University, Hampton Institute, and Atlanta University through exhibits featuring their undergraduate scholarship. As visceral demonstrations of African American intelligence and being, they contributed to the redefinition which this new generation of black males and females sought for themselves and their race. Significantly, the seed of the black feminist intellectual tradition emerged that was hypothesized in 1987 and substantiated through narrative and analysis in this study.[20] With the exception of armed revolutionary conflict, emigration to Africa existed as the ultimate political expression of protest, yet it was slighted contemporarily and through time by the elite and intellectuals, the so-called *representative men*. The importance of the dialogue is noted here.

Use of a comprehensive approach furthermore brought clarity to questions about nationwide social stratification as well as the nature of the social structure found within black Chicago neighborhoods on the eve of the fair. The exposition provided African Americans in Chicago with an opportunity to express themselves at all levels within their own unique culturally and socially segmented society. Both as a backdrop and a battleground, the exposition opened the door to understanding the extent to which social grouping, color, leadership, gender, and ideology in Chicago intersected within African American life at this time. On the eve of the world's fair, sociologist St. Clair Drake described this society of between 17,000 and 20,000 persons in social terms as one in which African Americans lived their lives within a socially distinguishable, three-tiered (or possibly, three-chambered) arrangement attesting to the extent of their increased economic and cultural participation within the city's mainstream.[21] A small *refined* element of culturally assimilated African Americans existed, with an expanding *respectable* segment composed of churchgoing, laboring folk, dominating the mass of black society numerically. Also sharing this arrangement loomed both the criminal ranks and the chronically dispossessed. Whether contemporary observation, datum, analysis, or interpretation is consulted, there remains one certainty about class formation during the World's Columbian decade. Sociocultural distinction and not socioeconomic differences contributed most significantly to the social chasm developing among African Americans in Chicago at the dawn of the twentieth century.

Examining non-elite along with elite African American thought, behavior, and institutions further provided major avenues for research. Analyzing and interpreting the multifaceted dimensions of the fair also allowed reconciliation of what actually happened and the extent to which Africans from the Old World and those from the Americas participated in the activities that molded this event. Upon closer examination of extant documents, including more than two dozen photographs and illustrations, persons of African descent were far from being outside the "pale," as claimed by the *Defender*. From a population base of over 10 million persons landed alive in the Americas over the course of four centuries, many intermixed with various groups from Europe and disparate New World native peoples. Others, in contrast, remained basically isolated in both their bloodlines and their culture. To illustrate the existence of a multiplicity of voices, rather than those of a representative few, I have chosen to use several examples of ordinary people, such as Nate Shaw of Alabama and Wiley Cherry of Chicago, gentlemen whose lives exemplify the aforementioned, as models for this major segment of the African American southern and transplanted, northern population. Shaw was introduced into the world of historians and sociologists by way of oral history in Theodore Rosengarten's *All God's Dangers: The Life of Nate Shaw* in 1975.[22] Historian Leon F. Litwack has more recently referred to their stories as part of an interior life or history whose time for recognition has come.[23]

The presence in Chicago of visiting Africans, especially the cruelly maligned Dahomeans (actually the Fon people of present-day Benin, formerly named Dahomey) warranted further review. The constant derision of these visitors in printed materials contemporary to the period illustrated the pervasiveness of racism associated with the tenets of Conservative Social Darwinism. The Fon came to the Windy City because Harvard University anthropologist Frederick Ward Putnam wanted to enlighten fairgoers about diversity and different levels of civilization around the world. Impresario and showman Sol Bloom craved to duplicate the profits he had amassed several years earlier in Paris, so once again he presented the exotic outsiders to the Nordic multitudes.

As to the all-important contact between diasporans and continental Africans, it is probable that the latter's presence in Chicago served to increase diasporan interest, along with an attendant curiosity, in the emigrationist movement. Clearly the bridge between persons of African descent currently born and living on the continent in 1893 and those persons representing the progeny of the great dispersion, or Diaspora, to the Americas ranked as strong as it was weak. In many cases, it could even be nonexistent, a topic historian Tunde Adeleke has examined intensely in his recent work, *UnAfrican Americans: Nineteenth-Century Black Nationalists and the Civilizing Mission*.[24] *Continental Africans* appears to be a most descriptive term for these groups of

Africans represented by the Fon people of Dahomey (Dahomeans), Nubians, Zulu, and others who were mentioned so frequently in the literature of the fair and newspapers and who typified the heterogeneity of the population of the African continent. Obviously, they were also different culturally from most of their brethren in the United States. This weak bridge included nationalists whose closest tie culturally to continental Africans existed along religious and ideological lines rather than on a foundation of shared experiences, customs, and beliefs.

As a group searching for an identity in a nation which persistently denied it, or confused them about it, American Africans identified themselves by several names. When convenient to whites of all persuasions, books, journals, and newspapers connected these members of the African Diaspora to their point of origin as a dispersed set of peoples coming from throughout portions of West and West Central Africa. Occasionally I use the terms *diasporans* and *diasporan Africans* as a means of conveying the multifaceted linguistic images attached to persons of African descent because contemporarily they were referred to as blacks, Afro-Americans, AfriAmericans, Afric Americans, or Africans (as the *Chicago Daily News* reported) along with Colored Americans and Negroes.

Grasping the meaning of black thinking, sentiment, and action required constant deciphering of oral and written utterances and interpreting demeanor through the photographic record. Further, multiple layers of ambiguities, paradoxes, and dilemmas often obscured a clear understanding of black involvement at the event. Researching and understanding the multifaceted meanings of this event became reminiscent of Churchill's epigram about dealing with a riddle wrapped in a mystery inside an enigma. Eminent African American scholar W. E. B. Du Bois's admonition in his classic *The Souls of Black Folk* fortunately provided the definitive methodological guide. His cautionary aid on how to conduct research remains just as pertinent to today's twenty-first century research as it did to the early twentieth century's:

> We seldom study the condition of the Negro today honestly and carefully. It is so much easier to assume that we know it all. Or perhaps, having already reached conclusions in our own minds, we are loathe to having them disturbed by facts. And yet how little we know of these millions, — of their daily lives and longings, of their homely joys and sorrows, of their real shortcomings and the meaning of their crimes! All this we can only learn by intimate contact with the masses, and not by wholesale arguments covering millions separate in time and space, and differing widely in training and culture.[25]

ACKNOWLEDGMENTS

My interest in the World's Columbian Exposition of 1893 grew slowly over the last six years after I initiated a general inquiry into the character of Frederick Douglass's activities at the event. I contacted John McCluskey, Jr., at Indiana University, and we struck up a friendship that led to his suggestion of a full-length book on the subject not only of Douglass's involvement and the meaning of Colored American Day activities held on August 25, 1893, but also on the extent and level of involvement by all persons of African descent. From that level of inquiry, a near-comprehensive examination began.

Next, a chance meeting with a visiting doctoral candidate from abroad, Mathias Eberenz of Hamburg, Germany, who arrived in Chicago to study the exposition in its American cultural context, moved my investigation to even more substantive levels. Over the course of the last half decade, many scholars and lay readers with a keen interest in the fair, and others with a deep commitment to collegiality, assisted a colleague in need of timely, helpful criticism and encouragement. For their examinations of the manuscript in its various stages, I wish to acknowledge my colleagues along with friends of scholarly inquiry at Roosevelt University: Lynn Y. Weiner, Alice J. Zimring, Joel Chukwuogo Okafor, Heather Dalmage, Bruce Kraig, Willie Dixon, Leon Bailey, and Cheryl Ganz. Also, in Chicago, William A. Burns, the community historian for Morgan Park, lent his critical skills at an early stage, while Robert T. Starks did so at a later period. Deirdra Ann Lucas not only provided an analytic eye to ensure against errors in interpretation but undertook the arduous task of indexing the book. Around the nation, others rendered invaluable assistance: Clovis Semmes of Eastern Michigan University, Robert L. Harris, Jr., of Cornell; John Graziano of City University of New York; Willard B. Gatewood of the University of Arkansas; Chester Beattie, Jr., Esq., of Austin, Texas; William G. Andrews, village historian of Brockport, New York; Arlene R. Thomas of Vicksburg, Mississippi; and Yvonne Craft of Xenia, Ohio.

Librarians, archivists, and technicians contributed greatly to this endeavor: Andrea Marks Telli of the Chicago Public Library and B. T. Bryght, Sr. of Roosevelt University lent their expert technical assistance on reproducing photographs and illustrations, respectively; Anita C. Haskell of the Roosevelt

University Libraries took an interest in the fair that became a passion; John Chalmers, Constance Gordon, and Beverly A. Cook at the Special Collections of the Chicago Public Library showed nothing short of a total commitment to this project; and Jacqueline Brown of the Wilberforce University Library rendered yeoman service and interest in uncovering that institution's role and contribution to the fair. Throughout the nation, others who contributed to this endeavor were Minnie Harris Clayton at the Robert W. Woodruff Library of the Atlanta University Center and Michelle Henry of the Chautauqua County Historical Society, New York.

At other repositories, the unsung heroes and heroines who make every successful undertaking what it becomes labor without name recognition but deserve more gratitude than that gesture confers: at the Newberry Library, the State Historical Society of Wisconsin, the Arthur Schomburg Research Center of the New York Public Library, the Chicago Historical Society, the Fisk University Library, and the Center for Interlibrary Loan, I salute their tireless, productive efforts. My new-found friendship and admiration for the editorial staff at the Indiana University Press also has to be acknowledged. Their professionalism and interest in my work has made the task of transforming research and theory all the more enjoyable and, obviously, more positive. As for my family, their interest has grown as their support remained just as steady as ever.

Among those whose relatives participated in the fair, these persons in particular were especially willing to share their family treasures: Lorraine Cherry Heflin, Jean Boyer Jones, and Lloyd G. Wheeler, III.

INTRODUCTION

*American Negroes have made notable progress toward
first-class citizenship in recent years. But foreign critics—
not all of them Communists—point with great effectiveness
at many inequalities from which Negroes still suffer. Some of
the sincere criticism is based, in large part, upon ignorance
of greater inequalities during earlier periods in our history
especially that from the end of Reconstruction to the end of
the nineteenth century. This ignorance is understandable in
view of the fact that it is one of the neglected periods in American history.*

—Rayford W. Logan,
The Betrayal of the Negro, 1954

A city's dream fashioned—to be the host to the international exposition celebrating the 400th anniversary of Columbus' arrival in the New World. A
race's dream fashioned—to participate in the celebration as a sign of true
emancipation of body and mind. A city's dream realized—not a city built
upon a hill, but a "white" city of plaster and fiber *staff* constructed upon a
marsh. A race's dream realized—not a recognition of its humanity and advancement on terms it desired, but participation gained to a degree significant
enough to lay a firm foundation for a brighter future. Yet this future foretold
of an ambivalence in thought and action as much as it offered clarity in what
Logan termed a most neglected period of American history.

The city's dream was manifested in the World's Columbian Exposition of
1893, a monumental event that qualified as a defining point in American
history.[1] Pre-modern, agricultural America culminated its transformation into
the last phase of becoming modern, urban, industrial America on the shores
of Lake Michigan. With this metamorphosis came international recognition
of Chicago's economic prominence and its grand effort at reviving classicism
in urban architecture at a time when a modern American form was evolving,
along with stimulating an appreciation of the *beaux arts* among all classes.
Held in Chicago between May 1 and October 30, it represented a watershed
in the evolution of American cities overall and, of course, for Chicago in

particular. After having beaten out Washington, D.C., St. Louis, and New York City for the honor of hosting this international fair, Chicago still had to endure constant jibes from the latter's boosters on real and imagined problems such as the quality of its drinking water, a menacing crime rate, violent labor strife, and insufferable midwestern parochialism in cultural affairs. The civic and commercial leadership of Chicago, like some of its African American citizens, seemed to have a point to prove, both to itself and to outsiders.

On a parallel plane, a plethora of African American dreams began to take form as the fair's managers announced the exposition's imminent opening. Little did white Americans realize that, seeking acknowledgment of their group's worth after two centuries of humiliating bondage, African Americans would place the event under a racial microscope as to the role their brethren and sistren of African descent would assume. Intricately linked to the success and grandeur of the World's Columbian Exposition, a set of highly differentiated African American *expectations*, influenced by region, class, gender, occupation, transgenerationalism and ideology moved forward toward consummation. The multifaceted influences and demeanor of both diasporan and continental Africans confirmed their breadth, while a treasure trove of written, photographic, and illustrated records revealed their depth.

SOME PERSPECTIVES ON THE FAIR: THE DIASPORAN AND CONTINENTAL AFRICANS

According to St. Clair Drake and Horace R. Cayton, "for the Negroes, the occasion [the fair] was a sort of silver jubilee celebrating a generation of freedom." The world's fair was significant, to be sure, and featured an African American seemingly as visible at the extravaganza as socialite Mrs. Bertha Honore Palmer, who reigned as the fair's unofficial queen. From Washington, the venerable abolitionist and racial egalitarian Frederick Douglass came to oversee the state of race relations in the age of new technology. The "Sage of Anacostia" embodied the dream that inclusion within the American mainstream was a possibility as no other Colored American could, and he spent the entire summer of 1893 in Chicago. So, *symbolically* in the eyes of African Americans, he might be likened ironically to a king in a soon to be legally *separate and equal* America.

Apart from Douglass as the black person most watched, the most over-reported event was the celebration of Colored American Day. It began in the controversy over whether or not African Americans should even observe a designated day. It escalated into another debate over its content and significance. When the celebration finally took place, it exemplified the status transformation occurring in many parts of the nation but was obviously unfamiliar in certain areas of the American South, where a highly Africanized culture held preeminence. However, it quickly faded into obscurity. The most significant contradiction followed in the aftermath of Ida B. Wells's spirited denunciation of the celebration. After good reviews by the liberal white press, she poignantly admitted remorse at not having participated.[2] On balance, Colored American Day represented just one of a plethora of activities in which African Americans engaged.

The most overlooked event over the last century was the Congress on Africa, variously called the Congress on African Ethnology or Congress on the Negro, which was also the most publicized event involving diasporan and continental African participation. It had an importance all its own irrespective of the presence of continental Africans in Chicago because few continentals but many diasporan proponents and opponents of African emigration participated in the late nineteenth century's most spirited ideological dialogue. During mid-August, an eight-day conclave on the status of the African at home and abroad ensued. The entire spectrum of the national African American intellectual and political leadership participated. The ubiquitous Douglass appeared, despite his ideological bent opposing African emigration. Quasi-nationalist spokesman Episcopal Bishop Alexander Crummell and active emigrationist A.M.E. Bishop Henry McNeal Turner attended. While diasporan and continental Africans spoke frequently, so did white explorers and missionaries. This event proved timely because the raging controversy in the year preceding the fair, apart from the Memphis lynchings of Ida B. Wells's fellow citizens, focused on emigration to Africa. On this issue, Wells exhibited sympathy to the nationalists' cause although she remained ardently in favor of remaining in America.

The issue of African emigration offered alternatives to African Americans, but they always assumed the shape of a dilemma. Remain in America, face the struggle for the basic rights of citizenship, and be labeled malcontents and whiners. Leave the country, resettle in Africa, and be labeled quitters. At this juncture, to the African American nationalist element, emigration to Africa presented the ultimate solution to the dilemma of this nation's racism. According to historian Edwin S. Redkey, this was not surprising because "emigration to Africa in the 1890s was not a new idea; rather, it drew on a long tradition of colonization plans."[3] Remaining steadfast in their opposition, the assimilationist diasporans remained adamant that anything other than an unswerving loyalty to America spelled disaster for their race. Part Four, entitled "All the World Is Here!," contains three chapters that examine the conference, the role of the Fon people of Dahomey at the fair, and activities at the Haytian Pavilion.

With this dichotomy over remaining in or leaving America manifest amid others, the influential nature of a plethora of ambiguities, paradoxes, and dilemmas seemed almost conventional. Throughout the duration of the fair, ambiguities existed among the African Americans both about their thought and actions. Whether the issue involved methods and strategy, personality, or ideology, uncertainty and division prevailed.

Sometimes seeking advancement and showing off the level of their racial achievement since emancipation, or merely in enhancing their economic status through securing work, persons of African ancestry born and residing in the United States regularly encountered racism as they positioned themselves to enjoy, participate, and benefit from this monumental event. Overall, the expectations of African Americans in other sections of the nation varied immensely, for example, in the South, or in the plains states of the West. These varying ideas reflected the diversity of interests and backgrounds found within this racially proscribed citizenry of ten million souls. Some of these well-educated, highly assimilated African Americans sought not just representation, but membership, at the highest level of planning and decision-making. They confidently envisioned themselves as planners of an event for which they finally utilized their administrative skills as college-trained Americans. Chapter 2, "Participation and Protest," attempts to capture much of this pre-fair energy.

Further, they carefully prepared themselves to participate in major intellectual and cultural events, such as the myriad parliaments and congresses, which included dialogues on such disparate topics as religion, women, dentistry, education, labor, and Africa. Across the spectrum, some African Americans proposed full participation in nearly all of the activities, such as joining in celebratory activities, namely Haytian Day and Colored American Day. A smaller segment volunteered to consult on the exhibits designed to proudly display the achievements of African Americans in the quarter century since emancipation, thereby controlling their prized racial image. As bona fide Americans, these persons, recently referred to by historian and Du Bois scholar David Levering Lewis as "Afro-Saxons,"[4] laid proud claim to the fullness of their American and Anglo-Saxon cultural heritages.

Yet, if a single Caucasian viewing the painting "The Underground Railroad," on display in the Art Palace, failed to comprehend the source of African American solicitude when the latter pondered the attainability of the American dream, Afro-Saxon faith in Anglo-Saxon genuineness seemed misplaced. The painting which evoked so much pathos showed Quaker abolitionists Levi Coffin and his wife, Aunt Katie, as they aided several African slaves fleeing slavery and crossing to the northern banks of the Ohio River. As the viewer described the scene, the refugees were "trusting to the future, and dare[d] not turn to look at what [might] be behind. They must have this one moment of freedom."[5] Afro-Saxons dared dream of a future, but one in which freedom was perpetual, not merely momentary. Chapter 6, entitled "'They Met at the Fair': Linkages," explores these activities.

Paradoxes abounded, and with good reason. Chief Justice Roger Taney's pronunciamento in 1857 invalidating African Americans' claims to the full rights of citizenship seemed to gain renewed popularity in the rarefied atmosphere of the 1890s. The enthusiastic embrace given nationally to Social Darwinism only served to affirm their worst fears. In 1883, the disillusioning decision by the U.S. Supreme Court invalidating the Civil Rights Act of 1875, coupled with the failure of the Congress to pass the Lodge Federal Elections

Bill, seemed to substantiate those fears. Then there was the increase in lynchings and lawlessness in the South, the advent of disfranchisement through the adoption of the Mississippi Plan in 1890, and the rise of debt peonage, which presaged the emergence of a new slave regimen. Much like a rising tide, the assault on African American rights seemed unstoppable.

The African Americans' reaction to egregious injustice could reach a breaking point, one demanding extreme responses. To many, it seemed they wanted to grasp and hold America more than the nation wanted to reciprocate their embrace. *The Reason Why the Colored American Is Not in the World's Columbian Exposition* and Charles Morris's *Negroes and the Fair: A Complaint against the Policy of the Columbian Exposition* articulated their deeply felt animus. In Chicago in 1892, a most unusual thing happened at a public gathering: black Chicagoans refused to sing the nation's unofficial anthem, "My Country 'Tis of Thee."[6] That the host city's diasporan population had reached a point where they would show disrespect for a national symbol, equaling the treatment they endured, is covered in two chapters in Part Two, "In Host City Chicago."

SOME PERSPECTIVES ON THE FAIR:
THE MOODS AND SENTIMENTS OF WHITE AMERICA

Although the central focus of this book is on participation of African Americans at the fair, white scholarly and lay perceptions, both contemporary and modern, influenced how persons of African descent were to be viewed. It is therefore appropriate to consider the mentality and sentiments of whites at the time of the fair. Whites flocked to the fair by the millions, some from Chicago and its hinterlands, many more from throughout the contiguous forty-four states comprising the United States and from Europe. Most were rank and file native Americans—Hoosiers, Suckers, Buckeyes, Jayhawkers, and Yankees. Some were Populists, others urban liberals slated to become progressives. Single-Taxers, Socialists, Utopians, Klansmen, and Southern Bourbons were also present on the fairgrounds.

Some brought sensitivity to the fairgrounds themselves, to the Midway Plaisance adjoining the northwestern entrance to the fairgrounds, and to Buffalo Bill Cody's Wild West Show directly west of the fair's expanse. Others were remarkable for their racial arrogance and nationalistic chauvinism. White Southerners came to Chicago with racial baggage they were not willing to shed as they enthusiastically celebrated their state and sectional heritages.[7] Some visitors evinced callowness, while many were simply curious about anything new or anyone new. The latter trait—curiosity—often emanated from a salutary core. Journalist, sometimes novelist, and son of the famous Nathaniel, Julian Hawthorne described his fellow Americans this way: "We are an orderly and well-behaved people, very tractable and yet with an underlying independence which explains our short but significant history. We are inquisitive, and we have a sense of humor and love of fun, but we are not demonstrative, and though we are willing to learn, we are somewhat skeptical and not particularly appreciative. Our vocabulary is largely idiomatic, but otherwise limited or reticent." So to what extent did a conscious predilection to the pejorative as manifested through a heavy reliance on the idiomatic and frequent use of such adjectives as "fierce, savage, barbaric, and ugly" to describe continental Africans lend itself to transformation internally into an unconscious or latent approval of the scorned?

"It is the cheapest and most exhaustive journey over the earth that was ever made," wrote journalist Jonathan G. Speed for *Harper's Weekly*. Speed was somewhat cynical about the educational results of this experience:

> there will be villages representing life [everywhere] . . . . To see all these things will be something of an education to those who cannot travel abroad and to those who have seen them with their native surrounding it will pleasantly recall memories of them. But it must be confessed that the primary purpose of the features of the Midway Plaisance is not educational, but rather to amuse. And no doubt a certain very large percentage will go rather for amusement than instruction. It is well, therefore, that these should be provided with the lands of things that are likely to please them, for there are many men and women in the world who will take instruction incidentally as children do in a Kindergarten."[8]

In this erratic setting, in which the power of the visceral reigned, any attempt a century later to explain thinking and behavior along conventional lines should objectively expect the unanticipated. So it was with skepticism that was then both prized and prevalent. White Americans "say they know what's fake," Hawthorne wrote, "possibly to guard against the contingency of being taken in. It is a pity that we cannot believe that the world contains anything except the things we are familiar with; and one of the best uses this Fair can serve will be to disabuse us of that idea." As to the possibility that they might be fooled in their prejudices, when promised continental Africans, white Americans abhorred being deceived into thinking that the Colored people that they were accustomed to seeing in their country were the *genuine* ones.

The Midway Plaisance—seven-eighths of a mile long and 600 feet wide—became the venue most noted for its combined celebrity, notoriety, and popularity in bringing exposure and information, if not knowledge, about the Earth's immense cultural and racial diversity. On the Midway Plaisance, familiarity did the unusual; it often bred sensitivity. Novelist Hawthorne observed it; as a journalist for *Cosmopolitan* magazine, he described the interaction among strangers as one in which the "ends of the earth [were] meeting, and finding one another good fellows."[9] Novelist Teresa Dean wrote that "after 11 o'clock the theaters and villages (on the Midway) are closed to visitors, and the natives come out on the Plaisance to enjoy a rest, and see each other and the friends they make in this country. Between you and me, I don't know but that it is just as much of an amusement to study these "friends" they make—the Americans who hobnob with them."[10] Mrs. D. C. Taylor noted that we "see people of every nation under the sun, black, brown, yellow and white, old and young, beautiful and homely, rich and poor, intelligent and ignorant, all brought to the same level, and crowding one another in this wonder Midway."[11]

While Hinsley posthumously uncovered a humor "that revealed deep uneasiness and uncertainty about [racial] boundaries . . . [and] was a humor evidently intended to encourage a sympathy with the exotic and simultaneously to keep a certain ironic distance,"[12] there was contemporary evidence to suggest that another course could be pursued. A Quaker visiting the Midway observed a recently married African American couple wandering the Street of Cairo and admiring the camel rides. For the young bride, her interest turned to envy as she watched another young woman sway back and forth on a "ship of the desert." Gaily dressed—overdressed, in fact—she took her turn, much to the amusement both of the crowd and herself. As they laughed, she also laughed, and the Quaker wrote: "There was an acre more or less of people, with mouths stretched from ear to ear. It was not a provoking merriment, not sarcastic, not that mean mirth that ridicules weakness. It was all sympathetic, good hearted, and good natured." As the young woman stepped from the prostrate animal's back, "the crowd began to cheer. Poor Dinah at first did not know whether to be offended or delighted. . . . The crowd was laughing in such a generous-hearted way that she wisely thought it best to join in."[13]

Interactions of this type became commonplace through diverse activities, including mock battles and swimming contests, with continental Africans assuming a different status in the glare of countless, inescapable Caucasian eyes. This study treats the Midway as something other than a freak show, because it was, in fact, a venue in which "the student of the races of mankind [could] have ample opportunities in a stroll along this wonderful street, where he [might] examine and criticize without fear or favor."[14] The Midway did not exist as a panorama of ethnic or racial shame, and the foreign visitors were "not a part of a show—they [were] the essence of] the people themselves," just more parts of a highly differentiated global humanity.[15]

As for the intentions of those who assembled the world's humanity to allow them to perform their daily routines as they did in indigenous settings, their thinking varied. Academician Frederick Ward Putnam of Harvard University's Peabody Museum, a leading institution in ethnological study and presentation, initially assumed responsibility for deciding how foreign visitors were to be presented to the white American public as well as the world on both the Midway and at the Anthropology Building. His views as a pioneer American ethnographer constituted those of a well-intentioned, benevolent racist mixed with those of the purported scholar, whose objectivity was unfortunately skewed by Social Darwinian presumptions of Nordic racial superiority buttressed by findings in physical anthropology. Yet the results of his efforts were neither predictable nor completely deleterious because of interference with his plans from the fair's directorship, which was all too eager to expand the profitability of the exposition.

The work of his assistant, Franz Boas, whose future contribution to human understanding would change the way the Western world viewed humanity, was constructed on this experience. Boas' primary interest in working with indigenous North American peoples would not have prevented him, in his secondary work with the foreign contingents, from gaining some awareness of the Fon of Dahomey. He shared his knowledge on Negro civilization and achievement in Bilad-as-Sudan within ten months of the fair's closing before the Section of Anthropology of the American Association for the Advancement of Science. In his seminal address, "Human Faculty as Determined by Race," he introduced the concept of African intelligence that undergirded his twentieth century breakthrough on the equality of racial potential.[16] Although the Fon arrived in Chicago under the auspices of American impresario Sol Bloom, a link between their lives and the meaning of their culture was likely of interest to Boas. Within a decade, Boas' star rose and he headed the newly organized anthropology department at Columbia University. There he pioneered an objective course of research that stressed inductive reasoning based on intensive, comprehensive examination of extensive field data. Equally as important—although this occurred slightly over a generation later—he helped obtain financial backing so that his protégés in cultural anthropology, Melville F. and Frances S. Herskovits, could take his scholarly, humanistic interest in Africa, and obviously in Dahomey, to salutary heights he only imagined in 1893 and 1894.[17]

As for showman Bloom, he had profited financially at the last Paris exposition by presenting foreign peoples to curious minds. He reasoned that America's fair would serve a similar purpose and claimed years later that no sinister racist agenda, academic, commercial or otherwise, existed or was being carried out on the Midway. Under his machinations, the Midway existed simply as popular and profitable entertainment.[18]

The complicated and contradictory set of images of the Midway and the fairgrounds often clashed with the interests, motivations, and prejudgements of the onlooker. The interests of the plethora of writers—journalists, novelists, satirists, and creative specialists (such as music critic Henry E. Krehbiel and composer Antonín Dvořák)—as well as dozens of photographers attest to more than just a condescending curiosity or a need to affirm racial superiority. As to the meaning of the recorded word, Carl S. Smith saw profundity in what offhandedly might be presumed to be simple: "The literature of the Columbian Exposition is important in what it tells us about how the Fair looked and felt, of course, but it also demonstrates that such events resonate in expected and unexpected ways in the minds of those trying to explore and explain what these events mean in and of themselves and in relation to other developments."[19]

Of Chicago's many dailies, the *Inter Ocean* and the *Evening Post* presented the most objective, informative, and comprehensive coverages of the diasporan and continental African presence. But there were no newspapers so virulently racist as to deviate from this basically liberal manner of reporting on non-white participants and visitors to the fair. James Weldon Johnson, in the city as an Atlanta University student, penned a series of articles for his institution's newspaper which reflected directly on this subject, writing, "We are enjoying a degree of newspaper notoriety of which we had never dreamed. Every day we figure quite conspicuously in the columns of the great dailies, in prose and poetry, sometimes in caricature. Generally the articles are very fair. Some of us have even had the honor of being interviewed by reporters."[20]

Moreover, the presence of radical racial egalitarians among the whites proved that the abolitionist mentality of the antebellum through Reconstruction periods had a life of its own, retaining great vitality near the end of the nineteenth century and into the new one.[21] Coupled with advocates of the Social Gospel and the more secular Reform Social Darwinists, these proponents of fair play interacted effectively and placed their agenda of inclusivity and tolerance squarely before fairgoers. Strategically positioned, they molded the agendas, directed the activities, and chose the speakers at the World's Congress of Representative Women, Congress on Labor, World Parliament of Religions, and Congress on Africa. Identified by name and persuasion, the Revs. Jenkin Lloyd Jones and Celia Parker Woolley of the Unitarian faith, journalists Albion Winegar Tourgée, Henry Demarest Lloyd, and Phoebe Couzins, and Congregationalists Joseph E. Roy, Frederick Perry Noble, and Isabella Beecher Hooker fit solidly in the nineteenth century's liberal, humanist tradition to which much progressive legislation, moral initiatives, peace efforts and broad-minded attitudes on race, belonged.

Among persons of both races who labored with their hands in the vineyards, the artificial boundaries of skin color often broke down more quickly than they did elsewhere. The frequency of interracial statutory marriage, common law marriage, and casual courtship proved this as did the existence of Chicago's Manasseh Society, a club consisting of more than one hundred mixed-race married couples. So, despite the prevalence of tenets of Social Darwinism on race, multiracial America lacked a caste system and a unified view on darker-skinned persons encountered on the fairgrounds.

Unfortunately, the fair also afforded an outlet for the more unsavory sentiments of white Chicagoans along with their American counterparts who latently, covertly, or overtly espoused and practiced racism. Most notable was the spate of bias, misinformation, and falsehood produced by the media of the period—journals, magazines, souvenir books, novels, and newspapers. Most egregious were the souvenir books and photographic collections, numbering over six hundred.[22] But even with their biases, *Scribner's, Independent, Atlantic Monthly, Cosmopolitan,* and *Frank Leslie's Illustrated Weekly* did inform its readership. *World's Fair Puck* announced its intention early to ridicule anything or anyone that it found to be silly or weak, so throughout the fair it operated as an equal opportunity offender. If there was a low point, it had to have come in the unanticipated racist drivel of host city mayor and former Virginian Carter G. Harrison, who greeted an African American conference with comments more appropriate for a meeting called by an antebellum planter.[23]

In sum, the Midway, along with the entirety of the fair itself, offered the observer an opportunity to see the human existence through a prism permitting as much light in and out as was desired. So, no definitive commentary on racism or racial intolerance is possible, and that, in and of itself, produced hope in the hearts of many African Americans.

*"All
the World
Is Here!"*

Part One

AROUND THE NATION

*Paul, like everyone else, was talking about the World's Fair.
. . . The Herald told Paul he could do another article, "Dayton at the Fair," if he went. . . . All of a sudden Paul realized
he was not just going to the fair. He was going to Chicago —
the Big City, the Wicked City.*

—Virginia Cunningham,
Paul Lawrence Dunbar and His Song

*When we left Atlanta . . . it was with no small degree of
anxiety and anticipation. Our hopes were bright and perhaps, highly colored, but I do not think that there was one of
us who did not fully realize the responsibilities of the undertaking we were about to make. . . . We reached Chicago . . .
[and] our reception surpassed any expectation we had had.
We were treated just as though the question of color had
never been brought up.*

—James Weldon Johnson,
The Bulletin of Atlanta University

Disparate sets of expectations, aspirations, hopes, and fears arose from the
national African American community on what the fair represented, each reflecting particular experiences and leaving an indelible imprint on its con-
stituents and on the shape of the event. One set originated from the ranks of
the middling and elite classes, especially from the northern states, who com-

prised the Talented Tenth. They envisioned the event as a setting in which they could demonstrate their recent educational achievement as they participated with whites in decision-making. Their quest for involvement in the administration and operations of the fair pitted African American against Caucasians who wanted absolute control based on what they perceived as a manifesting racial birthright. Their interest rested on the acquisition of civic spoils related to the attainments of economic class and those of gender interests.

Another set emanated from the demographically dominant laboring class, especially that segment found in Chicago, to whom the fair symbolized a source of employment. Still another group of black Southerners composed of the middling and elite leadership sought salutary representation of their race through exhibits that demonstrated the rising level of African American intellectual competence since emancipation. Exhibits, either included in larger demonstrations of progress or presented separately, would notably prove African American advancement in the arts, letters, and crafts. Meanwhile, a large mass of African Americans scattered throughout the nation wanted to visit Chicago and enjoy the scientific and cultural wonders of the fair. Perhaps the most important function of the fair for African Americans was to show "to the world, not only what America has done for the Negro, but what the Negro has done for himself."[1]

1

EXPECTATIONS

*The Chicago World's Fair of 1893 more than any World's
Fair that preceded it, either in Europe or America, demonstrated and displayed on a more colossal scale the development and progress of the human race. It more than anything
else illustrated the wealth, culture, education, and economic
high reaches of the white race, and yet there were brown,
yellow and black spots on that huge white avalanche of wonder to astonish and amaze.*

— Dr. M. A. Majors, 1893 Colored American
Day Committee Vice-president, writing in 1929

*Theoretically open to all Americans, the Exposition practi-
cally is, literally and figuratively, a "White City," in the
building of which the Colored American was allowed no
helping hand, and in its glorious success he has no share.*

— Ferdinand L. Barnett, *The Reason Why the
Colored American Is Not in the World's
Columbian Exposition,* 1893

Once the World's Columbian Exposition opened on May 1, 1893, it would
attract more than 21 million persons as visitors,[1] and among their ranks
would be thousands of African Americans, diasporans, from around the
nation. Heeding Du Bois's advice on understanding why these diasporans
showed interest in the event and attended in impressive numbers, an examination of certain attributes of, and trends among, this group seemed imperative. Key measuring points provide a locus from which to start: What did
diasporans expect to result from the event and, where appropriate, what provided fulfillment to them—in time, in space, and through experience? Not
surprisingly, their collective interests and corresponding experiences were
anything but homogeneous and differed greatly by region.

The overwhelming majority of African Americans resided in the former
slave states of the South where they marked time experientially from the beginning of mass emancipation in 1865. Then, and only then, could their advancement as freed people begin.

1. The Sage of Anacostia: Frederick Douglass, the leading voice of racial justice and assimilation. Courtesy of the University of Kansas Library.

2. Rev. Alexander Crummell, the beloved "Father Crummell" of Washington, D.C., erstwhile voice of emigration and now of remaining in America. Courtesy of the University of Kansas Library.

As one moved to the older sections of the country in the South and up along the eastern seaboard, populations existed so diverse in regard to their wealth and accomplishments that a traveler encountered a readily discernible class structure based on both sociocultural and economic factors. Circumstances existing nationally simply belied any impression gleaned from the more insular Chicago experience. In this vein, historian Willard Gatewood has described a national aristocracy among African Americans that met all the criteria to be recognized as a "Black 400." In terms of their wealth, education, social status, and cultural interests they were bona fide Afro-Saxons. What they anticipated from an international exposition depended on their individual preferences, but differences surely abounded. As the destination for a fun summer's excursion, Chicago ranked as the first choice. As a lyceum to hear the latest theories on what ailed the nation, the race, and humanity, Chicago was the destination of choice. Groups with an interest in the latter were targeted by the World's Fair Committee of Colored Men, a Chicago venture which was organizing excursions to the city. Thinking on a grand scale, the committee proposed to bring 10,000 persons based on their efforts alone in the upper South and southern Ohio.[2]

In the District of Columbia, where North sometimes met South, but where power and influence always reigned, two venerable leaders, Frederick Douglass and the Rev. Alexander Crummell, readied themselves for their separate sojourns northward. First and foremost, Frederick Douglass had plans to attend the October 11, 1892, inaugural ceremonies in which he was prepared to assume the mantle of national spokesman for Afro-America. Serving as a fulcrum for both diasporan thought and action, the "grand old man" would live out his greatest triumph and culminate his life as the dominant African American personality at the exposition. A living paradox, he had become Afro-Saxon America's ambassador to the nation. Born into slavery of mixed heritage, baptized among the righteous of New England's abolitionist stalwarts, committed to the realization of the promise of a color-blind American democracy, Douglass often criticized the land of his birth but never renounced her. His unwavering adoration for the best that America offered completely overwhelmed any animosity that he held toward her many imperfections. While he forgave, he could never forget America's moral obligation to publicly profess its past sinfulness and what he grew to consider as world's fair snubs rooted in the nation's slave past.[3]

As an Afro-Saxon seeking validation of his very being from white America, Douglass's condemnation on several occasions of the purported barbarity of the Fon people of Dahomey simply demonstrated that he had succumbed to the same racist notions of Afrophobia that white Americans held. He challenged the sincerity of the exposition leadership's true commitment to African American representation and participation, excoriating them severely. "Apparently they want us to be represented by the music and by the civilization of Dahomey," he criticized. "They have filled the Fair with the sound of barbaric music, and with sights of barbaric rites, and denied the colored American any representation."[4]

Douglass, of course, was only rejecting the origins of his maternal ancestry while embracing that of his slaveholder father. As he answered critics at the time of his second marriage to his Caucasian secretary in 1884, he explained his views on race. "I am not an African, as may be seen from my features and hair, and it is equally easy to discern that I am not a Caucasian . . . [and he elaborated further.] I conceive that there is no division of races. God Almighty made but one race. I adopt the theory that in time the varieties of races will be blended into one."[5]

When Douglass became the subject of the effort to categorize persons of mixed ancestry by their positive and negative racial attributes, the results, not unexpectedly, reached paradoxical levels. Former Kansas U.S. Senator John J. Ingalls responded to Douglass's racial self-assessment but culled from the situation a somewhat unflattering evaluation. In the senator's estimation, Douglass was "an eloquent, accomplished, and dignified gentleman. His father was a white man and his mother a slave. It is perhaps not invidious nor uncivil to affirm that the distinction of Douglass is not on account of this African blood, but in spite of it. The intellectual traits, qualities, and characteristics which have given him renown are due to his Anglo-Saxon reinforcement. . . . Whether justly or unjustly, African blood is regarded to the Caucasian as a taint to be abhorred."[6] Just as bizarre, a Douglass visit to Ireland produced this anecdote, often told by members of his own group for their amusement. As to the extent of his brilliance as an orator, a resident of Dublin remarked upon learning that Douglass was only "half-Negro": "Faith, an' if half a Naigar can make a speech like that, whut could a whole Naigar do?"[7] The Pan-Africanist theorist, scholar, pioneer, statesman, and Negrophile, Liberian leader Edward Wilmot Blyden, also admired Douglass. In 1880, he wrote in a West African newspaper: "He shows polish of society and the culture of extensive reading. He is strongly Negro, although of mixed blood. His genius and power come from the African side of his nature. He reminds me in his manner and bearing more of some aristocratic African chief such as I have seen in the distant interior, rather than of any cultivated European I have ever seen."[8]

When African Americans reacted to their African bloodlines as Douglass did, their responses merely highlighted the absurdity of both the circumstance and the moment. To the chagrin of a reporter for the *New York Times*, Colored Americans had no cause to silently ridicule these continental Africans at the fair. The reporter explained: "I willingly add that I saw several Afro-American ladies and gentlemen regarding these savage prototypes with much the same expression which the proud Caucasian wears when he is looking at the monkeys in Central Park, though candor compels me to say that the difference between the spectators and the spectacle was less marked."[9] A local reporter saw in the Fon people of Dahomey much of what was commonly seen in black America. He reported that the Fon carried their heavy baggage on their heads "with as much skill as the Southern Negroes 'tote' smaller bundles."[10] Then there was the headline in the *Chicago Daily News* that read: "Colored Belles to Come: Chicago's African '400' Agog over Prospective Visit of the Leaders of Colored Society."

Once again, if Afro-Saxons felt they could succeed in pleasing white America, this observation showed that they would invariably fail. Any satisfaction that appeared came in backhanded compliments. One author wrote: "Perhaps one of the most striking lessons which the Columbian Exposition taught was the fact that African slavery in America may not have been, after all, an unmixed evil, for of a truth, the advanced social condition of the American Africans over that of their barbarous countrymen is most encouraging and wonderful."[11]

The Rev. Alexander Crummell presided over St. Luke's Episcopal Church in the nation's capital, where for two decades he had tended to the needs of his African American flock and an occasional president. By moral standing and principled attitudes, he was Father Crummell; by intellect, he was Afro-Saxon America's sage.[12] A New York native by birth, Crummell was reared by free parents and considered himself directly linked spiritually with the Temne people of West Africa, his forbears. He was educated in New York, New England, and Great Britain, attending the African Free School, the Canal High School, Noyes Academy in New Hampshire, and Queen's College, Cambridge, where he received his A.B. in 1853. Crummell, however, failed in his attempt to matriculate at General Theological Seminary in New York because of racism. Remarkably, he consistently demonstrated intellectual acuity amid rigorous competition, racial slights, and social proscription. Not surprisingly, this intellectually and ideologically imposing religious leader seemed to embody the indomitable spirit of his race in that he perpetually resisted all forms of bondage—physical, emotional, intellectual, and spiritual. However, with his commitment not just to learning but to intellectual excellence, this "civilizationist" forever felt uncomfortable about associating with the masses—whether white, diasporan, or continental African—and underrated their abilities.[13]

Crummell resembled Douglass in many ways. Both men advocated a cautious approach to their race's advancement as they slowed with age, reaching beyond the biblical three score and ten years. In the year of the great fair, Crummell admitted unhesitatingly that "the shades of evening are upon me. Age is fast relaxing my powers."[14] They also recognized economic self-help as a viable means toward improving the race's status in America and called upon the masses of Afro-America to avail themselves of the civilizing benefits of living in a nation such as this one.

On the other hand, Crummell's emphasis on race as a determinant of his race's future led him to the belief that "we are a nation set apart in this country."[15] Accordingly, if only as a tactical measure, he promoted nurturing a strong sense of racial identity even if this contradicted any emphasis on seeking the rewarding citizenship benefits that life in America proffered. According to Meier, he counted "two great heresies: 'That the colored people of this country should forget as soon as possible that they ARE colored people'; and 'That colored men should give up all distinctive efforts, as colored men, in schools, churches, associations, and friendly societies.'"[16] As to persons of mixed blood and interracial marriages, he eschewed them both.[17] Crummell also began to see Douglass's emphasis on the slave past as obsessive, nonproductive, and irrelevant to the cause of black advancement.[18]

Despite his strategic interest in Africa's eventual elevation to prominence in the world community, as the world's fair approached, he had cultivated two decades of animus to the stratagem of emigrationism. Its mistaken emphasis on actual mass relocation and the enormity of the task of raising, as he saw it, the continental African to Afro-Saxon standards was nonsensical. However, he still believed intuitively in the chosen position of the downtrodden African. Of his ties to Africa through cultural retentions, he wrote "I wished last year [1892] to enlist two or three friends of mine in the attempt to organize an 'African Society' for the preservation of traditions, folk-lore, ancestral remembrances, etc., which may have come down from ancestral sources. But nothing came of it. The truth is that the dinning of the 'colonization' cause into the ears of the colored people—the iteration of the idle dogma that Africa is THE home of the black race of this land; has served to prejudice the race against the very name Africa. And this is a double folly:—the folly of the colonizationists, and the folly of the black man; i.e.[,] to forget family ties and his duty to his kin over the water."[19]

As to visiting Chicago for the forthcoming Parliament of Religions and

Congress on Africa, Crummell surely relished this trip. The expected intellectual discourse at the latter conclave promised a meeting similar to a Sanhedrin, that biblical assemblage of the most learned and concerned among the Hebrews. This appealing exercise of the cerebral just might have sparked the final decision in the priest's mind to organize the American Negro Academy two years after the fair.

As inconspicuous in the nation's capital as the two African American sages were prominent, the twenty-four-year-old, Virginia-born Louis B. Anderson toiled in the newspaper field. Anderson arrived in Washington, D.C., in 1889 and began work for newspaper man Major Moses P. Handy, who assumed duties as head of the world's fair Department of Publicity and Promotion. The young journalist eagerly prepared for his assignment as exchange reader,[20] perhaps sensing that a journey to Chicago might change his life forever, as in fact it did.

In the New South, on the District's southern border, which claimed a fresh role in America's industrial future, stood the Commonwealth of Virginia's Hampton Institute, located on the scenic Chesapeake. Excitement built as the opening day of the fair approached. Robert Sengstacke Abbott, a twenty-five-year-old who was then unsure of his career, but was destined within several decades to become a newspaper magnate, prepared for a trip north to sing with the popular Hampton Quartet.[21] Meanwhile, apprehension dominated the thought of the advance staff in Chicago. Would the school's educational exhibit be ready on time? "Carpenters work all night, so there is not a hour in the whole week, day, or night, that the sound of the hammer and trowel is not heard in the land," wrote one staffer. The Hampton exhibit was assigned a place in the impressive, yet unfinished, Liberal Arts Building, where the one comforting factor was the personage of "a benign old colored gentleman [who] guarde[d] the door with a firm but smiling face." What Hampton wanted most was the opportunity to show the world the enormous strides in education the children of the freedmen had made. Indeed, they would have their day "way to the southeast [in] section 1, column V . . . [where any visitor could] behold the forty-eight much belabeled boxes bearing the Hampton name."[22]

Farther south, a Georgian physician and his wife, Dr. Alberry A. and Mrs. Caddie Whitman, were putting the finishing touches on original poems they would deliver before fairgoers in September.[23] At Atlanta University, 500 students spread through five departments experienced a similar sense of anticipation. The institution's faculty, staff, and students were determined to show through academic creativity and craft production the best they had to offer to skeptical white fairgoers. With written materials from their classrooms, iron and wood products from their shops, and James Weldon Johnson among a group of Atlanta's best students, this caravan headed north. Johnson, in particular, would personify the Atlanta University ideal as he and his fellow students worked as "chairboys," joining scores of white college men in pushing

3. Bishop Henry McNeal Turner of the African Methodist Epsicopal Church, a proponent of African emigration. Courtesy of the University of Kansas Library.

sightseers in four-wheeled chairs around the expansive fairgrounds. As a bonus, Johnson served as scribe for the school's newspaper, writing with the insight and accuracy that marked his later literary years. On his initial experience with midwestern race relations, Johnson observed, "Our reception surpassed any expectation we had had. We were treated just as though the question of color had never been brought up."[24]

Georgia had a son of note that it could not disown, despite his fearless and unrelenting rhetoric denouncing American racism and embracing racial separation that would be accomplished by emigrating to Africa. Bishop Henry McNeal Turner of the A.M.E. Church had returned from trips to Liberia in 1892 and 1893 thoroughly convinced of the need to abandon the U.S. along with any hope that the American Dream would be extended to African Americans. When the fair opened, Turner was still in West Africa replenishing his ammunition cache with first-hand information with which to answer critics of emigration.

Turner's experience as a free person of color in antebellum South Carolina who worked alongside slaves in the cotton fields and was rescued through work in a law office as sweeper left him disgruntled as to this nation's sense of fair play. He evangelized for the white Southern Methodists before he discovered the liberating influence of the A.M.E. church in 1858 and the ideological rhetoric of emigration coming from the lips of a visiting Rev. Crummell. During the Civil War Turner recruited black troops in his church yard to help his people lay claim to having helped emancipate themselves. As the Reconstruction era dawned, he entered politics and was elected to the Georgia legislature. He was soon convinced that the white population was hopelessly trapped by its cowardice and greed. After whites expelled black members from the state legislature in 1868, Turner denounced the action and pledged never to support a nation that treated him and his race in this manner.[25] If African Americans remained in America, their lot would seemingly be to relive this tragedy repeatedly. His appeal to the masses in the South of the 1880s and 1890s reached a level of high acceptance for the message, if not for the solution of leaving America. But "contrary to some of the misinterpretations by his critics," Redkey has written, "the bishop did not urge a wholesale migration of all Afro-Americans to Africa; he recognized the impossibility of unloading millions of black paupers into a new land. . . . 'Five or ten thousand a year would be enough.'"[26]

At Tuskegee Institute in Alabama, educator Booker T. Washington[27] considered, then accepted, an invitation to speak on southern labor proffered through the efforts of labor reformer and erstwhile *Chicago Tribune* editor and writer Henry Demarest Lloyd.[28] As Washington made his plans to speak before the Congress on Labor which would convene in early September, he studied the data he would use to denounce the economic situation in the South in the most unequivocal of terms. A man with little leisure time, immediately before he left for Chicago he found himself struggling with Tuskegee's recurring exigencies, the latest being how to pay Montgomery storekeepers in cash for provisions needed during the upcoming fall term.

Still, Washington had another worry. Not wishing to offend influential whites who were acknowledged friends of the race, he sought to explain why he had failed to fulfill important speaking commitments in Chicago before his scheduled appearance there in September. Ever the diplomat, but with enervating responsibilities, he wrote late in August to one Chicagoan, "I regret it very much and fear they will not appreciate my situation or the condition of the South. It is hard for those away from here to understand matters. The situation is constantly changing and no one knows what the next day will bring."[29] Without a doubt, he probably also readied himself to personally measure the level of success northern blacks had attained in the host city.

The Tuskegeean already had made his mind up on the futility of internecine squabbling over separate exhibits and integrated displays of African American progress, so in Atlanta in 1895, a separate Negro exhibit hall, designed and built by African Americans, would stand first and foremost as an example of his race's accomplishments.[30] This span of time corresponding to the holding of the fair became known in historical circles as the last years of "the Era of Frederick Douglass,"[31] but it was soon to be dubbed "the Era of the Ascendancy of Booker T. Washington." Without a doubt, Washington shone as a man on the rise. In Washington's thinking, and more importantly, in that body of thought most popularly identified with his ascendance to national prominence among both Caucasians and African Americans, the only proper focus for his race was one with self-help, racial pride, and progress through collective racial initiative at its core. Significantly, at any given time of the week, any major spokesman of racial progress, including Frederick Douglass and the Rev. Alexander Crummell, could be heard supporting the benefits of pragmatic institutional separation.[32] Meanwhile, in Tuskegee, Alabama, the Institute's Lady Principal for Girls, Hallie Q. Brown, also busied herself preparing for a trip northward. She had only recently accepted her position in September 1892 and after several months in the Deep South probably felt somewhat isolated in Macon County's most successful and vigilant town. Renowned nationally as an accomplished elocutionist, Brown would have found herself culturally stifled in this rural milieu, but could look forward to a new appointment which she had already negotiated at Wilberforce University near Xenia, Ohio, and which was scheduled to begin at the conclusion of the fair. Never intellectually stagnant regardless of the circumstances, Brown's skills placed her high on the list of attractions wherever she was scheduled to speak, and she would do so several times on the fairgrounds and in various Chicago neighborhood churches. Having pled both for her race's inclusion in the administration of the exposition and for her hiring as a fit guardian of her race's interests, either within the Board of Lady Managers or on some other administrative unit, her name had become well known among prominent whites.

In Mississippi, where the political rights of African Americans had been almost completely eroded in 1890 through sleight-of-hand constitutional means, the black population held fast to the possibility that the American Dream could be attained through economic and educational channels. Meanwhile, the social life of African Americans received the kind of scrutiny reserved for quasi-slaves. Nonetheless, fraternal and secret orders proliferated to meet the special needs of a people undergoing the rapid social change associated with the incipient stages of emancipation.[33] The upcoming world's fair sparked an interest that extended beyond simply preparing for a visit to the fairyland of White City. Actual participation as bona fide citizens seemed possible with the cooperation of fellow Knights of Pythias and Masons already active in host city Chicago.[34] The former planned to send more than one thousand marchers[35] to join in the October 1892 inaugural ceremonies, and the latter organized a national conference.

Still in the Deep South, two Arkansas sharecroppers, George Crawford and Alex Williams, labored long and hard during the planting and cultivating phases of crop production to win a prize of a two-week, all-expense-paid trip to Chicago for the exposition. When the "lay by" period came in August, they claimed their prize and prepared for a deserved respite.[36] The oddity of southern race relations was reflected in the fact that they would travel north in the company of the white family that owned the land they rented. Basically, theirs was a journey north to simply enjoy the wonders of the world as placed on display in Chicago.

As a region, the white South of the Confederacy era fared poorly in representation at the fair. The legislatures of Georgia, Mississippi, North Carolina, South Carolina, Tennessee, and Alabama constructed no pavilions, probably because of the expense involved. They acceded instead to presenting exhibits in the Women's Building. The white women of Texas, Arkansas, Mississippi, and Louisiana despaired of the situation and immediately organized efforts to promote their respective states' interests. Black efforts were deliberately overlooked for being distinct, separate, and obviously unequal to what whites' standards demanded. In the case of Atlanta University, that institution represented the entire state of Georgia, willingly or not. The custodian of Atlanta University exhibit faced this question: "We are not coming from Georgia very much, are we?" One writer for the *Atlanta University Bulletin* described the fairgrounds as awe-inspiring, but in regard to his native state he admitted, "Georgia has no interests here. Having no state building, no pubic school exhibit, nothing in the line of agriculture or minerals or woods, the people of that state naturally care little about it, and those who do come are naturally ashamed of the state."[37] The Cotton States Exposition two years hence would give Georgia and Alabama a better venue to show their progress and gain national attention, thanks to a black Alabamian-by-choice named Washington.

In the northern states, comprising the East and Old Northwest (Midwest) during the antebellum period, life could be as pleasant as it was cruel and oppressive. Accordingly, northern African Americans delineated time in different spans—the Revolutionary era with widespread manumission in New England, the post-Revolutionary phase in which the emancipation thrust spread down the seaboard, the antebellum period that brought race riots, disappointing proscription, and yet hope. During and after the Civil War, the northern experience was replicated by the population of the plains states of the West.

Out in the Far West, the richest black man in America, Montana mine owner Charles P. Grove, with an estimated wealth of $4 million, sought a wife and planned a vacation for both. He chose Chicago so that he and his new bride could jointly see and experience the wonders of the world at their feet.[38] Also by 1893, Detroit-born Pullman porter Jesse Binga, an embodiment of African American restlessness in the era of the "New Negro,"[39] tired of employment in personal service on the 280- to 300-mile train route between Ogden, Utah, north to Pocatello, Idaho, and Butte, Montana. At age twenty-seven, Binga was typical of many African Americans of his generation who were born into freedom and acquired wide-ranging, sometimes insatiable, aspirations extending into many fields of endeavors despite formidable racial constraints. He loved money making, and after a profitable sale of twenty lots in Idaho that probably freed him of his latest debt and possibly provided a small treasury, he departed east for Chicago and the opportunities the fair offered.[40]

In the Mississippi Valley, Missouri became only one of two, or perhaps three, states[41] willing to afford an African American the opportunity to represent the state's citizens at the world's fair. Appointed Commissioner at Large, Hale G. Parker claimed Ohio as his birthplace but St. Louis, Missouri, as his permanent home. His family was comfortably off, thanks to the business and scientific achievements of his father, John Percival Parker, who owned and managed the Phoenix Foundry and Machine Works in southeastern Ohio.[42] A graduate of Oberlin in the liberal arts in 1873, Parker turned his attention to law and attended St. Louis Law School, from which he was graduated in 1882. He subsequently passed the bar in both Missouri and Illinois. At the time of his appointment he served as a high school principal and was well regarded as an administrator. Placed on a path to success early in life, Parker developed a mindset that locked on high achievement as the only acceptable standard for African Americans. In the light of extant circumstances nationally, it would lead him to provocative rhetoric in behalf of racial advancement and isolation from the realities of the day.

Also in Missouri there lived a lesser light in terms of fair politics and racial ideology, but a person recognized in the area of the crafts. He was Gary Price, "one of the most artistic carvers in the country, [who also wa]s preparing to come to the World's Fair" to show off his creations.[43] If any endeavor demonstrated racial advancement in the eyes of whites who would visit the fair, it would be the presentation of craftsmanship.[44]

In Iowa, botanist George Washington Carver contemplated which of his four prize-winning paintings, previously displayed at the Iowa Teachers' Association meeting in the winter of 1892, would accompany him to Chicago. He eventually selected the one he could physically manage best, that being the painting "Yucca gloriosa."[45]

In Illinois, Decatur resident George Price, advertised as "one of the greatest artistic wood carvers in the country," began preparations in spring 1892 to have a cane ready by the time of the fair's opening. Farther north in the state, African Americans in the host city, Chicago, prepared for an intense level of involvement. Dr. Daniel Hale Williams readied himself for his responsibilities as a member of the World's Columbian Congress on Medicine.[46] His close friend, Dr. Charles E. Bentley, had the duty of monitoring all of the dental sessions planned for the summer as part of a national dental congress. S. Laing and Fannie Barrier Williams prepared to open their home to visitors, the eminent voice of Afro-Saxon America, Frederick Douglass, being one such guest. When Douglass resided with any other black resident of the city, it was likely to be Lloyd Garrison Wheeler, merchant-tailor and Ward McAllister or social arbiter of black Chicago, who also readied himself for the festivities.

Had the fair taken place earlier in the city's history—for example, in 1876, along the shores of Lake Michigan instead of in Philadelphia, which entertained America's first world's fair—Chicago's African American citizenry would have had neither an appreciable interest in the event nor the resources to participate. The small size, limited wealth, and lack of occupational differentiation of the population would have relegated it invariably to the sidelines. By contrast, the possibilities of involvement in 1893 seemed nothing short of phenomenal. As the result of a rapidly expanding population with its ranks exceeding 16,000 persons, three times the total for 1876, it exhibited a vital structural differentiation and, with it, a desire among some for participation in the very mainstream of the fair's activities. Importantly, with or without the involvement of the local citizenry, the appetites of African Americans throughout the nation were whetted at the opportunity to show the world their progress since the end of chattel slavery in 1865.

During the post-Reconstruction era or Gilded Age, the nature of race relations seemed to define the possibilities for participation. Racial prejudice assumed such an unusual form in Chicago that transplanted professional Chicagoans from northern climes, such as former upper New York state resident Fannie Barrier Williams, wrote in a national publication that she had "experienced very few evidences of race prejudice and perhaps had more than my share of kindness and recognition."[47] One prominent African American attorney of the early twentieth century could pleasantly recall nearly four decades later that "before the fair in 1893 there was very little prejudice within or between the races."[48] Both recognized problems, but compared to the plight of their southern brethren, they appeared minor and therefore tolerable.

Several factors contributed to this anomaly in American race relations in which racial prejudice and discrimination seemed manageable. Chicago's New England heritage played a major role, earning the city the sobriquet of "sink hole of abolitionism" during the antebellum period. Moreover, the small size of the African American population rendered the group almost invisible in the midst of a perpetual population boom associated with rapid European immigration and its slow assimilation.

Chicago on the eve of the fair was truly an immigrant's city in terms of its demographics, but a WASP enclave in terms of its immense wealth and power. If any non-WASP group caught the dominant group's immediate attention and its subsequent public wrath, it was the Irish and then the Germans. Likewise, when the WASPs' sense of noblesse oblige was awakened, as it was in 1889, a Hull House could result. During a time of labor-capital confrontation, while the immigrants engaged in revolutionary or reform efforts aimed at ameliorating their economic plight, the ostracism of African Americans from a political economy that was built on an industrial and commercial base eliminated the possibility of interracial labor conflict or cooperation. In the world's largest livestock market, which was compressed into a single square mile containing a work force of 20,000, a solitary African American found employment by 1890. According to Herbst, "the few [African Americans] who entered the larger packing houses in the early nineties introduced no elements of conflict or competition. Negro butchers were an oddity; even unskilled Negro laborers were few. To stand beside a black man was an unfamiliar experience which at first created an element of curiosity and interest rather than of conflict."[49]

In this setting, it is not surprising that both races appraised race relations during this period as relatively free of the virulence found in the South. Historian Rayford W. Logan's research on the Chicago media revealed a press that accorded the African Americans of the city a level of basic humane consideration, if not a modicum of respect, which differed from their proscribed status nationally.[50] This research confirmed the observations of the *Chicago Conservator*, the leading paper among Chicago's African Americans, that "Chicago was a pretty fair place for Negroes to live and that there was little friction between the races."[51] An examination of the careers of some of the more successful and prosperous African American professionals illustrates a similar evolution. Dr. Daniel Hale Williams trained under a white physician, had an interim practice among whites, and later distinguished himself at Provident Hospital and Washington, D.C.'s Freedmen's Hospital. Attorney Edward H. Wilson trained under a noted white lawyer and later distinguished himself in Chicago's courts. Dr. Charles Edwin Bentley was welcomed into the all-white Chicago dental profession, and soon laid claim to a mixed, but predominantly white, clientele in the downtown area called the Loop.

When Illinois passed a Civil Rights Act in 1885 that guaranteed access to public accommodations throughout the city and state to all its citizens, it lent additional credit to its reputation as the land in which Lincoln's spirit of tolerance lived. Notably, the Act's introduction had been the work of an African American legislator, J. W. E. Thomas, who represented a racially mixed district in Chicago. In general, the high level of racial tolerance at the polls paved the way for African American election to political office, there being "too few [African Americans] to elect a county or town official if race lines had been drawn as tightly then."[52]

For the average African American, racial exclusion was the rule in employment, but not in housing, education, and social interchange among persons in similar economic circumstances. Chicago's municipal work force included four African Americans on the police department in 1886, twenty-three by 1894. The Fire Department employed one all-black unit, Company 21, which was headed by a white officer and situated immediately south of the Loop. In education, the Chicago Public Schools system permanently opened its doors to all youngsters in 1874.

Residential restrictions by law did not exist, so there was no "ghetto," even though African Americans clustered in an elongated pattern extending south from the Loop. Lucy Parsons, "Black Lucy," the widow of Arthur Parsons, who was executed as a Haymarket Square conspirator, lived on the north side among the German population. Many working class African Americans, such as the family of Wiley Cherry, lived on the west side adjacent to Italians along what was to become the Lake Street corridor with the completion of the elevated line in 1896. Virtually the entire city was open to African Americans, who also lived in enclaves and in its "suburbs" before Chicago's massive territorial annexation in 1889. Public parks were legally open to all citizens, with constraints being contingent on neighborhood preferences and hostilities. Both parties opened their ranks to African Americans, with the bulk claiming an allegiance to the Republican Party because of the Lincoln aura.

As to social matters, especially social interchange, the words of one of the South's most famous world's fair visitors, offered two years after the fair, rang with remarkable perception. In all things purely social, African Americans were free to enjoy the intricacies of their subculture. Their separate churches, lodges, fraternal orders, literary societies, clubs, and the like did not offend whites and provided them, just like their ethnic, immigrant counterparts, a source of individual and group solace. But in all things of benefit to the metropolis as a whole, such as providing a labor base or enjoying the diversions of the fair, they were expected to participate.

In northern Ohio's fabled Western Reserve, the *Cleveland Gazette* reported regularly on Chicago African Americans and preparations for the fair, from the prices of excursions to the availability of south side housing. With a distribution within Chicago combined with its coverage of the activities of African Americans throughout the Buckeye State, the *Gazette* bound the African American community closer and closer together. To the southeast, at Wilberforce University in the town sharing the same name, faculty, staff, and students prepared for their summer sojourn 300 miles west to Chicago. A.M.E. church luminaries Right Reverend Daniel A. Payne, Chancellor at Payne Seminary across the road and affiliated with Wilberforce, and Right Reverend Benjamin A. Arnett, D.D., president of Wilberforce, saw the exposition as an opportunity to convince the nation of the value of higher education for African American youth through demonstrated scholarship and professional pursuits such as taxidermy and geology. In the meantime, Professor of Classics William Scarborough prepared to pack while thinking about a paper he would deliver for Bishop Tanner on black journalistic accomplishments. For Scarborough and the others, the wind-cooled shores of Lake Michigan offered a delightful summer substitute for the isolation and humidity of the Miami Valley.

Little more than a two-hour carriage ride away, along winding roads, across creeks, and over bridges, lay Dayton where aspiring poet Paul Lawrence Dunbar happily accepted his assignment from the *Dayton Herald* to write a column called "Dayton at the Fair." Although his task was minor, it afforded him the chance to journey to a place where big dreams were realized more quickly than in small-town Dayton. Chicago seemed to be attracting more and more Daytonians, and Dunbar's brother and sister-in-law also made plans to travel north. "Eugenie Griffin, one of Paul's many girl friends, began boasting that she was going to Chicago, too, and that her relatives there would introduce her to big-city Negro society."[53] With his mother's blessings and big dreams, Dunbar headed northward.

In the Empire State, African Americans also readied themselves, preparing to participate as fully as possible. The rural village of Brockport straddled the Erie Canal to which it owed its birth, snuggled firmly in the "burned over" district of upper New York state. There, thirty or more miles west of Rochester, and with less than 1,000 inhabitants, its first and, for a short period, only African American family, the Barriers—mother, son, and daughter—lived. Proud patriarch A. J. had died in 1892. The remaining family members now eagerly anticipated the news of daughter and sibling Fannie Barrier Williams's proud involvement in the operations of the fair. Significantly, she held the distinction of being scheduled to speak at two of the most important of a myriad of international conferences at the fair. No other African American was scheduled to lecture in two major conferences. So it was not inappropriate to consider her one of the most prominent African Americans, regardless of gender, to represent the race at host city Chicago. Barrier made preparations to speak in September 1893 before the World's Parliament of Religions on the subject, "What Can Religion Do to Advance the Condition of the American Negro?" and, at the World's Congress of Representative Women, on the topic, "The Intellectual Progress of the Colored Women of the United States since the Emancipation Proclamation."

Moreover, zealously attempting to contribute to the uplift of the women of her race in April 1893, Williams tackled the seemingly impossible task of coordinating the myriad desires of her group as they planned exhibits on the fairgrounds. Whether because of her temperament, background, education, and appearance, or in spite of them, she won a prized appointment as "Clerk in charge of Colored Interests in the Department of Publicity and Promotion."[54] As the only African American holding any type of administrative appointment in the operations of the fair, and with a salary of $50 per month, the position's strategic placement might have appeared at the time to overshadow its paltry compensation and clerical features. Foremost, it allowed monitoring of the role African American women would assume at the fair, and Williams was committed to insure that and a minimizing of any intended exclusion.

Holding this position also allowed Williams the opportunity to mold, in a limited sense to be sure, the image of her emerging group. So stark were economic conditions that the lot of African American women stood in dismal contrast even to the demoralizing status of their gender counterparts within the race. African American men worked in menial positions and endured chain gangs, but they also won elective offices in political races and secured appointive ones in government after defeat or retirement. Moreover, in the growing professional pool, men dominated everywhere. In juxtaposition, racism and oppressive economic forces relegated 90 percent of African American women in 1890 to agricultural and domestic service nationally.

Three hundred miles to the east of the somnolent hamlet of Brockport, with its bragging rights to a native citizen's world's fair involvement, lay frenetic Manhattan. Pre-Harlem, pre-annexation (1898) New York City of the

1890s encompassed only the island of Manhattan. Its diasporan population of West Indians, old-time New Yorkers, and recent southern migrants totaled 20,000 in 1880. With continuous inmigration and the consolidation of the five boroughs of Queens, Bronx, Brooklyn, Staten Island, and Manhattan, it reached 60,000 by 1900. Despite Manhattan's centuries'-long prominence, most well-to-do black families claimed Brooklyn as home immediately following the Civil War draft riots of 1863; however, some semblance of the elite's influence was also felt in Manhattan.[55] For this group, the summer of 1893 loomed on the horizon, forming a part of the mysteries and dreams that shaped their childhoods. Expectations they forged about the fair might differ by degree, but not dramatically in substance, from those of others of their race by region, class, generation, and education: They envisioned the world as seeing and accepting a new image of the Colored race.

Of the social elements within the African American population most diligently endeavoring to showcase the progress of their race in Chicago, the *refined* "400" and the churchgoing *respectables* led the way. Collectively sensing the opportunity at hand, African Americans secured a seat on the New York Board of Women Managers in 1892 for Miss Joan Imogene Howard, and actively supported Howard's effort to accumulate exhibit items showing the intellectual and material progress made by the Colored women of New York state. Howard began immediately to travel throughout the state in her free time to collect a massive display of exhibits for the Women's Building, the only one that either African American women or men nationally would mount. When she was not engaged in her personal, extensive travel, "she sent written and printed appeals all over the state to arouse the women of her race to a knowledge of the importance of the occasion."[56] By pedigree, academic preparation, and personal resolve, New York state's finished product validated the faith New York placed in Howard and the effectiveness of her efforts.

Historian Willard Gatewood wrote, "The Howards were an old and highly respected Boston family whose members had figured prominently in the Underground Railroad and in the city's cultural and social life in the antebellum era."[57] Her brother was the well-known, Harvard-trained physician Dr. Edwin C. Howard, of Philadelphia Boulé fame. With her parents' encouragement she attended Girls High and Normal School in her native Boston, the first of her race to do so. After graduation, she quickly entered the teaching field in Boston and then moved to New York City. She continued teaching and in 1892 was graduated from the New York University with her degree of Master of Pedagogy.[58]

For the New York City theatrical crowd in mid-Manhattan's "Black Bohemia," a trip to Chicago meant a chance to reunite with the cast of "The Creole Show," which had been performing before white audiences since 1891 at white owner Sam T. Jack's Opera House in the downtown area. The Creoles, as the cast members were designated, presented a new phase in black theater life that moved beyond minstrelsy and the plantation to modern scenes, dance, dialogue, and costumes.[59]At the offices of the fledgling eight-year-old *New York Age,* T. Thomas Fortune pondered the contents of a speech he was to deliver at the Congress on Africa, also known as the Congress on the Negro, scheduled for August. As an opponent of African emigration, which to his dismay was gaining increasing popularity among the masses, he sought a persuasive argument to combat it. National leaders besides Frederick Douglass made plans to visit the city. Former Mississippi Senator Blanche K. Bruce and former Virginia Congressman John Mercer Langston joined the throngs heading to "White City," the Midway, and the enlarged environs of the Windy City.

It could be imagined that in Boston what remained of the Howard family and friends busied themselves for a visit to Chicago to see in actuality the fruits of kinswoman and friend Imogene's endeavors of the past year or so. Meanwhile, in Philadelphia, Florence A. Lewis prepared to view the results of her joint efforts with other Pennsylvanians on the Woman's Auxiliary Committee.[60] One certainty had to be evident: given the rising consciousnesses of race and class among these African Americans living in the older eastern cities, their participation was a foregone conclusion.

Across the Atlantic, two emerging voices of twentieth century African American leadership concerned themselves with the spate of activities and opportunities that existed abroad. In Germany, twenty-five-year-old W. E. B. Du Bois busied himself with his studies after having arrived there in August 1892. Having completed his doctorate at Harvard, he sought a more highly prized possession, a "coveted Heidelberg or Berlin doctorate[, the] ultimate seal of professional standing, a personal triumph and a racial marvel."[61] While his fascination with things German dominated his thinking, even to the point of encouraging African American academicians to emulate his exposure to invigorating Western European thought, many of them would be absorbing elements of a similar experience in Chicago.[62] Du Bois' intellectually rewarding stay in Germany was, at least in his mind at the time, nothing other than preparation for his contribution to liberate his race. As he celebrated his twenty-fifth birthday away from home, he reflected, "I am striving to make my life all that life might be—and I am limiting that strife only in so far as that strife is incompatible with others of my brothers and sisters making their lives similar. The crucial question now is where that limit comes. . . . I therefore take the world that the Unknown lay in my hands & work for the rise of the Negro peo-ple, taking for granted that their best development means the best development of the world."[63]

Meanwhile, in the British Isles, journalist Ida B. Wells of Memphis and New York City lectured as part of a racial mission to expose the American barbarity of lynching to a receptive, influential British audience. Such was her passion for the struggle that had to be waged in behalf of her race in the United States on the fairgrounds that she counted the days before her anti-lynching crusade would conclude. Significantly, according to Paula Giddings, it was "her antilynching campaign [that] not only helped launch the modern civil rights movement, but brought black women into the forefront of the struggle for black and women's rights."[64]

A model of principled thought and behavior related to Wells's deep Christian beliefs, and she instinctively balanced those attributes against her impetuosity and zeal used in the cause of societal righteousness. But in pursuit of justice she always distinguished herself more as the pragmatist than the ideologue. Finally, sometime in the spring, she boarded a steamer for home so that she would not miss the entire fair. She arrived in Chicago in late June.[65]

Everywhere throughout black America a like-mindedness evidenced itself, facilitated through an extensive network of churches, bonded loosely by conference and associational affiliations, newspapers, fraternal orders, national women's and men's groups, constant travel over the nation's extensive rail system, along with national civil rights organizations such as the Afro-American League and the Colored Men's Protective Association. Overcoming regional differences began to seem feasible as a mounting sense of national excitement cascaded to the heights of euphoria.

2

PARTICIPATION AND PROTEST

*The most effective weapon [against racism] in the present
emergency is participation. . . . The most common form of
defense is, "I am not going where I am not wanted." Of all
the pernicious policies, this one is most responsible for proscription on account of color and servitude. In it lurks the
poisonous germ of an engrossing sociability which is allowed
to trespass upon the domain of education . . . religion . . .
business, and to swallow up the serious duty and necessity
of the hour. Standing behind this shibboleth, many men
move forward or backward at the bidding of a [white] smile
or frown. Manhood dances to the caprice of the weathercock,
and colonization by choice is the logical result.*

> —Hale G. Parker, Alternate Commissioner
> at Large (Missouri), National Board of
> Commissioners, December 1892

*Members of the race, only 30 years removed from the status
of slavery, felt keenly that proud America's record of achievements and progress could not be completed unless it included on history's impeachable scroll the matchless triumph
of the former slave. The Race, however, from the start was
doomed to bitter disappointment, for during the preliminary
arrangements [emphasis added] our people were given to understand that so far as active participation by them was concerned they were "outside the pale."*

> —Albert G. Barnett, *Chicago Defender*, 1933

THE NATIONAL EFFORT TO ENSURE FULL AFRICAN AMERICAN PARTICIPATION AT THE FAIR

In a remarkable series of maneuvers for a group only two decades removed from bondage, African American men and women sought inclusion at
the national level in this international event of monumental historical impor-

tance. Well-educated and highly trained persons were in the vanguard of this effort, which appeared to assume the stature of a movement, as early as 1888. They announced to white America that they had indeed arrived at a level at which they could legitimately demand full participation in the fair's operations. This gesture, however, represented more than an attempt at satisfying a collective group ego. It signified organized self-affirmation of achievement under the most grueling of circumstances that usually demanded recognition by whites in leadership positions. Against the obstacles of gender and race, African Americans were poised not just to confront but to overcome the discrimination that they had encountered throughout their nearly three centuries in America. This social elite, residing not only in Chicago but throughout the nation, gained the support of middle-class, respectable citizens to initially press for representation in strategic matters affecting the shape of the fair, specifically in decision-making and planning.

Although the direct descendants of slaves who, slightly over two decades previously, were excluded from the pinnacles of power, this generation easily pinpointed the locus of power from which African Americans could best attain the "just representation" at the fair to which they felt entitled. With experience in Reconstruction-era politics during which time they held seats in both the U.S. Senate and House of Representatives, their strategy led them to the nation's capital. In Washington, petitioning and lobbying served as their major tactical approaches. They based their claim to representation as a distinct group on more than two centuries of unrewarded toil along with an unwavering loyalty to the highest ideals of the nation. From coast to coast, they were convinced of the rightness of their cause. Channeling their initial efforts at the office of the chief executive who authorized the holding of a world's fair, and then to the Congress, which appropriated money for its support, they were prepared to persevere.

In March 1889, President Benjamin Harrison assumed office, and, rightly or wrongly, immediately drew the ire of African Americans because of his all-white choices for membership on the National Board of Commissioners, the governing board of the fair. The African American leadership perceived a reluctance on Harrison's part to champion the cause of racial fairness on the issue of representation. Yet, upon cursory examination, Harrison's record on race relations appeared impressive, if not exemplary. He had soothed the leading African American politicians through his political appointments, while he vigorously pursued the rights of African Americans, personally sponsoring the Federal Elections Bill and Federal Education Bill. However, historian George B. Sinkler found that the president tended to act on matters of race with great circumspection, being aware that the nation had embraced a near contentious, if not overtly hostile, Social Darwinian attitude.

Harrison so angered some Indiana black Republicans that by the summer of 1891 former U.S. Senator Blanche K. Bruce of Mississippi was forced to journey to Indianapolis to restore political tranquility. A loyal party man, Bruce ended up praising Harrison in the most lavish of terms, lauding him as a party leader who "has done more for us than any President ever has done," and railing against "a few disappointed individuals . . . who have been given nothing [in the way of appointments]."[1]

With this backdrop, appointments to the highly prestigious Board would have involved the president in choosing African Americans over their socially scrambling Caucasian counterparts. Any hesitation that he exhibited probably had more to do with his reluctance to challenge the covetousness of his friends and party favorites in a time of spoils politics and social climbing than anything else. In a period described by historian Rayford W. Logan as "the nadir in American life," Harrison also proved vulnerable to southern racial etiquette and "lily-whitism" as well as northern class elitism.

Harrison's first missed opportunity occurred in 1890 when he failed to intervene in the appointments of representatives to fill a National Board of Commissioners which would be responsible for administering the fair. Each state and territory selected two delegates along with alternates to this body, which also included eight delegates at large. In addition, one alternate was appointed for every commissioner. Their all-male ranks would total 208 members. In a complicated structure reflecting the national aspect of the fair, individual states and territories had as much input on the granting of positions from which decisions were made as they had over appointments to key boards for men and women. From the African American perspective, Ferdinand L. Barnett examined the scenario: "The Colored people of our country number over seven and one half millions. In two of the states of the south the colored population exceeds the white population, and so far as the productive energy of the southern states is concerned, almost the entire output of agricultural products is the work of Negro labor. The colored people therefore thought that their numbers, more than one eighth of the entire population of the country, would entitle them to one Commissioner at Large, and that their importance as a labor factor in the South would secure for them fair representation among the Commissioners appointed from the states."[2] Despite their efforts and hopes, when African American men sought representation on the national board, it was not until 1892 that they realized any success. A lone African American was appointed as part of the Missouri delegation to serve as an alternate member on the national board. St. Louis high school principal and attorney Hale Parker was the choice; this coincided with the end of the Republican Party convention when promises made invariably had to be kept.

Parker, to his credit, had lobbied previously for total inclusion on terms most African Americans could accept. Nevertheless, with his appointment, certain African Americans remained dissatisfied with their group's role at the fair. Rejecting the idea of being swallowed up into a melting pot, they envisioned an identification extolling their distinctiveness. This notion appeared as anathema to Afro-Saxons who saw their future insured best in a color-blind yet egalitarian nation. For his part, Parker lambasted his fellow blacks for exhorting racial pride and a racial destiny as viable means to achieve the end of full recognition as American citizens.

Previously, an aroused African American citizenry had lobbied both houses of Congress. Intense pressure was exerted both through the offices of three sitting African American members of Congress in the House of Representatives and through selected white representatives. Of the former group, Henry P. Cheatham of North Carolina served during the 51st and 52nd Congresses (December 2, 1889–March 3, 1893). Two other Southerners, the well-known John Mercer Langston of Virginia and Thomas Miller of South Carolina, served almost identical terms between September 23, 1890, and March 3, 1891. (Both were disputants over election returns and lost a portion of their terms during the 51st session of Congress.) Of the three, Cheatham did most to protect African American interests during the proposed world's fair. When he attempted to act, however, more high-profile issues thwarted his efforts. A Democratic tumult over a Republican-sponsored National Election Act to protect African American rights submerged Cheatham's bill to pay for an exhibit on Negro art, industry, and agriculture. "It seems that whenever the Colored people of this country ask for anything," he lamented, "something unfortunately intervenes to hinder their getting what they ask."[3]

Additional pressure came through petitions and direct pleas from white congressmen at the time Chicago sought an additional $5 million to finance the fair. In 1892, a spate of bills appeared calling for black representation through federally sponsored exhibits. On July 15, in the Senate, the petition of thirty organizations, including that of Baltimorean Thomas L. Hall, Right Worthy Grand Supreme Ruler, Order of Galileans, requested that "the appropriations for the World's Columbian Exposition be withheld unless ample provision be made for the representation of the colored people's interest at said Exposition." The next day in the House, an Iowa congressman submitted a resolution from Chicagoans "urging that $200,000 be set apart by Congress for the purpose of gathering statistics of the colored race." In August, in the House, another white congressman presented a petition from the bishops of the A.M.E. Church and the A.M.E.Z. Church requesting that "the moral, intellectual, and industrial progress and development of the colored people during the first quarter century of their freedom should be made to form a part of the Government exhibit at the World's Fair."[4]

Not all efforts emanating throughout the nation reached the halls of the Capitol, but an extensive network of interest developed among African Americans that found its strength in local and regional activities. According to Cassell, "as early as 1890 a Colored World's Fair Association had been incorporated in Georgia with the purpose of assembling an exhibit at Jackson Park. . . . In March 1891 black leaders from Virginia and North Carolina convened in Norfolk, and passed resolutions supporting their idea of a separate black exhibit."[5] In the end, nothing tangible came from these efforts, but they did alert many people to the growing influence and potential power of African Americans.

At the point that African American men could not gain the fullest representation they sought for their race, the mantle of leadership in this matter of perceived racial entitlement voluntarily passed to the women. It seemed by design and indicated acknowledgment among some African Americans of a once latent, but now potent, ideological agenda that progressive elements of both genders could endorse. That African American women acted both collaboratively across the chasm of gender and separately when responding to particularistic gender interests merely attested to the decade of the 1890s as an era of feminist/womanist agency.

The genesis and onset of black feminism can be delineated clearly in the post-Reconstruction era. It incubated as African American women began to articulate a need for redefining themselves. Maligned, along with their men, by whites who adhered to Victorian-era sexual standards, some of these women reasoned that the salvation of the race's image, and ultimately of the race itself, would come only through women assuming vanguard status for their race's liberation. While recent scholarship has questioned both the possibility and feasibility of cross-gender cooperation at a time when the exploitation of black women seemed to be in the combined interests of white males, white females, and sometimes black males,[6] these women deliberately set out on a course of their own.

Both Paula Giddings and Evelyn Brooks Higginbotham located this attitude in the writings of educator Anna Julia Cooper, who spoke these telling words: "Only the BLACK WOMAN can say 'when and where I enter, in the quiet, undisputed dignity of my womanhood, without violence and without suing or special patronage, then and there the whole . . . race enters with me.'"[7] Giddings elaborates:

> [Because of their] experience [as] black women [they knew all too well] the relationship between sexism and racism. Because both are motivated by similar economic, social, and psychological forces, it is only logical that those who sought to undermine Blacks were also the most virulent antifeminists. The means of oppression differed across race and sex lines, but the wellspring of that oppression was the same. Black women understood this dynamic. . . . Of course, Black women could understand the relationship between racism and sexism because they had to strive against both. In doing so they became the linchpin between two of the most important social reform movements in American history: the struggles for Black rights and women's rights. . . . Throughout their history, Black women also understood the relationship between the progress of the race and their own feminism. Women's rights were an empty promise if Afro-Americans were crushed under the heel of a racist power structure. In times of racial militancy, Black women threw their considerable energies into that struggle—even at the expense of their feminist yearnings. However, when militancy faltered, Black women stepped forward to demand the rights of their race from the

broader society, and *their* rights as women from their men. The latter demand was not seen in the context of race *versus* sex, but as one where their rights had to be secured in order to assure black progress.[8]

Thus, the history of African American women at the World's Columbian Exposition was basically one of cooperation with their racial and gender counterparts. For example, an advisory panel of seven men, including Dr. Daniel Hale Williams of Provident Hospital and lawyer-publicist Ferdinand L. Barnett, supported the Woman's Columbian Auxiliary Association. Further, analysis of the "Aim and Plan of Action" of the Woman's Columbian Auxiliary Association indicates that this organization subordinated gender to group advancement as it took a "race first, gender second" position.[9] Underscoring this fact, the opening paragraph alone contains five references to the importance of advancing the race above all other considerations. With a strategic advantage based on geography, the women of host city Chicago proffered their agenda for inclusive representation and a Negro exhibit as early as November 1890.[10] After a successful mass meeting at Bethesda Baptist Church, the Woman's Columbian Association, led by Mrs. Lettie Trent, a schoolteacher, was organized. Importantly, it appears to have been formed without elite support. These African American women first sought seats on the Board of Lady Managers, a body organized in March 1890 after successful protest activities by white women against gender discrimination by white males. Second, along with policy-making involvement, they proposed an exhibit to demonstrate racial progress since emancipation. Finally, they proposed the employment of African Americans in quasi-administrative or clerical positions at the women's headquarters on the fairgrounds. Within several weeks, the Woman's Columbian Auxiliary Association, led by Mrs. R. D. Boone, organized, representing the second major group led by African American women. This group had more substantive backing.

The timing at first seemed to favor these black women who sought a sympathetic hearing, since the white women had already won their battle over equality of representation in administering the fair. Their separate approaches, on the other hand, merely augured trouble in the future. With victory in hand over the "dominant sex," the white women split into two groups, with one segment, which sought complete equality between the sexes, pitted against the other, which sought autonomy for women within the domestic sphere. Identified respectively as the Queen Isabella Association or Society, and the Chicago Women's Department, these groups had organized within two months of each other in August and October 1889. The former was reformist, but in comparison to the latter appeared thoroughly militant as it advocated an activist role for women. The "New Women" of the 1890s found their home at the fair, but it would not be a comfortable one.

After political maneuvering, the narrow-based Chicago group led by Bertha Honore Palmer, wife of the Chicago retail and hotel tycoon Potter Palmer, assumed hegemony over the Board. The Chicago Women's Department, under Palmer's control, virtually represented her kingdom, or queendom. Conceding the necessity for compromise, she agreed to expand Board membership to include two female delegates and two alternates from each state and territory, as well as from the District of Columbia, and eight members at large. As president, Palmer immediately filled the Board with nine prominent white women from the Chicago area. As to the Board's final composition, the names of Susan B. Anthony and Jane Addams were conspicuously absent.[11]

Promoting Palmer's ideological bent, the Board espoused the cause of enlarging the women's sphere. Part of what Palmer and her faction wanted was an emphasis on the total productivity of women worldwide. In industry, in the home, and in the sciences and arts, the productions of women were featured in a building especially designed by and for them. Assessed by posterity, "the Board of Lady Managers celebrated the beauty and techniques of the more traditional handiwork of women."[12] The locus of this exemplary showing by women was their own building on the fairgrounds, designed by a female architect and filled with the material evidence of women's contributions to societies and progress around the globe.

In addition to the struggle in the larger world of gender conflict, Palmer responded to the wishes of Chicago's white "400" and their associates, comprised primarily of upper and upper middle class women who thrived outside the professions and political involvements. As an upwardly mobile white female married to one of the city's three major civic movers, Bertha Honore Palmer cherished her social power and her upcoming role as unofficial American Queen of the Exposition. Fittingly, Badger has referred to her as the "Lady Astor of the Middle West."[13] At this point the African American women approached the Board for inclusion, but a recognition based primarily on race and not gender. Energized to advance as individuals with control over their domestic affairs, these white women regarded the matter of requests from a proscribed group very lightly.[14] Concerns of minority group advancement failed to impress these social climbers and the social cost of shunting the African American women to the side was minimal during an era of both racial and material self-indulgence.

While white women split into ideological camps along the fault line of gender self-definition, African American women, already committed across gender lines with black men on the need for racial advancement, divided too. However, their division was procedural, over the best course to take for racial representation. Would it be as a separate, distinctive group, or as part of the mainstream of American society? Lettie Trent sought a separate exhibit in the spirit of promoting racial distinctiveness in a nation and world where race mattered all too much. Her husband, Hannibal H. Trent, had joined an enterprising group of African Americans who organized under the banner of the World's Fair Committee of Colored Men and who planned to transport thousands of excursionists to Chicago.[15] Also, Trent had shown a willingness to work through a white woman with strong liberal credentials, Mary Logan.[16] Mrs. Boone expressed an opposite position, showing the complexity of the issue, to Mrs. Palmer and the Board of Lady Managers: "We do not in any way suggest a separate department in the coming exposition, but we do believe there is a field of labor among the colored people, in which members of the race can serve with special effectiveness and success."[17]

Both of these Chicago-based African-American women's groups seemed directly reflective of the personalities and status of their leaders, so disagreements erupted almost naturally. Boone appeared to be the more acceptable culturally to Palmer and her friends. She was supported by an advisory panel of seven, including Dr. Daniel Hale Williams, Ferdinand L. Barnett, Mrs. J. C. Plummer, and an overall organizational membership of one hundred persons.[18] Less assertive in tone than Trent, Boone appeared to be more aware of African American traits, tendencies, and conditions that the Palmer group discerned in everyday life throughout the nation. Her approach was the cautious one usually reflective of the Afro-Saxons. She ultimately wished to ride on the boat, but was unwilling to rock it.

Boone's organization proposed to represent "the earnest efforts of Colored women who desire to secure for the coming World's Exposition the best possible representation of art, science, industry and various achievements of the colored race." The group believed in self-help and evinced its sense of agency by stating, "The race must work for itself: we must originate our own plans of action and depend upon no one else to make our exhibit . . . it cannot expect the American white people to expend their energy and tax their best efforts to help any one class of American citizens . . . [despite prejudice against us] we are most satisfied if we are allowed a fair field in which to direct our efforts."[19] As to the question, "shall we have a separate exhibit or shall our work take its place in the department in which it belongs? Upon this question the Association takes no uncertain stand. We are unalterably opposed to a separate exhibit."

What is most important, Trent exhibited a single-mindedness in regard to purpose that found its match only in the persona of a prominent visitor from Memphis in 1893, Ida B. Wells.[20] She also evidently appeared to whites as a sometimes baffled racial advocate. Moreover, she lacked the acceptable social credentials to get even a preliminary consideration from Mrs. Palmer and her cohorts. Her base of institutional support seemed to lie among the respectables, and as such she was always in danger of not gaining white recognition. The simple matter of failing to own a telephone in an age when status was conferred by such a possession, along with two undeliverable telegrams to her south side address, would also serve to irritate Mrs. Palmer and her staff.[21]

Much to the dismay of the African American women, the intense level of intraracial parochialism apparently provided the perfect excuse for their eventual exclusion by Palmer and her supporters. There were now four African American women's groups talking with Palmer. Coupled with Palmer's suspicions that white women in opposition to her leadership were helping the black women, the chances of inclusion continued to dwindle just as economic resources did.[22] Bertha Honore Palmer, southern-born and intimately aware of that region's racial protocol, first suggested that the interests of African Americans could be just as well served by white representatives already on the Board who were sympathetic to African American interests. Palmer subsequently relied on Mary Cecil Cantrell of Kentucky, her major supporter for the presidency of the Board of Lady Managers. In the greatest of ironies, a white southern woman from a former slave-holding state sought to represent black women who, in turn, saw themselves as speaking for the entirety of a proscribed race recently liberated from bondage. The gap between African American expectations and Caucasian arrogance was exemplified by these exchanges. One letter read: "[A]s I have lived in the South (in New Orleans) all my life, [I] have always been friendly to them," and one Board member interviewed an Atlanta railroad station matron to ascertain black wishes.[23]

In another irony, Palmer, installed and sustained amid contention between competing white women's groups, cited disagreement between the two African American groups as a major reason why, along with her distaste for promoting racial distinctiveness, the request of the black women could not be met at the national level. According to Palmer, "Nearly all of our members thought that it would be making a distinction which the Negroes themselves would not want, as there was no reason why their exhibit should not be collected and entered in the general collection."[24]

While African Americans were charging exclusion, they were relying on their truest white friends, found in the personages of Phoebe Couzins, Isabella Beecher Hooker, Mary Logan, widow of Civil War hero General John Logan, and a handful of others of the abolitionist stripe. These women readily spoke out against the exclusion. Formally, the Board of Lady Managers responded with an explanation that they had not intended to be discriminatory. Replying only to the charge that they discriminated on the opportunity to place an exhibit as opposed to opening a seat on the Board of Lady Managers, the white women cited the improbability of such an occurrence: "It can be readily seen that this action would not only be unjust but would be impossible to carry into effect, as it can not be known whether applicants for space are white or colored unless they voluntarily reveal their identity." They continued, "It may be definitely stated that the Board of Lady Managers has no desire to make any such discrimination. It is endeavoring to show the work of industrial women for all countries without discrimination as to race or color, and it will certainly feel an especial interest in securing such a representation from the colored women of the country as will fully illustrate their rapid advancement since the emancipation of their race."[25]

Palmer on another occasion did suggest that the African American women seek representation on the state boards. The fairness of the Empire State and the perseverance of one New York City resident, Miss Joan Imogene

Howard, resulted in her gaining a seat on the New York Board of Women Managers. The outcome of her successful efforts in behalf of the women of that state will be discussed in chapter 7.

Efforts by individuals who lived outside Chicago complemented the activities of organized groups, both in the host city and elsewhere in the nation, to meet the black agenda. As early as October 1891, Wilberforce College instructor Hallie Q. Brown sought a paid position, seeking the aid of former President Hayes.[26] She also had Palmer's support because of her "intelligence and her 'dramatic and telling' rhetoric," but the resources necessary to pay for her full-time position never materialized.[27] Shortly thereafter, in December 1891, Fannie Barrier Williams of Chicago "argued logically and eloquently" before the world's fair National Board of Control for two positions to be filled by African Americans to oversee the display of exhibits.[28] For this action, taken individually, Williams incurred the wrath of Trent's Women's Columbian Association.[29]

Meeting a series of early and late rebuffs, the women eventually enjoyed only the slightest of success in these efforts. After a four-year struggle, two African American women acquired positions of note; both were Chicagoans. Mrs. A. M. Curtis had previously served as solicitor for Provident Hospital where her husband was surgeon. Once hired by the Board of Lady Managers, she filled an office position, being assigned "a desk in Mrs. Palmer's office." Her responsibilities included securing adequate space and locations for African American exhibits and communicating matters of interest to black citizens throughout the nation. Described as a "woman of remarkable intelligence and energy," she benefited from her reputation of providing civic leadership and humanitarian aid to the African American community.[30] Within two months, however, she left her position and was succeeded by Fannie Barrier Williams, whose tenure was also of brief duration. Williams, described as a "handsome and refined colored woman," had a background similar to Curtis's which included an affiliation with Provident Hospital and marriage to a professional man, Attorney S. Laing Williams. In their efforts, these men and women laid the groundwork for further African American involvement at the fair once it opened.

THE PROTEST AGAINST INJUSTICE AT THE FAIR

Before the fair opened in May 1893 a small group of African American journalists, imbued with a sense of mission fervently buttressed by ideology, became convinced that only an international declaration would suffice to carry their grievances against the American nation. Frederick Douglass and Ida B. Wells proposed publication[31] of a pamphlet explaining their racial complaints and assumed leadership of the four-person team of publicists, which now included I. Garland Penn and Ferdinand L. Barnett. They viewed the fair as their window of opportunity, and from these circumstances emanated the idea for a controversial pamphlet highlighting injustices entitled *The Reason Why the Colored American Is Not in the Columbian World's Exposition.*

Along with Douglass's articulate disapproval from the very beginning of the fair, expressed in both speeches and written statements—the assimilationist African American position on race relations in general and African American hopes in particular—the pamphlet was to set the tone for civil rights advocacy in the twentieth century. Not all African Americans, however, agreed that it should see the light of day. Two countermovements emerged, one headed by newspaper editors, the other by persons of a more gradualist persuasion who hesitated to offend powerful whites, especially in the North. Both challenged the need for such a statement at such a time and questioned the motives of the writers.

One Pine Bluff, Arkansas, writer stated: "The world likes heroism, and it appears to me that the proposed memorial would be too much upon the order of a whine to have the desired effect. Our condition and the wrongs that are imposed upon us cannot be altogether unknown to the masses of noted visitors expected at the World's Fair."[32] He suggested instead showing the world the African American's ability to rise above segregation and discrimination through the presentation of impressive exhibits. The editor of the *Indianapolis Freeman* advised Douglass to use his national credentials to prepare a statement to the American people, which he was sure the Associated Press would carry. Or, he suggested, Douglass could write to the president and recapitulate the race's grievances.[33] As opposition accompanied by disinterest mounted, fundraising for the pamphlet languished. Ida B. Wells blamed herself in July 1893 for her tardy return to America to promote the pamphlet, but the fault lay with the message, not the messenger. In order to publish in several languages, the team needed $5,000. As of August, having acquired less than $500, an English-only printing was all that could be managed.[34]

A second important segment of the protest scenario included contrary views on supporting a separate day on which racial progress could be demonstrated, a special tribute designated as "Colored American Day." This day earned unwarranted recognition because of the controversy surrounding it and the documentation it garnered subsequently. The dynamics of cultural orientation, color, and leadership roles forced African Americans to line up either in support of, or in opposition to, a separate day celebrating African American achievement. The decision resulted from a conscious effort by the fair's white management to recognize the distinct achievements of African Americans as sought by certain segments of the African American population as well as to defuse African American protest about racial exclusion. With this gesture, the fair's leadership expected that adverse publicity for this very public, monumental, international event would subside.

African American acceptance of the offer was lukewarm, causing the abolitionist-liberal media, represented locally by the *Inter Ocean* and Albion Tourgée, to question how well African Americans grasped the meaning of their own objectives.[35] Tourgée possessed impeccable credentials in matters involving racial equality, so he was able to speak candidly and be heard. Thrice-wounded on Civil War battlefields, but a latecomer to the abolitionist cause, he nonetheless gained recognition for his unswerving loyalty to African American liberation. Since he stood steadfast for immediate, unconditional access to citizenship rights for African Americans, he questioned the need to celebrate its denial.[36]

As a historical episode of some, but not great, note, Colored American Day sparked the formation of two massive organizing efforts, both approximating crusades and assuming ideological dimensions, and commencing almost from the time the management of the fair offered African American groups an opportunity to demonstrate the progress made by their race since the emancipation. The intensity of the struggle convinced the *Indianapolis Freeman* to report on the activities and exchange as division between conflicting camps. A similar scenario developed nationally, with both opposition and support forces attempting either to dissuade or to persuade African Americans to ignore or celebrate the special day. As to the day itself, they perceived it either as opportunity or pitfall, compliment or insult, recognition or denial. Depending nationally on the grouping involved—elite, middle, or working class—approaches differed. The existence of "social grades" in Chicago, with refined and respectable elements, also produced divided opinions.

All along the assimilationist spectrum the event produced comment and reaction, ranging from enthusiastic support to outright condemnation. Those integrationists who viewed the event positively saw the designated day as conferring a long-sought recognition of their group in an activity that they would control. With this hegemony over time, space, and content, they possessed the ability to illuminate their group's achievements since the end of slavery. Essentially, they viewed this act of fairness and generosity from the fair's leadership in complimentary terms. As the friendly *Chicago Inter Ocean* opined, "It rests with the colored people alone whether this shall be a day that will properly represent them as they would stand before the public. It especially rests with the more intelligent colored people who too often are sensitive about criticism and the disposition of thoughtless white people to treat all gatherings of colored people as something of the minstrel order." The newspaper continued, placing Colored American Day in perspective, as something other than the primary event of the fair as historians and other writers have sometimes imagined it: "The Colored people of culture and refinement cannot afford to leave the representation of their race to the servant class."[37] For the national working class, within the respectable category in Chicago, they could just as easily ignore or endorse the day. If they chose the former, it could be that they felt that their wishes would not be considered in its planning, execution, and enjoyment. On the other hand, if they chose the latter, perhaps they sensed the possibility of entertainment or fulfillment at a level to their liking.

If it was half a loaf, Douglass recognized that for a group engaged in perpetual struggle for its elevation and liberation, it was an opportunity that could not be squandered.[38] Despite the protest by assimilationists, on the one hand Colored American Day was not an unusual event. There were a Norwegian Day, a Maine Day, an Irish Day, and a dozen or so other special days. However, for elite or refined African Americans it offended their sense of inclusiveness, and appeared as a deliberate racial affront. Ironically, the very existence of a Colored American Day at the fair was proving divisive among the refined and the respectables, with members of each group speaking for and against having such a day in the first place. In and of itself, the program for Colored American Day conveyed an important statement about the level of assimilation among the members of the nation's "400's." The opportunity was one not to be ignored, some warned. To the racially less sensitive, it would show how much cultural distance the race had put between itself and the slavery of the mind and culture of 1865.

Opposition arose from those local and national segments of African Americans who considered the offer of a special group day as a slight. In the vanguard stood Chicago's Lettie Trent and Ida B. Wells of Memphis, notable for their early rejection of the idea as representing a retreat from integration. Another major voice in opposition locally was Wells's future husband, Ferdinand L. Barnett, who wrote that after Congress failed the diasporan cause, "in consideration of the color proof character of the Exposition Management it was the refinement of irony to set aside August 25 to be observed as 'Colored People's day' . . . [The exclusion of Colored Americans from employment is near complete] and yet in spite of this fact, the Colored Americans were expected to observe a designated day as their day—to rejoice and be exceedingly glad."[39] In this instance Wells and Barnett had many supporters, including Douglass, who reversed himself to take advantage of perhaps the only opportunity that African Americans would have to completely mold a celebratory event in his own image. Opposition to a separate day along ideological grounds related to Caucasian exclusion of fellow citizens along racial lines. For Colored Americans seeking entry into American society, it was seen as an insult. National condemnation among African Americans grew. The National Colored Peoples Protective Association of America, a broad-based civil rights organization, rejected the opportunity to participate, both immediately and repeatedly. At its annual convocation on the fairgrounds on June 25 through June 27 one spokesperson after another denounced the separation of the races through observance of such a day.

Perhaps one very tangible factor worthy of consideration is the role of fading racial memory, once rooted firmly in experience, but now a passing and obsolete feature of a new generation's reality. Paralleling the special nature of Colored American Day was Washington, D.C.'s annual Emancipation Day celebration. Emancipation of the total slave population of this city occurred on April 17, 1862, by an act of Congress, and it continued to overshadow, with good reason, the partial presidential emancipation of January 1, 1863, which is accorded so much more attention. Every April 17, the diasporan population of the nation's capital paraded along Pennsylvania Avenue, passing the White House to presidential review, and ending at a bronze statue of Lincoln. For years every class, social grouping—high brow, aspiring socialite, and rank and file—and racial mix—mulatto, quadroon, and pure blood—marched together. As the years passed, prosperity and demographic regeneration took their course, and by the Gilded Age, unrestrained, broadbased enthusiasm gave way to diminished support and even cynicism. The well-to-do of whatever generation saw the event as an embarrassment; the young who knew of slavery only through tradition began to ignore its significance in an age of expanding social mobility and opportunity along the eastern seaboard. The perceptive assessment of one observer warrants a full recitation:

> It always puzzles strangers to Washington, who happen to be here on the 17 of April, to find that the colored people of the District of Columbia have an Emancipation Day of their own. . . . If they never knew it before, they will never forget it, if they are here on what is known as "Mancipation Day" by most of the old-time colored people in the District, . . . For on that day there is a procession of colored militia and other more or less uniformed citizens in the street and on either sidewalk . . . With all their musical ability, the people in these processions are like children in their love of the drum, so that there is always noise enough to engage the ear even if there were not enough color to attract the eye. . . . [over the years] Frederick Douglass and Blanche K. Bruce dropped out, followed by the richer and more respectable among them, until the celebration was left largely to the lower classes, especially as it was not taken up to any great extent by young graduates of the public schools.[40]

A third area of contention rested on the question of exhibits. There was strong interest in the idea from the very beginning; however, a dichotomy appeared between those who viewed any exhibit displayed outside of the mainstream offerings as exclusionary and those who saw separate exhibits as offering the greater opportunity for black visibility amid thousands of other exhibits. Supporters of mainstream inclusion, both white and black, stated that their stance originated in the principle that "merit knows no color line." However, the promotion of African American exhibits, conceived by African Americans, appealed to those who were "especially interested" in the endeavor. Once received, the exhibits "should be impartially judged and assigned to their places as classified."[41]

Supporters of separate exhibits feared that both the limited resources of their group and their level of achievement over the last quarter of a century placed them in an untenable position of appearing inferior or deficient. One Chicago newspaper reported in 1890 that one black Chicagoan finessed the argument by calling for a separate exhibit but no denunciation of them for their separate existence. His argument was this:

[African American exhibitors] do not wish to be swallowed up in the great Exposition Buildings as would be the case were they to exhibit in common with the white exhibitors, but they are desirous of being afforded opportunity, by means of a separate apartment, to substantially and thoroughly display, in properly classified and installed shape, just what progress has been attained by their race. . . .

The colored people are outspoken in their condemnation of any precipitation of race discrimination into the question and want their feelings in the matter clearly conceived on all sides.[42]

The question of what was to be proven, to whom, why, and how was never sufficiently addressed, but it could not be done along rational lines. Mounting either a separate or a mainstream exhibit placed African Americans in the predicament of being compared to the white world and fighting their stereotype in the white world's eyes. After all, what could an exhibit possibly demonstrate to a nation committed to racial hegemony and currently maintaining control over the image of black males and females through lynching bees and sexual fabrication about their morals?

THE INAUGURAL PARADE AND CELEBRATION

Although technically the four hundredth anniversary of Columbus' arrival in the New World should have been celebrated in October 1892, preparations for the fair were not expected to be completed until spring 1893. Nonetheless, historical accuracy dictated that some observance be held, and the fair's managers planned and carried out a gala celebration as part of its inaugural ceremonies. Hundreds of thousands lined the streets, ten persons deep in some places, to catch a glimpse of the parade of 75,000 which then headed south from the Loop to Jackson Park. At its terminus in the mammoth Manufacturing Building, the paraders were met by 100,000 more who listened to celebratory speeches.

As Bancroft described the parade, "Here were assembled people of all nationalities, ages, and conditions of life, from grizzled veterans of the Civil War, bearing aloft their country's banner, to rosy-cheeked boys and girls, waving their miniature flags. . . . Here in the same line marched the Teuton and Slav, the Orangeman and Catholic, the African Negro and the American Indian. Foes by heredity became as brothers."[43] African Americans from around the nation marched with an enthusiasm that infected the crowd who, in turn, shared in the fervor of the moment. One contemporary account recalled that "if anything, the Colored troops, more than any other marching organization, seemed to feel the importance of the occasion, and their martial bearing and strict attention to movements and evolution won them many rounds of applause along the line of march."[44] Another noted that when Companies A and F of the Ninth Cavalry Regiment (the U.S. Army's famed Plains Indian fighters known as the Buffalo Soldiers) appeared, they were well received. As "it [the regiment] passed at a gallop, it was wildly cheered."[45] Strong memories of valiant service in behalf of the Republic persisted to this time, and, in fact, beyond. When two black law students graduated from the Kent College of Law in Chicago in 1897, the law editor made a peculiar reference to the graduates, writing: "It was worthy of note that when the column of sixty-nine students formed in line and marched upon the stage . . . to make a final charge for their diplomas, that the column was led by two colored graduates, Louis B. Anderson and John R. Auter. It was not the first time the colored troops led in a desperate charge."[46] Most African Americans marched, however, as part of the Tenth Division of parade participants. Regular U.S. Army units were joined by African American fraternal orders that traveled to the city from afar. Over a thousand young marchers of the Crispus Attucks Division, Number 1, the Knights of Pythias, came from Mississippi and paraded with the Chivalric Division, Number 2, with its fifty fully uniformed officers and men. Marching along State Street to martial strains, they thrilled thousands of spectators, most of them white.[47] To the African Americans, the significance of this involvement cannot be overestimated because of its effect on their morale. Representative of the many fraternal orders that dotted the south side landscape, these uniformed marchers no doubt stirred the same pride among blacks that the victorious Union army (without African American troops) did for whites in its grand march down Pennsylvania Avenue in 1865.

At the inaugural ceremonies, the ubiquitous Frederick Douglas scolded the leaders of the fair for their exclusion of African Americans, the very group he pointed out whose labor had provided the initial economic basis for the progress that was being celebrated.[48] At a reception held at the Auditorium Theater during the city-wide gala, Douglass's presence stood out. One exposition memorial appraised the situation as one where "social equality was evident" for the first time in U.S. history.[49] As to the living accommodations afforded the Douglasses, they resided at the ultra-exclusive Palmer House.[50]

3

RACE, CLASS, AND GENDER

The dangerous mistake of sacrificing great opportunities for advancement on a mistaken "race pride," in the vain attempt to build a "race history" and to work out a "separate and distinct destiny" in this democratic country, must be defeated.

> —Hale G. Parker, Alternate Commissioner at Large (Missouri), National Board of Commissioners, December 1892

When asked if she preferred the term "Afro-American" as a name for her people, [Ida B. Wells] said it accurately described the position and had become a popular designation. "Negro leaves out the element of nationality, and we are all Americans, nor has the Republic more faithful and loyal citizens than those of our race. Some of the 'colored' people are not distinguishable from whites, so far has their Negro blood been diluted, but they are all Afro-Americans—that is, Americans of African descent."

> —Ladies' Pictorial (London), May 1893[1]

Revolting as the theory may appear to some present, I believe that all humanity started black—that black was the original color of mankind.

> —Bishop Henry McNeal Turner, Chicago, 1893

RACE AND CULTURE

On the eve of and during the fair, the state of African American thinking on the subject of race assumed a complexity noticeable by its avoidance by scholars of succeeding generations. At various levels, the very nature of the African Americans' *being*, race, culture, social grade (or class), gender, ideology, and politics intersected, sometimes in a most convoluted fashion. Nell Irvin

Painter has said that for Kansas during this period, "Race functioned as the idiom for discussions of class."[2] Obviously, the meaning and influence of this mesh differed between individuals and within cities and regions, defying simple categorization. Yet, in tackling the issue of categorical interpretations, it seemed as though Lewis Carroll's Alice had reappeared as she questioned Humpty Dumpty's determined effort to stamp a brand of legitimacy on a particular interpretation to the exclusion of all others:

> "When I use a word," Humpty Dumpty said in a rather scornful tone, "it means just what I choose it to mean, — neither more nor less."
>
> "The question is," said Alice, "whether you *can* make words mean so many different things."
>
> "The question is," said Humpty Dumpty, "which is to be master—that's all."[3]

Clarity is what is needed, rather than obfuscation employed in the name of convention or theory. More recently, Wilson J. Moses wrote that "divid[ing] black American social and political thought into categories . . . seemed too neatly discrete, and sometimes downright false."[4] While an accurate set of ideological categories is impossible to construct, some labeling has proven useful where a search for understanding absolutely requires it. Hopefully what concepts are offered here on the subject do not cross those bounds of illogic, contradiction, and impropriety.

The thinking and sentiments of the rank and file merit examination although they are perennially ignored in favor of the more commonly accepted conceptualizations of what the elite thought and felt. The feelings of ordinary folk were not usually expressed through the spoken or written word, but through their actions, such as exemplified by the journey of two hundred hopeful African Americans to New York in 1892 to reach an Africa-bound ship. Their inaction, sometimes interpreted as apathy by the condescending and unknowing, spoke volumes—obviously unwritten but also misinterpreted and misunderstood, but still worthy of consideration as to understanding the general state of affairs at any time and place.[5] Commissioner Parker's awareness of these tendencies convinced him of the necessity to address them in his message calling for full participation in the nation's affairs despite pervasive racism. He opposed withdrawal in the face of injustice and exclusion, accommodation to unjust conditions, and separate development whether advocated by nationalist strategists or integrationist tacticians. But what he advocated carried little weight beyond those who shared his beliefs on race.

With race, whether its construct is artificial or substantive, biological or cultural does not concern us here as much as the pervasive adoption and use of the construct in daily living. Unequivocally, persons of unmixed African descent at the mass level identified themselves exclusively by the construct of race and affinity for the perpetuation of their way of life. St. Clair Drake wrote on the historical bases from which this identity derived: "The people of the Diaspora in North America never developed an *African-American* culture in the sense that the people of the Caribbean and South America did. Rather what might be called an *Afro*-American sub-culture evolved."[6] This was not a culture independently constructed away from the indigenous African home world with an authentic core clearly intact, but rather one quite similar to the garden-salad variety found in America among immigrants from Europe, Asia, South America, and the indigenous peoples of North America. Within this subculture, persons sought an internally produced affirmation for their being, rather than one that was externally developed and required a hegemonic sanction from a dominant, outside group. This permitted them to develop a consciousness free from wondering what whites thought about them during their every waking moment.

One important effort to illuminate the character of this subculture was defined throughout a series of interviews in the 1970s that revolved around a *core black culture* for its urban, northern component. John Langston Gwaltney's *Drylongso: A Self-Portrait on Black America* defined Drake's Afro-American subculture at several levels. According to ethnologist Gwaltney:

> Core black culture is more than ad hoc synchronic adaptive survival. Its values, systems of logic and world view are rooted in a lengthy peasant tradition and clandestine theology. It is the notion of sacrifice for kin, the belief in the natural sequence of cause and effect. . . . The expectations and canons of core black culture are arbiters of black intra-communal status and style. . . . In black culture there is a durable, general tolerance, amazingly free of condescension, for the individual's right to follow the truth where it leads. . . . [And, not surprisingly,] the sense of nationhood among blacks is as old as [blacks'] abhorrence of slavery. Black nationhood is not rooted in territoriality so much as it is in a profound belief in the fitness of core black culture and in the solidarity born of a transgenerational detestation of [black] subordination [to whites]. The tradition which is so vital in shaping black culture was founded and fostered by those slave foreparents who are so widely respected for their refusal to accept, in their hearts, the Euro-American definition of them as things.[7]

Another work from the 1970s that uses the interviewing process to recapture the essence of ordinary people from the rural South is historian Theodore Rosengarten's life of Nate Shaw. In direct contrast to stereotypes of persons lacking a positive sense of self and social and philosophical moorings because of alleged racial inferiority, the near contemporary, fair-era reflections of Nate Shaw offer rich insight into the thinking of the average African Americans whose presence in the city was growing.

On August 25, 1893, Colored American Day, an anonymous African American was photographed at the fair (see Frontispiece) to represent "Everyman" in black Chicago. He resembles this writer's own slavery-era maternal great-grandfather—tall, almost gaunt, yet sturdy; not well educated but intelligent, experienced, and observant; deserving of humane recognition beyond that accorded a cipher. He appears quietly confident, like one of those Civil

War veterans who resided in the city and marched triumphantly in the October 1892 inaugural parade. Nate Shaw could easily be a rural relative of this man.

Shaw also fit into the mold described by Robert Russa Moton:

> [Suddenly,] great change followed emancipation. This act released the Negro's energies for self-improvement, ambitions repressed by slavery found immediate expression in efforts toward education, the acquisition of property and the cultivation of religion. . . . Thrown wholly on his own resources, he was not long in recognizing that whatever of good was to be realized from his new status as a free man must come ultimately from his own will to profit by its opportunities and advantages, and from his own efforts to improve his condition. . . . Anyone who would understand the Negro of to-day must take account of this continuous progress of the race, most rapid since emancipation and accelerating with each decade.

With a confidence and perhaps a hidden smugness paralleling that of his subjects as they treasured their secrets, Moton concluded, "Of the nature and extent of this progress the overwhelming majority of white people in America are, practically speaking, entirely ignorant."[8]

Rosengarten's description of the Nate Shaw he had grown to know is illuminating: "Shaw demonstrates that a person is, at every moment, everything he always was; his current role can eclipse his past but not deny it."[9] As Shaw remembered the source of his consciousness as a person with both human agency and destiny, the latter reinforcing the growing strength of the former, he delved into the past at that point where historians commonly recognize a historical beginning for African Americans, the Civil War, with its vibrant emancipatory legacy.[10]

> Grandma Cealy said many a time, tellin people who came in there while she was there, "Why, Hayes, that's my baby, that's my baby. He was fifteen years old when it surrendered." Well, I didn't have no knowledge of what surrendin was. But it didn't come to me like this: that was in the days of freein the colored people. . . . But really, I was too little to *know* anything, only what I definitely heard em say and I never did hear nobody say what the surrender was. I just decided it was the beginnin of the days of freedom.

Shaw recognized the impermanence of any oppressor's reign and with it, the usefulness of silent acceptance of that which is temporary while change is anticipated. He recalled, "The Bible says, 'What has been will be again.' And Grandma Cealy said a right smart [thing] about this: that that day was comin. Colored people once knowed what it was like to live under freedom before they got to this country, and they would know it again. . . . I got to be a little old boy, when I was old enough to catch on to what people said, and even to the words of the old people, and the Bible, it was instilled in me many a time: the bottom rail will come to the top someday. I taken that to mean a change in the later years, durin of my lifetime maybe. I believe, if that day come, the poor generation on earth will banish away their toils and snares. But won't nobody do it for em but themselves."[11] In terms of thinking about race, the distance between Commissioner Parker's world and that of Shaw and the man in the Frontispiece must be measured in light years.

According to Charles S. Johnson's *Shadow of the Plantation*, there were other blacks with an unconventional lifestyle residing in the Deep South of the 1890s and in the midst of Alabama plantation life in the twentieth century. In his objective exploration of African American life, Johnson took care to mention these "Salt-Water Men": Africans captured and transported illegally after U.S. participation in the Atlantic slave trade had ended. Arriving late in the antebellum period, their presence and influence constitute a hidden treasure trove of information on consanguinity to Africa. In his depression-era field studies, he noted:

> Another class of Negroes in relation to whom there is retained, in the memory of the community, an active social distinction is the "salt-water nigger." They were the freshly imported Negroes from Africa toward whom the Negro slaves felt a pronounced superiority. Cass Stewart, now over eighty-five years of age, could remember some of these. Said he: "I was wid de Africans. Dey couldn't understand what dey was saying deyselves. I seed dem salt-water niggers down my home near Selma. I knowed a man down dere working 25 acres, couldn't work wid half of 'em 'cause when you made one of 'em mad you made all of 'em mad."
>
> The older slaves kept themselves aloof from the African, partly out of contempt and partly out of fear. In the community today there are contemptuous references to certain families as springing from "salt-water niggers." This situation provides an unexpected link with Africa which might indeed yield traces of other transplanted culture traits. (One old resident, in quoting remembered expressions of these Africans, used terms strikingly similar to the African West Coast pidgin English, which was all the more unusual because West Coast pidgin is not common in the dialect of the Negroes in this part of the South).[12]

In dramatic contrast, however important the influence of core black culture was on the many, a sentiment toward a countervailing national identity as Americans, or Colored Americans, grew stronger among the few. These were the educated, articulate elite of both mixed and unmixed racial heritage. As white Americans slowly began to recognize their claim to the benefits of citizenship, the likes of which were tested by the level of inclusion or exclusion from the operations and management of the World's Columbian Exposition, this group's hopes of inclusion into the American mainstream were buoyed. From this source, the Afro-Saxon mentality sprang, one that comported itself antithetically to that of the Afro-American, so the world views of the elite and masses grew dialectically disparate.

The racial duality W. E. B. Du Bois described so eloquently in *Souls of Black Folk* (1903) fit the experiences of the ultra-assimilationist elite perfectly. The African American, according to Du Bois, was aware that he was both a Negro and an American, meaning that he sought refuge in the black world among African Americans and their institutions while concurrently pursuing the full enjoyment of his citizenship rights among the dominant, majority white American citizenry. This duality opened the possibility that African Americans would often act in contradiction to any "true believer's" commitment, such as that of Commissioner Parker, a purist integrationism that rejected any voluntary grouping, voluntary separation, or drawing of the color line among African Americans themselves.[13] According to Arna Bontemps and Jack Conroy, even a mulatto like Chicago legend John Jones "never lost his identity as a colored American."[14] Chicago dentist Charles E. Bentley, originally a native of Cincinnati and of mixed racial ancestry, promoted the American Union Club, an all-black investment and mutual aid club capitalized at $12,000. Significantly, it advertised itself as "a valuable enterprise to the colored people of the city, and something that no young man who has the interest of the race at heart and desires elevation of society should fail to cooperate with."[15]

As to the dilemma posed by Du Bois of a warring American-ness battling a Negro-ness and manifesting itself in a racial duality, its influence on the rank and file segment of Afro-Chicago as well as Afro-America is conjectural and unsubstantiated. Despite the importance of racial duality in the lives and mindsets of *some* African Americans, David Levering Lewis has shown that it should never have been considered the only choice of persons of African descent in America, Chicago, or anywhere else on the globe.[16] Further, Gwaltney postulated that "to the prudent black American masses, however, core black culture *is* the mainstream [culture]."[17] The question of establishing a racial identity for those persons of unmixed blood and loyalties has rarely been addressed, but will be later in this chapter.

Yet another idea emerged during this period. It concerned assuming an identity resting either solely or significantly on gender rather than race. Derived from the strong sentiment for racial orientation in interpreting the vicissitudes of life for African Americans, black feminism/womanism placed an emphasis on an intergender struggle exacerbated by race, class, and other influences. Complementing Giddings's position a decade later on the importance of gender, but not its absolute primacy in relational spheres, was that of Higginbotham, as she warned of a "narrowness of vision on this crucial issue."[18] She criticized the white-led feminist movement which promoted a racial notion along with those of class and gender, all resulting in the detrimental treatment of African Americans, female and male. Higginbotham argued that since "white America's deployment of race in the construction of power relations inherently disadvantaged all African Americans who were suffering from protection of white privileges along the axes of race, class, and gender, some black women scholars have largely refrained from an analysis of gender along the lines of the male/female dichotomy so prevalent among white feminists. . . . At the threshold of the twenty-first century, black women scholars continue to emphasize the inseparable unity of race and gender in their thought." She warned, however, that "we should challenge the overdeterminacy of race *vis à vis* social relations among blacks themselves and conceptions of the black community as harmonious and monolithic."[19]

DISPARATE RACIAL SENTIMENTS

The traditional approach of linking race, culture, and ideology has recognized a basic dichotomy in black thought between integrationists who wanted to remain in America and nationalists, or emigrationists, who wanted to leave. Yet in its simplicity, this unnatural binary choice could never capture the diversity of mindsets pervasive in the late nineteenth century. That the period nurtured diversity in thinking about the place of the African American in American society was fully illustrated in a forty-year-old study dealing with Georgia politics. Black Georgians chose among many alternatives as they sought to remedy their oppressive lot: some considered emigration to Africa, others migration to the North, a number planned colonization to the West, and quite a few practiced "stayhereation." "Each of these plans was to have its proponents, who, by propaganda and forceful arguments, expected to realize their dreams."[20]

Bishop Henry McNeal Turner of the A.M.E. Church gained prominence as the leading advocate of emigration in Georgia and nationwide. Since there were Georgians who knew of the hardships that New Yorkers, Philadelphians, Bostonians, and Chicagoans were experiencing in the North while gaining access to political rights at the expense of economic opportunities, they rejected a northward exodus.[21] Other Southerners thought likewise, and with the rise of debt peonage throughout the Deep South, many African Americans now lacked any opportunity to make a decision at all.[22] Further, even within the latter group favoring "stayhereation," divisions appeared throughout the nation. Assimilationist proponents of self-determination through separate racial institutions found themselves at odds with ultra-assimilationists who decried any surrender to segregation, voluntary or involuntary.[23]

As he attempted to check what he considered excesses in divergent African American thinking, exposition commissioner Hale G. Parker's denunciation of race pride, race history, and race destiny clearly illustrated his concern. When the full text of Parker's pronouncement is examined closely in light of extant circumstances, it is evident that he was only addressing one of several sets of ideological exchanges pervading both Chicago and the nation at this time. Parker was not placing himself "above" the rest of his fellow African Americans, as one historian has imagined.[24] Rather, he was clarifying his position for those with whom he identified both racially and ideologically, while seeking to restrain those actions and principles which he felt jeopardized racial advancement. Basically, like Washington, his ideological opposite, Parker sought a strategic advantage from which to ensure maximum black participation in the fair.

Prominent at the fair, he being one of only three African Americans holding official positions, the ideological sentiments of Commissioner Parker, along with those of Haytian Commissioner Frederick Douglass, carried special importance. Both men held a strong belief in the inevitability of African American triumph over racism in a competitive, Darwinian environment. Involvement in that arena was a requisite, and a demonstration of competence remained a continuous responsibility. If the major problem of the late nineteenth century was the color line, the solution required a maximum commitment to improve self and nation along with a stronger dose of faith in American ideals and institutions. Consistently Parker and Douglass challenged any form of compromise with the national promise of equal opportunity for all or with inequality both in thought and practice, whether it manifested itself in social isolation, voluntary separation, or emigrationism. In their minds and over the long haul, it was a matter of the inability of the immovable object of white racial supremacy to withstand the irresistible force of the American Dream as encompassed in the promise of equal opportunity for all citizens.

High standards and competitive zeal became essential ingredients for national, but not racial, progress, according to Missourian Parker. Chicagoans who reached the American standard set by New England institutions in education and the professions included Fannie Barrier Williams, her husband, S. Laing Williams, Dr. Charles Edwin Bentley, Drs. Daniel Hale Williams and A. Wilberforce Williams (unrelated), Ferdinand Barnett, attorneys Edward H. Morris from Kentucky and Edward Wright from New York City, Lloyd Garrison Wheeler, and John G. Jones. Their motivation to experience America's opportunities to the fullest originated, significantly, in their positive experiences as youth, young adults, and mature individuals.

The leading local ideological counterparts to Parker and Douglass were Drs. Charles E. Bentley and Daniel Hale Williams, journalist Fannie Barrier Williams, and attorneys Edward H. Morris, S. Laing Williams, and James Madden. Staunch ultra-assimilationists, the two medical practitioners supported and led African American efforts to organize Provident Hospital and Training School in 1891 as an interracial institution serving all the city.

The views of Bentley closely paralleled Parker's as the Chicagoan rose in influence both among blacks and whites because of his success in mainstream America. From the time of the fair to the first quarter of the next century, Bentley maintained a predominantly white dental practice in the heart of the Loop, much to the chagrin of some African Americans living in the south Loop and near south side. As to his accomplishments in the newly professionalizing field of dentistry, Bentley could take pride in having conceived of and organized the almost all-white Odontographic Society of Chicago in 1889.[25] Viewing the health needs of the indigent and working class, he offered a solution rooted firmly in the era's thinking reflecting William Graham Sumner's influence—avoid charity, and hope for economic improvement that would provide a wholesome work environment. Yet, because of Bentley's sense of racial commitment, he could work tirelessly alongside Williams at Provident in the slowly expanding black south side, filling the positions of oral surgeon and Secretary of the Board of Directors of the Training School Committee.

Daniel Hale Williams distinguished himself in 1893 during the fair when he became the first surgeon to complete a successful suturing of the human heart. In the heat of July, a knifing victim brought to Provident Hospital would certainly have met his Maker had Williams not demonstrated his surgical skills. A man who avoided controversy outside the operating and examining rooms, Williams supposedly bucked an ideological maelstrom among the elite to establish Provident Hospital. As one Chicago historian wrote, "Many of Chicago's long-time residents were very much against the establishment of a 'segregated' hospital, which they immediately deemed Provident would be despite evidence to the contrary. Williams maintained the hospital would be staffed, owned and supported by white and black together, and only competent personnel would be utilized in all areas of hospital administration and service."[26]

At this time in her life, Fannie Barrier Williams appeared a totally committed ultra-assimilationist, and conducted her affairs accordingly. She and her husband, S. Laing Williams, strived to hone the interests and skills of their African American friends in intellectual and literary discourse to prepare them for their entry into respectable WASP society, even as token representatives of their group. The couple worshiped at predominantly white, high-status All Souls Church, which was Unitarian. They did not reside within the neighborhood surrounding the Dearborn Street corridor; rather, they lived near predominantly wealthy, and white, Grand Boulevard. Clearly, the Williamses were the most American couple in black Chicago's ranks.

The views of this elite on racial identity revolved primarily around the question of how closely its members would align with or distance themselves from the sentiments associated with the majority of persons of African descent. The elite deviated by choice from the derivative African- and southern-based cultural practices and heritage that comprised Afro-American culture. Like many persons of color in color-conscious America, the elite's concern with skin color bordered on the obsessive. While it was common for white America routinely to denounce a dark complexion as ugly and to extol the virtues of a fair one, the same was true for many Afro-Saxons.[27] Certain racial sentiments held by Chicago's refined paralleled white attitudes. Cultured northern whites could tout a Paul Lawrence Dunbar, visiting the city for the fair and a favorite of theirs, as a pure Negro, showing their awareness of the difference.[28] Similarly, they could chide mulatto Frederick Douglass because of his African bloodline and features.[29] Repeated references to Douglass's mane being reminiscent of a lion's are telling. Whether this prejudice about skin color existed in Chicago to the extreme, the way it did on the East Coast, and in the South in cities such as Charleston, New Orleans, and Washington, D.C.,[30] is conjectural. However, awareness of color distinctions pervaded every corner of Afro-Saxon America and Afro-America.

The role of persons of mixed racial ancestry has recently revived the interests of academicians, but to the contemporary mind, especially that perspective associated with unmixed Colored people, "passing" and claims to high status based on skin color routinely evoked criticism or raised eyebrows.[31] This struggle over identity grew to be recognized as the problem of the "internal color line." In Chicago, the editor of the *Broad Ax* accused Dr. Bentley of being "willing to give up his little white Jesus, and all the good things in the world, if he could be a little whiter."[32] Fannie Barrier Williams would, at another time in her life, protect her right to first class railroad accommodations in the South by claiming French blood, a claim the overwhelming number of rank and file African Americans could not make.[33] Dr. Daniel Hale Williams's reddish hair and Caucasian complexion were whispered about by African Americans whenever they were not touting his accomplishments.[34] Captain Charles L. Marshall of the Eighth Illinois passed for white in La Salle, Illinois, to keep a position as bricklayer, and supposedly exhibited antiblack attitudes in order to curry favor and protect his identity.[35] So the elite found it necessary to distance themselves not only from the criminal element of Black America, but also from Africans and other African Americans who looked too Negroid.

Culturally, the twenty-five-member Prudence Crandall Study Club typified the kind of organization that nurtured the elite by committing itself to intellectual enlightenment and perfecting social decorum. Organized in 1887 with the prompting of Fannie and S. Laing Williams, it has been described by Gatewood as the earliest in a succession of high-status social organizations, to which most of the first families of black Chicago belonged.[36] Families with refined tastes also joined the Fellowship Club and the Lotus Social Club. These clubs and the literary groups usually formed under the auspices of the older Protestant churches.

Church participation in the nine religious institutions in Chicago played an integral role in African American life. The formal edifices in which these bodies were situated reflected the permanency and aspirations of their congregations. Inside each, the required demeanor often appeared foreign to southern migrants, accustomed to traditional church services which embraced emotional and personal responses to the Spirit.[37] Newcomers either conformed, as hundreds had done before them, or ignored this variant form of black church life to join smaller, mission churches. For a few African Americans, such as S. Laing and Fannie Barrier Williams, membership in predominantly white churches beckoned, since by 1887, Unitarian minister Rev. Jenkin Lloyd Jones had opened All Souls to all Americans.[38]

Along with others of their race, the refined often articulated a desire for a speedy realization of the "American Dream" that late twentieth century African Americans still demand on an immediate basis. While this lent support to historian Allan H. Spear's thesis of an abolitionist, integrationist tradition being influential among African Americans in Chicago, by no stretch of the

imagination could their hegemony over popular belief be considered an established fact. One fact was obvious. They did confirm the accuracy of Ida B.
Wells's observations about the diversity of the racial mix and the importance
of race identification when attempting to clarify strategy and tactics.

Commissioner Parker tapped into the deepest feelings and sentiments of
the elite toward this nation which led them to embrace a hope that someday
they would become part of the American mainstream. During the Reconstruction era, this hope evolved into a strategy. It was a strategy, however, that
embraced methods and means linked paradoxically to distinctiveness and racial isolation. The appearance of inconsistency began with the widespread
exaltation of "race pride," "race consciousness," and "race solidarity" as *the*
means to achieve full recognition of citizenship rights and black humanity.
Parker, embodying the national spirit of assimilationist racial advancement,
looked askance at these means as counterproductive, if not altogether destruc-
tive of strategic value. Remarkably, the evolution of Dr. Charles E. Bentley
revealed the same thoughts as Bentley emerged from the obscurity of his
young adult life on the eve of the fair to reach the pinnacle of professional and
civic prominence in the next century.[39]

The expansive ranks of the assimilationists also included persons willing to counterbalance the desired end of enjoying full citizenship rights and
respect with means that were contradictory to that end. Nonetheless, even
if these cultural pluralists were, by degree, somewhat less than "true believers," they considered themselves just as correct and logical in their choice of
alternative means to promote their strategy. The means of race solidarity embracing some semblance of voluntary separation still seemed practical in a
world filled with so many paradoxes and ambiguities related to race. Wilson J.
Moses, in his historical examination of the time span between 1850 and 1925,
considered this period one in which "some of the best educated and most
gifted black men and women were associated with institutional separation."[40]

Virginia teacher and lawyer I. Garland Penn contributed to the "militant" pamphlet *The Reason Why the Colored American Is Not in the World's
Columbian Exposition* in 1893, but in 1895 with Booker T. Washington's
blessing he assumed the position of Chief of the Negro Department for the
Cotton States Exposition in Atlanta, with the responsibility of overseeing the
design, construction, and preparation of exhibits in the Negro Building.[41]
Publisher and attorney Ferdinand L. Barnett opposed Colored American Day
as an abomination, yet supported a separate African American exhibit.[42] The
difference between the two in his mind might have rested in the genesis of the
concepts. The former originated with whites and appeared as a salve on a
festering sore. The latter was conceived in the black imagination as a vehicle
to demonstrate African American achievement. Given an opportunity on the
fairgrounds to strike a blow against the pronouncements of emigrationist leader A.M.E. Bishop Henry McNeal Turner in debate, Barnett earnestly spoke in
opposition.[43] When at the beginning of the century Ferdinand L. Barnett at-

tacked Booker T. Washington's accommodationism with a vengeance, he aimed not so much at the Tuskegeean's methods but at the manner in which they were used in conjunction with an especially repugnant obsequiousness to white authority. Such behavior was something the average northern Afro-Saxon could never countenance.

OTHER RACIAL SENTIMENT IN CHICAGO

In Chicago, it became commonplace for members of the group classi-fied by historian Allan H. Spear in the twentieth century as "militant" integra-tionists to occasionally adopt methods and means more commonly associat-ed with the national advocates of separate development, southern regional accommodationism, or emigrationism. In the ranks of these pragmatic assim-ilationists, Lloyd G. Wheeler saw the same benefits to group solidarity in business enterprises as those on which Isaac Harris reported in 1885. In the twentieth century, he acted even more firmly in behalf of a separate econo-my as a means to integration. Dr. George Cleveland Hall arrived in the city in the 1880s, joined the staff at Provident, and was in attendance during Dan-iel Hale Williams's pathbreaking heart surgery in 1893. Hall identified with the practical element within the ranks of the integrationists and early in the new century closely identified with Booker T. Washington along with the Urban League Movement, both of which challenged the unquestioning acceptance of the ultra-assimilationist ideal. While Ferdinand L. Barnett ex-tolled the virtues of racial solidarity in the pages of the *Conservator*, Isaac C. Harris did the same in 1885 in the pages of the *Colored Men's Profession-al and Business Directory*, ministers preached about salvation as a racial blessing, and fraternal orders and social clubs exaggerated racial strengths and history.

On the eve of the fair, black Chicago proved itself capable of assuming many ideological postures as it sought advancement. Contrary to the assess-ments of some historians, the rudimentary formation of a racially conscious group identity began to make inroads in Chicago during the post-Reconstruc-tion era, not later. As a matter of fact, evidence has lain dormant as to the emergence of this African American thought in the commercial and social spheres as early as the 1870s. Its influence, perhaps deliberately overlooked at times, is important for this study and for every other endeavor examining ac-tivities beyond the ranks of the elite. While the idea that newly arrived Euro-peans with strong ethnic backgrounds acted normally in attempting to main-tain their own cultural identities in the social and cultural environment of native white Chicago, the notion was never extended to African Americans. Among rank and file African Americans who simply worked among the lim-ited occupations available, they shaped their world view influenced by a grow-ing racial consciousness built on racial solidarity and racial pride.[44] While in the world of the Afro-Saxon elite WASP hegemony dictated respect and emulation, in the world of the African American rank and file the wrongdoing and foibles of whites were all too well known to make anything but a negative impression. So while servants and other supposed subordinates proffered an outward recognition of elevated white status, it was based on fear and the power of economic manipulation rather than respect.

Some major documentation that illuminates the character of this often-overlooked social organization in pre-fair Chicago was remarkable for its content as well as antithetical sketches of an alternative side of racial adjustment. Isaac C. Harris's *Colored Men's Professional and Business Directory* (1885) was one such document. Of immense historical value, Harris's *Directory* represents the major extant guidepost of the late nineteenth century on African American life in Chicago. Comprehensive, objective, and accurate, it highlights a fledgling community energized by an internal dynamism. Even though the *Directory* promoted a cause—African American commercial advancement—its *raison d'être* never obviated the comprehensive glimpse of life it presented. It established the existence of a variety of activities and organizations, from literary societies to fraternal orders to small businesses. Contemporary to the period, based on direct observation and survey, and recognized as the primary document on the makeup of African American society nearing the end of the century, it has enjoyed far too limited use as a source of knowledge about black Chicago.[45]

Consistent with a national pattern among African Americans in which they embraced the virtues of a group economy,[46] Harris established that businessmen were proud to show how far African Americans had progressed less than a generation since emancipation, and that these individuals wanted to tap into an already existing African American market:

> I have frequently consulted with many of our leading citizens and well-thinking people upon the great need of a work of this kind, and they have earnestly admitted with one accord that a directory of the business, professions and prominent occupations of the enterprising colored people in the city of Chicago would be a work of vast importance, and a reliable medium of authoritative information, while its many advantages would be highly appreciated by all lovers of our race progress. . . . The unjust discrimination made on the account of color, by many writers, and their biased ideas, will not allow them to view and treat our industrial, educational and financial progress in the true light of merit, justice and reason; therefore, being actuated by a sensibility of race pride, and the great love and admiration which I have for the exemplary enterprise demonstrated by the colored people of Chicago, I have felt it to be an imperative duty to collect, with great care and discretion, a few facts and figures, in order to show to others of our race what the colored people in the great metropolis of the west are doing towards an honest accumulation of wealth, establishment of business, and acquiring that experience in the various professions and the branches of industry necessary to make life a grand success and the elevation of our race a true and constant aim.
>
> There seems to be a great degree of race pride, inspiring the better class with an inordinate desire to see each other succeed in whatever pursuit they may perchance engage in. This fact is demonstrated in many instances by the large patronage and

co-operation which they received from one another, it being occasionally sufficient enough to support different branches of business where the trade is entirely colored.[47]

Both viscerally and cerebrally, a significant segment of Chicago's African Americans acknowledged that Chicago and the nation were in the midst of a financial, technological, and machine revolution. African Americans participated as builders away from the fairgrounds as they constructed or opened new residences and places of trade. The *Indianapolis Freeman* reported that Adam G. Smith, one of the wealthiest Negroes in Illinois, was erecting "a large hotel at 2713 South Dearborn." It announced that the "saloon business, of course, has gone way up" and that S. J. Manning and W. M. Grant were the proprietors of a "mammoth grocery house."[48] Beyond racial constraints, they desired to participate fully in the expanding, urban market economy, if not in the world's fair decade, then sometime in the future.

Seven years after Harris expressed his support of the timeliness of promoting race pride, Commissioner Parker heaped scorn on the advocates of group economy and self-help. "The term 'colored merchant' is getting to be a numerous article and is lavishly applied to any citizen of color engaged in any pursuit," he wrote sardonically, speaking from his successful, competitive experience in the business sphere. "Tried by the ordinary tests of a legitimate commercial business he becomes less numerous and rises to the level of *merchant*, just as 'our colored leaders' when tried by the tests of leadership dwindle to a few who can be *called leaders of men*. And this is the consummation we insist on. . . . Out of this arises the imperative duty of all men to become patrons of the World's Fair."[49]

As to the fair and those alternatives to the full participation espoused by Parker, withdrawal symbolized anything but "a judicious method of redressing or reforming a wrong, nor of enforcing a right." He continued that it amounted to "a desertion of the field in the hour of actual engagement, in which public and private interests are ruthlessly sacrificed. . . . In an hour like this, when the great forces and agencies which have unfolded the life of the world are to be exposed to modern thought, to advise contempt of the opportunity to show identification with those forces will certainly be construed to the disparagement of the colored people." But such was the frustration in the heat of this battle that Lettie Trent and Ida B. Wells considered this approach preferable to experiencing any more racial slights. And of course every emigrationist gravitated to the position that physical withdrawal by the mass of African Americans represented the only true solution to continued oppression in America.

Voluntary separatism resulting in all-black institutions, relationships, communities, and towns fared little better in the eyes of Commissioner Parker. He considered "the dangerous mistake of sacrificing great opportunities for advancement on a mistaken 'race pride,' in the vain attempt to build a 'race history' and to work out a 'separate and distinct destiny' in this democratic country, must be defeated. There is nothing more incompatible with the manifest destiny of the republic. It is resistance to the logical current of *our* [emphasis added] history and to the noble efforts consecrated to the cause of freedom and humanity by the bravest souls of the century."

From the ranks of the respectables, a discernible social sentiment also emanated from families, fraternal orders, social clubs, and cultural organizations. These African Americans represented the majority will within the nation. They encountered less stress from duality, if they experienced it at all, and were acutely aware of racism as a threat to their ability to enjoy freedom and unfettered opportunity in America. Importantly, in their actions and in their thoughts they never sought a consciousness as Afro-Saxons. As to the question of their establishing a racial identity, these persons of unmixed blood had neither the need to ponder the meaning of the obvious nor an inclination to shed a God-given birthright.

Still, other segments of the respectables would have ignored all but their own immediate needs. They remained as indifferent to race as they could, which explains why so many of their contemporaries spoke of a nonsupportive mass of African Americans. They were also an integral part of the group who could withdraw at a moment's notice of racial opposition.

EMIGRATIONIST SENTIMENT

The existence of emigrationist sentiment and its proselytizers, who abounded locally, nationally, and abroad, further illustrated how yet another segment of the city's rank and file respectable element was thinking. Whether Bishop Henry McNeal Turner of the A.M.E. Church, Edward Blyden of Liberia, or peripatetic agents for various emigrationist ventures, both legitimate and dubious, they listened to the clarion call of the ideology of nationalism that loomed as a force with which to be reckoned by integrationists of all shades, from ultra-assimilationists to pragmatic assimilationists to southern regional accommodationists. The race consciousness and race pride that Parker so feared shone to these African Americans as a beacon.

W. E. B. Du Bois's name has not appeared as *participant* in this study until this point because of his absence from this country in 1893. However, his initial, signal contribution to this debate on race nationhood evolved a short time after the fair, in 1897. In "The Conservation of Races," delivered before the American Negro Academy, he articulated a view with pertinence to the year 1893. The visionary declared:

> We cannot reverse history; we are subject to the same natural laws as other races, and if the Negro is ever to be a factor in the world's history — if among the gaily decorated banners that deck the broad ramparts of civilization is to hang one uncompromisingly black, then it must be placed there by black hands, fashioned by black heads and hallowed by the travail of two hundred million black hearts beating in one glad song of jubilee.

> For this reason, the advance guard of the Negro people—the eight million people of Negro blood in the United States of America—must soon come to realize that if they are to take their just place in the van of Pan-Negroism, then their destiny is *not* absorption by the white Americans. That if in America it is to be proven for the first time in the modern world that not only are Negroes capable of evolving individual men like Toussaint the savior, but are a nation stored with wonderful possibilities of culture, then their destiny is not a servile imitation of Anglo-Saxon culture, but a stalwart originality which shall unswervingly follow Negro ideals.[50]

First and foremost, Du Bois spoke to and for a generation which knew the source of its cultural origins, at least in a regional sense. West and West Central Africa, home to Mandingo, Wolof, Ibo, BaKongo, and BaLunda, were the well-known regions of departure for the Americas for four hundred years. Interest in Africa pervaded the popular imagination, and if it was not the substance of everyday conversation, it was still the subject on enough infrequent occasions to be deemed a portion of popular thought. Whether it emanated from a family discussion, a missionary obligation from the church, the many public forums, other abundant newspaper accounts, or whatever fountain, the debate was real and lively. When the *Indianapolis Freeman* cavalierly reported on the discourse of the 1890s,[51] its notice of the debate provided the information necessary to allow a basis of discussion from which intelligent decisions could be made.

Then there was the matter of the presence of the "Salt-Water Men" and other groups in the Gulf region and the Gullah people of the eastern U.S. The peripatetic Edward Wilmot Blyden of Liberia had even visited the hinterlands of black America, traveling in the north to Chicago in 1880 and 1889 to promote the benefits of African resettlement.[52] Even earlier, in 1847, a missionary had returned from Liberia and reported on conditions to the black-influenced Wood River Baptist Association of Illinois.[53]

Once again Nate Shaw's remembrances, representative of many of the average person's, prove illuminating.[54] He recalled, "I heard talk when I was a boy of how the colored people come to America. Now the talk that I heard might not be exactly how it was but I have no reason to argue with the words. It all comes down to this: the colored people was transferred here from Africa just like you transfer a drove of stock. White man gathered em up in the distant countries; they didn't have no knowledge of where they was goin, they had to move by orders, had no idea of where they was goin. Passed em across the water in some fashion and they was put over in this country and sold just like you'd go out here and sell a hog, a horse, a cow, just so." As to their racial identity based on color, Shaw recounted, "They was black people—all of em was dark at that time—but they wasn't recognized as people." And for the poignancy of the memory that haunted Frederick Douglass, Ida B. Wells, and so many others, he probably sighed and stated, "Well, after they got over here—I has a hard time keepin myself together when I thinks about it—they was put under the possession of marsters and mistresses."[55] Black

America could never forget slavery, so the fair symbolized an important ritual of national redemption if white America acted with contrition.

Among the emigrationists who sought an answer to their dreams in West Africa, the homeland of their ancestors, their interests and commitments ranged expansively also. The "true believers" were Bishop Henry McNeal Turner as well as erstwhile emigrationist Alexander Crummell, along with the rank and file who soured on unkept American promises of equality of opportunity and protection under the law and who wanted to leave centuries-long memories of misery.

The national debate over emigration to Africa filled the African American newspapers of 1892, especially after Bishop Turner returned from a sojourn to Liberia and embarked on a crusade promoting emigration. Even Ida B. Wells saw something favorable in the Turner position, and in 1892, at least, she criticized T. Thomas Fortune's lambasting of Turner. Ironically, the next year at the Congress on Africa, her future husband, Ferdinand L. Barnett, would read Fortune's latest assault on the emigrationist position and add his personal denunciation. This conclave embodied the spirit of the ideological debate that became such an integral part of the Congress on Africa which is covered in chapter 10.

Nevertheless, for 1892, Wells argued that not only whites, but many African Americans, longed for blacks to return to West Africa. While she never considered emigration, she admitted that "the entire race is not sanguine over our possessions in this country." Malaria posed a health problem, but so did diseases in the American South. As to Africa's riches, the scramble of Europeans to control them confirmed their presence. Comparing the unknown dangers and problems of settlement in Africa to those encountered by the Puritans of Massachusetts Bay, Wells convincingly argued that African resettlement offered opportunities for those hardy and committed enough to seek them. From what Wells "gleaned from current history, the great need of Liberia is a strong, intelligent citizenship, to develop her resources and evolve a government which shall command the attention and respect of the civilized world. For any faction of our eight millions of Afro-Americans to devote its talents to the work with measurable success would be an example and inspiration for Afro-Americans the world over. The greater the obstacles the more pronounced the victory."[56]

The source of emigrationist sentiment, whether as a continuous attachment or a cyclical phenomenon, appearing at times of greatest discontent with American conditions, is debatable. At the cusp of the twenty-first century, it is refreshing just to have had a historical reality finally recognized as such.

Part Two

IN HOST CITY CHICAGO

> *The relationship of the Negro community to this event [the World's Columbian Exposition] throws some light on Negro-white relationships and the strength of Negro institutions during the nineties.*
>
> —St. Clair Drake,
> *Negro Churches and Voluntary Associations*

The scholarship of renowned sociologist St. Clair Drake, based on his activities as a participant-observer of the black Chicago social scene and chronicler of its peculiarities, provided the vital intellectual framework needed to link the character and role of Chicago's African Americans to the city and world at the time of the World's Columbian Exposition of 1893.[1] His focus on black institutional vitality revealed individuals pursuing dreams emanating from work, strong families, churches, and social organizations, and showed the dynamics of African American advancement and the bases for its myriad leaderships.

With the dawn of freedom in 1865, nearly three decades before the opening of the fair in Chicago, the African American population consisted of about 3,000 working class persons locked in the grip of uncertainty as to their contemporary status as citizens and without any substantial promises as to their future. By 1868 and 1870, they enjoyed, respectively, a guarantee of citizenship rights and, after a nudge to their state government, an extension of the franchise. By the last decade of the nineteenth century, host city Chicago in the heart of the American Midwest offered a set of opportunities notable for their dissimilarities. In the economic sphere, work as the essential element toward achieving personal independence seemed readily at hand, even before plans for the exposition were announced. But, "in the north, although Negroes were rapidly becoming mainly urban dwellers, and in spite of their highly industrialized environment, they experienced great difficulty in securing work in factories."[2] So, new work, as represented by the creation of a new venue, the "White City," raised hopes.

Work by itself could never completely dictate the limits of the African American lifestyle. Instead, the perception of what life should be and the thinking that buttressed it meshed with work to shape a *culture of work* that fit the African American lifestyle as much as a combination of external and internal realities warranted. The world of the respectables represented as much of what they could glean from life as it did what they had to accept or dared to expect. Chapter 4 addresses the character of this arrangement. The response of the refined element of society to its fulfillment through chosen endeavors paralleled that of the respectables as both labored to sustain not only their physical needs but also their nonmaterial desires. Chapter 5 explores the relationship between the finite nature of size of the African American population and its seemingly infinite capacity to break from prescribed roles in a Darwinian environment.

4

THE DOMAIN OF WORK

The labor of one-half of this country has always been, and is still being done by [the African Americans]. The first credit this country had in its commerce with foreign nations was created by production resulting from their labor. The wealth created by their industry has afforded to the white people of this country the leisure essential to their group progress in education, art, science, industry, and invention.

—Ida B. Wells, *The Reason Why the Colored American Is Not in the World's Columbian Exposition,* 1893[1]

We tell you to go to work; and to work you must go or die. Men are not valued in this country, or in any country, for what they are; they are valued for what they can do. It is vain if we talk about being men, if we do not do the work of men.

—Frederick Douglass[2]

The arduous task of reshaping the marshy landscape along the south shore of Lake Michigan at Fifty-ninth Street into the series of lagoons and canals intersecting the impressive white superstructures that made "White City" so physically awe-inspiring finally began with a groundbreaking ceremony in June 1891. At this point in time "a man stuck the nose of a plough into the sand of this plain . . . and before some scores of thousands of working men all over the country—day-laborers, like himself; iron-forgers, architects, truckmen, carpenters, painters, surveyors, glaziers, designers, moulders, joiners, masons, gardeners—men of every trade and art and handicraft, of every nationality, of every class and kind of humanity, working together in widely separate places for the accomplishment of one purpose."[3]

To the extent that this writer's description meant to convey that inclusiveness reigned—that is, that the work force was truly cosmopolitan or multiracial—then a begrudging systemic hope of new work opportunities held nationally by African Americans appeared justified. Figure 4 shows three workers rowing on the uncompleted waterway system, probably on a Sunday,

4. Three unidentified workmen enjoying a boat ride on the site of the still-to-be-completed fairgrounds. Courtesy of the Chicago Public Library.

and apparently enjoying themselves while viewing the extent of the work completed. When Paul Lawrence Dunbar arrived in Chicago, he joined thousands of other young and older men seeking, but not necessarily finding, work. His biographer wrote that "out on the fairgrounds he tramped from building to building, but no workers were needed. Finally he got a job, cleaning one of the big domes. That lasted only a few days. His next job was in a basement shipping room, uncrating exhibit specimens. Here dampness soon brought on a racking cough. The cough got worse, and Paul quit to look for work out of doors, or at least where there was good air."[4] James Weldon Johnson's easy access to the sphere of carpentry and guarantee of work as a chair boy seemed to be unusual. He wrote home describing how "by reason of our industrial training in Atlanta University, fifteen of us were employed to do work at the grounds as carpenters, at $3.25 per day of eight hours, and the other was employed as a plasterer at $4.50. There is more work here than men can be employed to do. Any price is being paid for workmen."[5] An analysis of photographs and pencil sketches of the work site suggests the existence of a cosmopolitan work force, but a shaded face by no means indicated with certainty that a worker was of African descent. Most trades such as designing, glaziering, surveying, painting, sculpting, and moulding were off limits to certain groups, particularly African Americans, and many immigrants possessed swarthy hues easily mistaken for the mixed hues of African Americans from a distance or from the use of a faint penmark.

5. The workmen who cleared the marsh and wooded areas for the fairgrounds. An African American worker with his horse team is visible at left. Courtesy of the University of Chicago Library.

6. A common scene on the site of the fairgrounds, as workmen remove debris. Courtesy of the Chicago Public Library.

7. These are the workers who prepared the fairgrounds for the construction of scores of structures. Courtesy of the Chicago Public Library.

Ferdinand L. Barnett saw a problem here, one with a clear intent to harm African Americans. He wrote in *The Reason Why the Colored American Is Not in the World's Columbian Exposition:* "In this wonderful hive of national industry, representing an outlay of thirty million dollars, and numbering its employees by the thousands, only two colored people could be found whose occupations were of a higher grade than that of a janitor, laborer and porter, and these two only clerkships. Only as a menial is the Colored American to be seen—the Nation's deliberate and cowardly tribute to the southern demand 'to keep the Negro in his place.'"[6] Barnett rejected in absolute terms a continued horizontal African American domination of the menial and service positions; instead, he demanded a vertical integration of the work force, with African Americans sharing positions along the pyramid of work, from the apex to its base. However, for the black working class in a nation on the verge of a major depression, work of any kind was cherished.

Assuming the absence of manifest racism in hiring at the unskilled level, some work appeared to have been available for all common laborers in the earliest days of preparation of the fairgrounds. Three photographs show crews at work, probably dredging and leveling the marshy areas on which the fair's buildings and lagoons would be situated. To build the canals and lagoons, 537,000 cubic yards of soil and filler had to be moved from place to place. In the first photograph (fig. 5), an assemblage of perhaps two dozen teams of horses with handlers has gathered. In the background in the upper left quarter, an African American with his team is clearly visible, with a look on his face that evinces immense satisfaction with his status as a worker. Two photographs (figs. 6 and 7) of the removal of soil and placement of it into horse-driven railroads cars show the African American presence again. Assuming the continued presence of manifest sexism and racism in hiring of black women at any level, almost no work would have been available to them.

Beyond seeking seats on the two influential governing boards over the fair, the National Board of Commissioners and the Board of Lady Managers, or holding positions that allowed African Americans to mold their group's image through exhibits, another perspective existed as to what the World's Columbian Exposition represented as a major event to the nation. Work as a sustaining and emancipating influence on personal betterment constituted an essential part of the African American working class ethos around the country. For the laboring class, the announcement of a world's fair meant possible job opportunities in host city Chicago. Conscious of their role in building the nation from its earliest days, they believed all too well the truth of what Ida B. Wells wrote about in 1893 in *The Reason Why the Colored American Is Not in the World's Columbian Exposition.* America's wealth had been extracted from their energies and therefore built upon their shoulders. No segment of the work force knew this better than the southern black labor force that was still concentrated in the agricultural production of that antebellum staple long deposed as king on the world market—cotton. Others in budding southern industries found themselves relegated to low-paying economic niches just like their northern brethren.[7] So, seemingly as part of a dismal national pattern, African American workers already residing in, or on their way to, Chicago faced an uphill climb as they sought employment parity.

Notwithstanding the documented, indispensable role of the African slave laborer as a major factor in the growth of the American economy between the late seventeenth and mid-nineteenth centuries, the time of the fair stood as the time of the industrial laborer. And racism in the North had precluded the entry of African Americans into that economic sector. Du Bois studied economic conditions in Philadelphia during this decade and concluded that while racism played a part in the exclusion of the African American worker from industry, "possibly a more potent part, is the natural spirit of monopoly and desire to keep up wages. So long as the cry against 'Irish' or 'foreigners' was able to marshal race prejudice in the service of those who desired to keep those people out of some employments, that cry was sedulously used. So to-day the workmen plainly see that a large amount of competition can be shut off by taking advantage of public opinion and drawing the color line."[8] Du Bois did not let capital off the hook cleanly. Employers also had to share a portion of the blame for racial exclusion. One exceptional experiment in fair play was instituted at the Midvale Steel Works by Frederick W. Taylor, hailed as the "father of scientific management." Taylor proved conclusively that race differences played no part in the push for efficiency that he so fervently and successfully pursued.[9]

In Chicago as early as spring 1891 five white labor organizations, including the Knights of Labor, met to discuss the control of work at the fair in anticipation of groundbreaking. Despite the image of the Knights as a conglomeration of organizations that embraced inclusivity in employment even in regard to African Americans, the matter of color-blind economic opportunity was never mentioned. Most important were the eight-hour day, employment of native-born Americans who were primarily local residents, and institution of a minimum wage to allay the invasion of low-priced, non-union labor. Without a guarantee of the right of non-whites to work, in Chicago, at least, the Knights as champions of the rights of the African American worker failed in their mission.[10] This setback occurred at a time when African Americans comprised at least ten percent of the Knights' national membership.[11]

Not unexpectedly, in 1892 friction between African American workers and the city's organized labor movement was exacerbated beyond repair as members of the Knights in Chicago endorsed the deportation of African Americans to Africa. The city's African American workers responded by staging a protest meeting, in whose wake a letter of indignation circulated which attracted sizeable coverage in the white press. Sadly, within six months of the fair's closing, the Knights again angered African American workers when the suggestion of lessening job competition by deporting black labor to Central Africa was made. American to the core, these African Americans reacted with the indignant suggestion that "if this country is too small for the Knights of Labor and the Negro, then let the Knights leave."[12] While nothing beyond these nonviolent actions took place, if the dominant immigrant groups in the city, the Germans and the Irish, had been involved there might have been a resort to physical confrontation. Given the strength of unions in the city and their exclusion of African Americans, union memberships guaranteed work for whites and a greater sense of isolation for African Americans.[13]

Although St. Clair Drake described African Americans who migrated to the city to find work and subsequently decided to remain permanently because of job opportunities,[14] it appears that the bulk of employed workers in the city at the time of the fair were already residents. Accordingly, Chicago's laboring force on the eve of, and during, the fair could have been described as basically resident and on the economic periphery. In 1892, *Scribner's Magazine* described working-class black Chicago in terms that might appear cryptic outside the period in which the article was written, but that resonated with clarity to its cosmopolitan readership: "The colored people have done and are doing remarkably well, considering the disadvantages and discouragements under which they live. They are industrious [performing energetically and devotedly] rather than hard working [performing robotically like the immigrants], . . . and economical [avoiding extravagance] rather than acquisitive [seeking wealth greedily]."[15]

On the eve of the fair, the class and occupational configuration of the African American population in Chicago rested primarily on this nonindustrial, service-oriented base of approximately 10,000 workers.[16] Contemporary analysis depicted restaurant and hotel workers, domestic servants, Pullman porters, foundry men, and dock workers as prevalent.[17] A smattering of carpenters, plasterers, musicians, and other skilled craftsmen could be found but were almost invisible, immersed as they were in a citywide labor force numbering one-half million. Except for a handful of specialized venues in which the need for crucial skills overshadowed racial preference, clerical positions remained out of reach for competent African Americans of both genders.[18] Jobs for black females were particularly limited; three-quarters of them were in the domestic and service sectors. Chicago's black municipal employees in offices and service capacities were scattered throughout the work force. Only one library clerk, a female, was on the city's payroll before 1893, with another to be added as a political gesture by Mayor Carter Harrison during the fair. The Chicago Fire Department still carried only one unit and the police department expanded its force to include twenty-three men in uniform because of the "liberal political administration of Mayor Washburne."[19] Federal employees at the post office numbered seventy-eight. Lastly, a predominantly male professional class, comprising well-trained physicians and attorneys, was slowly evolving.

Yet an abiding faith in the ultimate equity of the American labor system saw African American expectations of work rise by the very fact that the fairgrounds had to be constructed by spring 1893. This deadline meant work for 7,000 to 8,000 men who constituted, appropriate to the pervasiveness of the fair's pronounced martial air, a virtual "army of laborers with a staff of artists and architects . . . under the command of D. H. Burnham, . . . a man born for generalship."[20]

In a city basking in the reflected glory of its industrial might, the exclusion of African Americans from the manufacturing sector relegated them to an economic venue of circumscribed opportunity and limited expectations. The commercial sphere appeared almost as unpromising. Amassing a fortune through meat packing, steel production, transportation, or merchandising would have been unthinkable. As nineteenth century residents, the "old-timers," recalled, "no one dreamed that a member of our Race would [ever] be wealthy."[21] While white Chicago developed its upper class, a group from which its civic leadership emerged, black Chicago was prevented from building a comparable wellspring.

As members of a distinct and separate segment of the labor force, and accustomed to the need to maximize whatever advantages could be found under whatever conditions they encountered, working class African Americans availed themselves of every job opportunity. Acclimated to hard work, with "almost three-fifths of the Negro population ten years of age and over" as wage earners,[22] they sought employment before the fair opened as well as during its course of operations on the fairgrounds, along the Midway, in the Loop, and even in the near south side's notorious red-light district, the Levee.

Among these respectables, perhaps no occupational group approached their work with the sense of "industriousness" noted by *Scribner's* more than waitpersons, both male and female, the former sometimes referred to as "Commodores of the Dining Room."[23] Ordinarily, more than 1,500 males in Chicago[24] earned livable wages in these competitive and stressful workplaces. Working with agility, charm, skill, strength, and pride in their calling, their trademark—an effervescent smile—might have been a grin after all. An ability to interact amicably with patrons obviously produced bigger tips. With a demeanor commonly reminiscent to whites of their group's previous condition of forced obsequiousness just three decades before, this perceived acceptance of racial subordination was really a simple desire to give the customer, paraphrasing Marshall Field, what he or she wanted at the moment. An effective waiter conferred on a diner an elevated status, if only for an hour, whatever his actual social rank.

Within this culture of work, a unique structure evolved. Headwaiters directed a hierarchy that included assistants, a captain, and various grades of lieutenancy. They also derived great economic benefits from their positions. The family of Palmer House headwaiter Charles Jordan received one such benefit when, after Jordan's death in Arkansas, Chicago hotel magnate Potter Palmer assumed the expenses of embalming and shipping his remains home to Chicago for burial. Headwaiter C. C. Lewis displayed his power when, in May 1893, he challenged a strike called by the Colored Waiters' Alliance against at least three hotels, no doubt aware of the fact that his position carried a level of security that "mere" waiters could only envy in an owner-dominated workplace. His taking the side of capital against labor was probably typical for persons in control, who had the most to gain from labor's output of energy in the workplace.[25]

The culture of work for African Americans was shaped by additional circumstances. First, because of blatant racism, black workers earned their living outside the industrial sphere, so a sense of labor consciousness and solidarity was less likely to be nurtured. Several generations removed in time, historian Sharon Harley described African American women workers in the domestic segment as defying convention about the nexus of work and life,[26] but this attitude applied to their male racial counterparts as well. Harley cited May Anna Madison, who was interviewed in John Langston Gwaltney's *Drylongso: A Self-Portrait on Black America*. Madison proclaimed: "I don't know any black woman who is too proud to get out here and work . . . . [But] working for other people can't be but so good for you because you are working for them and not for yourself. See, the best work is work that you want to do that you do for yourself. . . . One very important difference between white people and black people is that white people think that you *are* your work. Now, a black person has more sense than that because he knows that what I am doing doesn't have anything to do with what I want to do or what I do when I am doing for myself. Now, black people think that work is just what I have to do to get what I want."[27] In the same vein, for the twentieth century southern worker, Robin D. G. Kelley described and analyzed variations and continuities as African Americans molded the sphere of work as much as it shaped their thinking, behavior, and lives.[28]

Second, a sense of personal mastery over a challenging task was possible on a daily basis with a job well done. In the spheres of work, family, and friends, this type of employment carried a heightened status unachievable by the worker whose work regimen was routinized. Association with the nation's elite in the grand hotels and restaurants in the nation's second largest metropolis placed the waiter, if only in his hidden thoughts, in close proximity to individuals at the pinnacle of economic power. For the few that were college graduates or with partial college training, serving their supposed racial and social "betters" probably allowed the opportunity for some internal group version of racial one-upmanship.

The experiences of a waiter on the dining cars of the Chicago, Burlington & Quincy Railroad illustrate several of these points. John M. Washington began working for the CB&Q in 1881 at age twenty-two, hoping to join the wait staff. Lacking experience or skills, he was relegated to managing and cleaning the gas lamps in dining cars, at which he excelled, until such time as an apprenticeship of observing was served. Once in the service, Washington distinguished himself for being able to take and serve twelve full orders at one time. Eventually, company officials recognized his value to the railroad and he was promoted to mail messenger and bank liaison which "brought him in[to] contact with many of the country's leading railroad magnates."[29]

Once home, anecdotes and reenactments of white posturing and pretense surely found attentive ears.[30] In the sphere of recreation within African American society, dominated as it was by the working class, the replication of what the white nouveau riches experienced allowed headwaiters to join Pullman porters and servants to the millionaires in acting as the arbiters of working class standards of conduct. This explains how Julius Avendorph, a private messenger, came to be called the "social arbiter of black Chicago."[31] The cakewalk, the African American dance caricature of Nordic pretense and arrogance, originated from this group and spread to the black theater. An embarrassment to the black elite, it fit the needs of working class African Americans as it provided relief from the tensions of laboring in a hostile white world and as a vehicle through which to sometimes challenge white authority covertly. On the other hand, having fun in and of itself often reigned as the prime motivation behind some of these activities. Paul Lawrence Dunbar witnessed this ability of the worker to transform drudgery and down time into a recreational episode. He wrote about young waiters in a hotel:

> When they were not busy they would gather around and talk, usually about girls. In order to keep an eye out for prospective customers, they always stood near the dining-room door, much to the annoyance of the busy waiters who had to pass through with heavy trays.

"Jump back!" would come the warning, and then with a teasing grin for the romantic topic, "Jump back, *honey*, jump back!"

The boys jumped, and then went on with their gossip—

"I seen my lady home las' night!"

"Uh-oh! An' then what?"

"I raise' huh lips an' took a li'l taste. *M-m-m!*"

In between came the repeated warning, "Jump back!"

It echoed in Dunbar's mind like a refrain, one he later turned into the poem "A Negro Love Song."[32]

Carving one's own niche in the workplace meant that compensation, at whatever level, adequate or inadequate, did not have to dictate the totality of a worker's attitudes. Earnings of waitpersons, for example, could climb as high as $75 a month for a headwaiter and explained why "a man would pride himself on being able to tell you" of his pecuniary achievement.[33] Wages could also fall as low as $15 per month for a water boy. Young Paul Lawrence Dunbar found work as a waiter in a hotel and met another aspiring poet, James Corrothers, "who eked out his earnings as space writer for Chicago newspapers by waiting on table during the evening rush hours. This 'dinner waiting' brought three dollars a week and dinner."[34]

Restaurant work had a dismal downside. David Katzman has written of waiters in Detroit that they felt constant apprehension about a possible reduction in force, long hours, and uncertain pay.[35] Such conditions were surely not unique to any specific locale and help explain the basis of African American protest in the workplace in Chicago. Differentiation in grades of service, responsibility, and remuneration often extended to "10 grades and pay runs."[36] Dissatisfaction with wages led African American waiters to stage several strikes in May 1893 which crippled operations at Loop restaurants, indicating a labor consciousness in advance of black entry into the industrial work force. These strikes were led and supported almost solely by African Americans (in one instance, they were undertaken in cooperation with German waiters). The issues of contention were working conditions, wages, and the matter of dignity.[37]

For waiters, the fair represented both increased work opportunities and increased wages as the restaurants on the fairgrounds, in the Loop, and in downtown hotels filled with the anticipated millions of visitors. At the fairgrounds, there were twenty-seven cafes and restaurants which made plans to serve 8,000 customers with a needed work force of 1,000 waiters and cooks.[38]

One story in particular showed how these workers, through their composure, dignity, and concern for humanity irrespective of color, could establish a link bordering on congeniality with whites. A conversation, rather than a formal, procedural demand for service, had taken place between a white female diner and a waiter on the outskirts of the fair at a Stony Island Avenue restaurant. It evolved into commiseration over the fate of a young, attractive, female victim of a disastrous fire that occurred in July 1893 in the middle of the fairgrounds. Both parties recognized that as humans they could communicate, and so they did, in a most humane fashion.[39] A contrasting view among pseudoaristocratic, condescending whites, as recounted by socialite Hobart Chatfield Chatfield-Taylor, saw these workers solely as "grinning waiters."[40]

The Pullman porters who provided hotel-type service on railroad coaches and on the luxurious Pullman Palace Cars were dubbed the "Ambassadors of Hospitality." This occupational group, along with their female counterparts working as maids, enjoyed unique status among African Americans because of their work experience, position in the burgeoning railroad industry, and expected workplace demeanor. As the era of industrialism proceeded to transform American society, a new economic opportunity evolved. The nation was becoming dependent on the rails for long-distance transportation, and expected luxury as a nonmaterial byproduct. African Americans could not be hired as conductors and engineers anywhere in the nation, and outside the South they could not work as trainmen and firemen, so jobs as porters and maids gave them an opportunity beyond farm work. William H. Harris wrote: "The Pullman Palace Car Company of Chicago employed many blacks as porters and maids on sleeping cars to perform personal services for the increasing number of passengers who traveled across the country."[41] But Pullman did even more than this. Blacks virtually monopolized this entire service sector.[42]

When choosing a work force, industrial magnate George M. Pullman was predisposed to recruit from the ranks of former slaves. He sought a particular personality type to satisfy his white customers, both in the North and in the South, and deference bordering on obsequiousness, whether feigned or ingrained, fit the bill. Pullman went so far as to insist that porters smile on all occasions when encountering passengers. In context, to this industrial magnate who made millions manufacturing his Palace Cars, "which provided the needed link between the sumptuous hotels that met the traveler in all of our great cities," servility was expected from all of his employees, whether they worked in the shop, in the rolling hotel suites called Palace Cars, or at his model, all-white employee town—appropriately named Pullman—located south of Chicago. As to whether the specter of racism was at the core of Pullman's demands, that point is conjectural, since African American leaders such as Frederick Douglass often effused about the industrialist's beneficence with apparent knowledge of or indifference to his demands as an employer. At the Congress on Africa, even Bishop Henry McNeal Turner found occasion to praise Pullman.[43]

Belying the sincerity of that ever-present smile, the Pullman porter's work schedule was grueling. A 100-hour work week was becoming all too common on train runs. Chances for promotion were virtually nonexistent. "If [a porter] enters the service at 18 he will likely be receiving the same pay at 48 if he stays in the service,"[44] reported Richard R. Wright. However, wages and tips could exceed those earned by a waiter or porter in private hotel service, which rendered Pullman jobs extraordinarily attractive.

As a newer generation of workers succeeded the original pool of former slaves, their expectations increased, but there was no appreciable change in their work demeanor. The image of the ubiquitous, sometimes overly courteous "George," with his obligatory smile, still dominated this service by the end of the century. Yet, for the later generation of porters coming into service around and after 1893, their public image belied their elevated status among African Americans of all classes who knew only too well the intricacies of wearing the mask in a white-dominated society.[45] To confirm this disparity between perception and actuality, one has only to reflect on the career of erstwhile porter Jesse Binga, who in the next century became the personification of African American assertiveness and success in entrepreneurial and then in business endeavors as a hard-nosed financier who could be broken only by a national economic depression.

In order to compensate for the drudgery and the sometimes excessive demands on their time, "Daddy Joe" stories evolved. While Daddy Joe was a real person, the exploits of this extraordinary figure outgrew reality and seemed appropriate remedies for all occasions when members of his race needed relief from their economic and psychological oppression. According to stories told in private in off hours around the Baker heating stoves, Daddy Joe's stature was Bunyanesque. His height and hands were so imposing that he could "walk flat-footed down the aisle and let the upper berths down on each other."[46] Whether encountering hostile red men on the Plains or malicious white men on the Palace Cars, Daddy Joe was master of any situation. Through it all, his demeanor established the standard to which all Pullman porters aspired: loyalty and dedication to the job regardless of the impediments.

Renowned sociologist E. Franklin Frazier both legitimized and elevated the status of these workers when, in 1932, his doctoral dissertation of the previous year was published. He maintained that "the occupational organization of the Negro community conform[ed] to the distribution of Pullman porters, who at one time represented on the whole the group that had a comparable good income and a high conception of [its] place in the community. 'Once in Chicago,' said a former Pullman porter, 'you weren't anybody unless you were a Pullman porter. We handled more money than most of the colored people, and led all the social life.'"[47] This comment had significance beyond the sphere of work; it extended into the social realms of recreation and leadership. The succeeding chapter incorporates the latter subject into a discussion of the nature of multiple leaderships in world's fair–era Chicago.

Pullman porters, waiters, and others had a demonstrated ability to translate their experience with fine living into something that the greater community could enjoy. In a social realm dominated by camaraderie and an escape into leisure-time activities, food and social interaction had the power to transform a people, especially members of the working class in the service areas. One example of how a supposedly dispirited group could use a menu to affirm self-esteem is the serving list at the third annual banquet of the Newport Hunting and Fishing Club on January 22, 1885. The menu featured Fillet of Beef Larded aux Champignons, Rabbit Braise, Stewed Bear with Jelly, Squirrel Larded, Quail on Toast, Roast Venison, Baked Red Snapper, and other delicacies.[48] The social clubs and fraternal orders that pervaded the city depended on these annual functions to ease the tensions of living in an increasingly hostile society. The desire to be left alone, free from white interference, to have "good times," much like the European immigrant groups, makes too much sense not to have been accepted and examined by earlier social analysts of African American behavior.

Wearing their uniforms as symbols of their knightly authority, Pullman porters assumed unto themselves a power never envisioned by their employers and customers and recognizable all too clearly in the black community. These "ambassadors" expanded their horizons individually as well as collectively, gaining knowledge of how the nation and the world operated through travel, eavesdropping on discussions of the nation's movers and shakers, and reflecting on what they said and heard in dialogues with compassionate whites.[49] In 1883, one Pullman porter, Floyd Thornhill, engaged in an informal conversation with a U.S. Senator that soon transformed itself into a formal interview used in a Senate hearing on labor conditions in the South.[50] Perhaps with knowledge of that incident or a similar episode on the rails, historian J. A. Rogers illustrated this newly emerging personality among the Pullman porters through his use of a composite character, Dixon, who bettered his southern "better" intellectually on a transcontinental train ride.[51] On a westbound train heading to the Windy City, one world's fair writer from New England expressed intense satisfaction at curbing the feigned fawning of an obnoxious porter. The porter was a tyrant, "the unresisted bully of the car" whose actions were stopped once "that dapper darkie's shoulder" was paralyzed by a firm grip.[52] Quite reasonably, for an African American to intimidate white passengers while simultaneously appearing to observe proper racial decorum demonstrated how well some of these men succeeded in being masters of their work environment.

Another challenge to the dignity of labor took place during the summer of 1893 when the Pullman Company placed its famous Palace Cars on display at the world's fair at the imposing Transportation Building. A rather servile "Mr. Fritsch" provided regular status reports to his "honored Mr. Pullman" on the number of visitors inspecting the cars, the number of important dignitaries who viewed the cars with a prospect of adding them to their railroads or personal travel accouterments, and the efficiency of his retinue of porters, who kept the cars spotless. On one occasion, Fritsch proudly wrote to Pullman, "We had a fine train to show today. It was cleaned well inside and outside, as I had made it pretty lively for the [work] force yesterday and am determined to return a well-kept train to Pullman [town, on] Oct. 31."[53] Porters on the rolling trains worked just as hard as this crew on the stationary exhibit, yet the prospect of decent wages never materialized for any of them, a feature all too typical for all employees of the Pullman Company.

The small number of African American musicians in the city and from around the nation who secured work in Chicago before the fair played in isolated settings, such as the red-light district, the Levee.[54] On the fairgrounds they faced complete exclusion. The overwhelmingly white organized bands in the city dominated the musical scene. When the Haytians celebrated their designated day at the fair in July, the highly regarded and all-white Iowa State Band provided the music. This band included among its instruments an oboe, some clarinets, and saxophones along with extensive brass instruments —French horns, trombones, and a tuba. Even the eagerly anticipated Colored American Day in August advertised the participation of the all-white Gilmore's Band. The many visiting African American musicians such as pianist and cornetist Scott Joplin of Sedalia, Missouri, were left to find employment where they could, in his case on the periphery of the fairgrounds where many visitors retired after their exhaustive strolls. In fact, Joplin may have headed a band.

As to the music played, classical initially dominated, as the fair's musical czar, Theodore Thomas, promoted music to the masses as an art form worthy of their acceptance. Within two months, white fairgoers rejected both the daily fee to hear the classics and Thomas himself. After Thomas's resignation in late July, popular and marching band music succeeded in capturing the public's fancy. March tunes of the Sousa variety and songs like "'The Bowery," "Reuben, Reuben," and Ta Ra Ra Boom-de-ay" were added to the repertoire of music by Wagner, Mozart, Liszt, and other classical masters. Renowned Bohemian composer and arranger Antonín Dvořák, while enjoying the classical offerings of Thomas and others, with which he was of course familiar, caused a stir by advocating that Americans seek the roots of their authentic national music in African American music. To the host of Anglo-Saxon music critics who questioned the composer's judgment, *The Presto*, a monthly musical trade journal, offered this response: "The future of American music seems to be an all-absorbing question since Dr. Dvorak rendered his famous opinion relative to Negro melodies. The critics do not agree with him that American inspiration must spring from such a common-place source. They think the worthy has missed the mark entirely, although they do not agree as to the substitute they would offer for the Negro airs proposed by Dvorak. It is apparently easier in this instance to tear down than to build up. Still, some of the opinions expressed afforded interesting reading."[55] Throughout the South, African Americans interested in maintaining this treasured cultural legacy from a trying past viewed the composer's statements as simple good sense.

8. The staff of Daniel Burnham included an African American. Courtesy of the Chicago Historical Society.

Despite restraints on the performance of both black performers and black music, some was undoubtedly played immediately outside the fairgrounds along Stony Island Avenue or near the Midway. Singing groups such as the Fisk Jubilee Singers and the Hampton Quartet sang extensively at African American functions both on and off the fairgrounds and were well received by both races. Another group, the Standard Quartet, performed at a concert in July 1893, singing "Negro spiritual songs while others contributed patriotic songs."[56] Significantly, the only authentic African-based music played on the fairgrounds occurred at the Dahomey Village, and it was apparently enjoyed by as many as it might have annoyed. Importantly, Will Marion Cook dated the birth of ragtime to the year and incident of the fair.[57] According to Cook: "About 1898 marked the starting and quick growth of the so-called 'ragtime.' As far back as 1875 Negroes in questionable resorts along the Mississippi had commenced to evolve this musical figure, but at the World's Fair in Chicago 'ragtime' got a running start and swept the Americas, next Europe, and to-day the craze has not diminished."[58]

While work on the fairgrounds for African Americans was finite, their presence could hardly have been said to have been invisible. The official World's Columbian Exposition photographs of the various staffs included African Americans along with their colleagues. Director of Works Daniel H.

9. Fair official Buchanan's staff, which administered the activities of the massive Agricultural Building, included an African American. Courtesy of the Chicago Historical Society.

10. This photo of the staff of the Hide and Leather Building shows another African American worker in the top row. Courtesy of the Chicago Historical Society.

11. The job of guarding the world's first Ferris Wheel was assigned to an African American. Courtesy of the Chicago Historical Society.

Burnham's staff photograph included E. Jackson, head janitor, along with his coworkers, dressed appropriately for the occasion (fig. 8). Chief Buchanan and his staff, including the dapper J. Shreeves, are pictured outside the Agricultural Building (fig. 9). When manufacturers and staff from the Hide and Leather Building posed for their place in history, included was an unidentified African American in the top row (fig. 10). The famous circular, steel-framed wheel of William Ferris relied on A. S. Johnson to perform his duties as official office guard (fig. 11). Washingtonian Louis B. Anderson landed "the job of exchange reader in his department of Publicity and Promotion. Among the archives of the Exposition the scrap-books containing all newspaper references to the Fair throughout the world represent his work in that department"[59] (see fig. 12). And we must not overlook J. E. Johnson, who was employed as a stenographer in the Bureau of Awards.[60]

The importance of this is found in the fact that, given the racism of the day, these employees could have been excluded or hidden, but were not. They are featured as integral parts of organizations, appearing dignified and representing neither themselves nor their race in a derogatory fashion. In at least one exhibit depicting slave-plantation Louisiana, the latter did occur.

Deliberate, calculated racial exclusion proved the rule for the Columbian Guard, however. Very early, hiring for this elite, quasi-military escort, police, and fire protective unit of the fair unfolded in a depressing, Machiavellian scenario. Exclusion of African Americans became the rule as 2,000

12. Two custodians at "White City" discuss the affairs of the day. Courtesy of the Chicago Historical Society.

openings were filled. When William J. Crawford, a seven-year resident of the city, applied for a position, the staff physician deliberately misread a chest measurement to make Crawford fall one inch short of a required expanded chest size of 36 inches. Even Crawford's immediate reexamination by another white doctor failed to satisfy Guard leadership. Two subsequent letters re-

13. This African American, seen walking toward us from the bridge in the company of another man, is dressed in a custodian's uniform. Courtesy of the Chicago Public Library.

questing reconsideration were ignored. The Guard remained lily white for the duration of the fair.

In contrast, the fair's custodial staff, which served in a unit initially falling under the jurisdiction of the Columbian Guard's leadership (until a week before the fair opened, when it became part of the Superintendent of Buildings' responsibility), did include African Americans. Anywhere from 1,000 to 2,000 janitors, watchmen, overseers and foremen, and stable hands had responsibility for cleaning up the fairgrounds during the day and the myriad buildings after closing.[61] African Americans were hired exclusively for the 140-person janitorial staff. Their responsibilities included *light* clean-up during the day, and their dapper gray uniforms (fig. 12) were similar in design to those worn by members of the Columbian Guard. They were assigned to the Guard stations and in the Service Building, which made them highly visible to the public. One such immaculately dressed custodian was photographed walking through the fairgrounds in conversation with a companion (fig. 13).

The *heavy* work of cleaning the fairgrounds and buildings was purportedly left to the predominantly white, possibly foreign-born, watchmen, who were responsible for mopping the floors, cleaning the buildings, and "caring for stoves and salamanders therein."[62] Their numbers fluctuated from well over 1,000 before the May 1 opening of the fair to 705 by the summer months. Since the low pay, $1.50 per day, combined with "conditions [that were] al-

ways discouraging," led supervisory personnel to wonder at "how little dissatisfaction and how much actual enthusiasm was shown by the men,"[63] conjec-
ture exists that some African Americans might have been included in their
ranks. This link between untoward labor conditions and compliant work attitudes represented circumstances under which the employment of workers
across the racial divide flourished.

At particular exhibits, such as Pullman's, company workers performed
custodial duties. Moreover, some African Americans were hired as "washroom
caretakers," lavatory attendants in pay toilets who provided toiletries and other
amenities to patrons. Demanding of his time, but not deleterious to his dignity, Paul Lawrence Dunbar took such work at a pay scale of $10.50 per week,
with Tuesday being payday.[64] The persons who engaged in the various types of
work described to this point constituted that segment of society referred to by
Drake as the respectables.

As to the variety of employment, Dr. M. A. Majors recalled: "The World's
Fair Commission graciously accorded our youths who came with students'
credentials from the various colleges and universities the monopoly of chair
rolling, messengers, dusters, caretakers and watchmen."[65] As for the students from Atlanta University and elsewhere at white institutions, they earned
their money as attendants who would roll moving chairs throughout the fairgrounds for seventy-five cents per hour, of which they received a percentage.
These student chair boys could expect to earn up to $40 a week, at a time
when some white and black adult laborers with families often earned less in
the city.

The miles of fairgrounds with the countless exhibits to be viewed by the
average fairgoer illuminated the importance of this conveyance service. "The
rolling-chairs that run about the grounds and through the buildings are the
salvation of many a fainting spirit. To thousands of human beings with nothing but a human back and human legs the fair would be a failure without
them. They are a support for the weary, strength for the weak."[66] In all, over
one thousand young workers were hired, and at least fifty presumably were
African American (fig. 14). According to James Weldon Johnson, writing for
his college newsletter, *The Bulletin of Atlanta University*, he and his class-
mates experienced anxiety and anticipation at having this opportunity to visit
the nation's second largest city, and at the same time to earn money toward
their school expenses. Whether this opportunity was unavailable to the adult
males of the city's African American community is unknown.

One of the more dramatic incidents the chair boys experienced involved
a strike protesting a drop in earnings. While the white chair boys faced the
issue with the air of labor consciousness, the blacks remained aloof deliberately, considering themselves favored to be earning what they did as well as
fortunate to be physically where they were. In their collective consciousness,
they realized they were students temporarily acting as workers. Their permanent affiliation with the academy placed them, however, at the very heart of

14. An African American collegian is seen on the left among his fellow chair boys. Courtesy of the Chicago Historical Society.

knowledge that allowed men to rule the world. What this division over challenging management wrought is unknown, but it could not have enhanced relations among the summer workers. The incident would have served to reinforce in the white mind the validity of the end-of-the-century caricature of the black worker as strikebreaker or, in this case, reluctant supporter of the just cause of labor against oppressive capital.

There were also instances in which the specter of racism raised its ugly face to spoil what appeared to be amiable relations between the college men. James Weldon Johnson noted that usually anything derogatory said about the members of his race was voiced outside earshot. As to relations with other whites who would have ridden in their "gospel chariots," they might have been captured accurately on an occasion or two by this assessment of human contact: "There is sometimes a contrast in manners and education between the occupant of the chair and the man behind that is not in the favor of the former. When one sees what is evidently a citizen with far more money than brains, and without the faintest appreciation of the beauties that encompass him, wheeled about at seventy-five cents an hour by a youth so far his superior that any comparison is impossible, it causes one to realize Fortune is indeed an irresponsible flirt, who is never so happy as when doing the wrong thing."[67]

The frivolity of the decade contributed to its sobriquet as the "Gay Nineties" and provided work beyond the pale of legality and accepted morality. A veritable menagerie of individuals willing to engage in nefarious activities awaited fair visitors who were easily tempted. For the white "swells" and "sports" who sought anonymous entertainment away from their normally sedate milieu of pretended Victorian morality, the fun to be had proved irresistible. The stratum of Chicago's African American community which Drake called the "riff-raff," and which Du Bois referred to as the "Submerged Tenth" when he encountered them in Philadelphia's Seventh Ward, made its contribution to this bacchanalian mood by virtue of its undisciplined social behavior and blindness to the responsibilities of home and self. In its ranks were found persons who were often unemployed and sometimes criminal in character. Many had only recently come to the city because of both the legitimate and illegitimate opportunities the fair afforded.[68] Sometimes the equivalent of today's "underclass," they frequented and operated gambling dens, working as card sharks, bouncers and enforcers, and thieves.[69] They contributed to the economic crimes of larceny, robbery, and burglary that Monroe Nathan Work documented in his 1896 study on the nature and causes of crime among African Americans in Chicago.[70] Du Bois' description of the contagion of antisocial thought and behavior is appropriate for the denizens of Chicago's Cheyenne section of the Levee:

> The size of the more desperate class of criminals and their shrewd abettors is of course comparatively small, but it is large enough to characterize the slum districts. Around this central body lies a large crowd of satellites and feeders: young idlers attracted by the excitement, shiftless and lazy ne'er-do-wells, who have sunk from better things, and a rough crowd of pleasure seekers and libertines. These are the fellows who figure in the police courts for larceny and fighting, and drift thus into graver crime or shrewder dissoluteness. They are far more ignorant than their leaders, and rapidly die out from disease and excess. . . . Their environment in this city makes it easier for them to live by crime or the results of crime than by work, and being without ambition and grown bitter with the world—they shift with the stream.[71]

Women operating beyond the pale of morality included two strong-arm artists from the Levee who roamed far from their normal haunts to outside the fairgrounds to rob a male visitor of $50.[72] As for dens of prostitution and related venues of moral depravity, "it was also understood by those knowledgeable in such matters that some 'boarding houses' catered to the more private and intimate recreational needs of their clientele," one writer found. So, "the Columbian Exposition was a boon to Chicago's economy, and the festive spirit it inspired took many forms."[73] In the city's red-light district, located in the Levee district south of the Loop, three African American brothels featuring "Colored Gay Ladies of the Night" made themselves available to free-spending Caucasian customers. Several madams of color maintained lucrative establishments and expected healthy profits from the clientele of the fair. The city's second "best known" madam, Vina Fields, met the increased demand of the fair by doubling her labor force to sixty women.[74] This large number was especially disheartening because it probably equaled the number found in Philadelphia, with a black population twice the size of Chicago's.[75]

Intelligent, perceptive, resourceful, and focused on her desire to make money, Fields demanded a commitment from her prostitutes that approximated work activities in the equally exploitative legitimate world. She posted rules and regulations in the rooms of her brothel that enforced decorum and adherence to a dehumanizing protocol. This madam also knew empirically that "girls [did] not take to the life from love of vice, neither [did] they remain in it from any taste of debauchery. It [was] an easy lazy way to make a living, and once they [were] started either by force, fraud or ill-luck there [was] no way of getting back." Her reputation among persons associated with the moral netherworld ranked high. "The police have nothing to say against her," Stead wrote in his timeless jeremiad, *If Christ Came to Chicago.* "An old experienced police matron emphatically declared that 'Vina is a good woman' and I think it will be admitted by all who know her, that she is probably as good as any woman can be who conducts so bad a business."[76]

As for her exploitation of black women in this field of dead-end, demoralizing labor, Fields justified the situation thus: "What brings [the] girls here? . . . Misery . . . . Always misery. Unhappy homes, cruel parents, bad husbands . . . I don't know one exception." Evidently Fields envisioned herself as providing a haven for the abused. And she was known to feed the hungry and homeless. Yet, as Stead observed first-hand, "in the brothel as in the factory the person at the top carries off most of the booty." As for her own child, Fields's daughter attended a convent, far away from the source of her parent's ill-gotten tuition payments.[77] The dispossessed segment of the immoral netherworld, self-stigmatized as well as branded by their contemporaries as immoral, also shaped their sphere of existence as much as they could. However, as the ultimate victims of economic deprivation and labor proscription, they fared no better than exploited creatures in the gilded cages of the era.

5

THE SOCIAL ORDER

The leading business among the colored people was railroad-
ing. The headwaiters were at the top of society. They almost
dictated social customs. A man prided himself that he was
Mr. So and So's valet. Next to the headwaiters were the por-
ters and then came the barbers. I have seen that whole thing
change. First there were four colored doctors. Very few col-
ored people employed a colored physician, they didn't be-
lieve in it. . . . There was great rivalry between the home
people and the strangers. I was known as an interloper. . . .

—From the manuscript "Autobiography of a
Physician," cited in E. Franklin Frazier, *The Negro*
Family in Chicago

Anyone studying black Chicago in the late nineteenth century immediately confronts a monumental quagmire involving the structure of its social order and the character of its leadership—origins, *raison d'être*, composition, size, influence, and power. Since an understanding of the configuration of a society allows interpretation of the demeanor and thinking of its members, an accurate description of the dynamics of stratification and its relationship to the civic, community, and social spheres is essential in presenting a history such as this. The nexus between social grade (or class), occupation, world view, and leadership is best examined by focusing, first, on the character of social stratification, both theoretical and actual; second, on the composition of the ranks of the various social groupings; and third, on the relationship between the multiple leaderships that existed vertically and simultaneously, paralleling and overlapping each other in the civic, community, and social spheres, rather than linearly or horizontally, in temporal succession.

The most notable scholarly influence over six decades has been sociologist E. Franklin Frazier, mentioned in chapter 4. In his use of certain data from the "Autobiography of a Physician," a manuscript he obtained from an anonymous African American, and subsequent commentary in his doctoral dissertation, Frazier encouraged acceptance of a thoroughly convoluted perspective on the composition, ranking, and leadership of early black Chicago society during the post-Reconstruction era. Historian Allan H. Spear, whose

Black Chicago has been used for three decades as the definitive study of African American life in Chicago between 1890 and 1920, has been yet another major influence on the structure and evolution of leadership. At first glance, Spear presented a compelling story of an evolving civic leadership similar to that in other northern cities such as Boston, New York, and Philadelphia. Then there is the contribution of St. Clair Drake, who, in a 1940 work, eliminated a socioeconomic basis for class differentiation since cultural affinities, rather than the manner in which African Americans earned their wealth, produced an arrangement, not necessarily pyramidal, in which three social groupings coexisted.

Five years later, the publication of Drake and Cayton's *Black Metropolis* described post–World War I society in a manner that suggested, but did not carefully delineate temporally, the transformation of a socially differentiated elite sometime between the Columbian World's Exposition and the advent of the war into one that was becoming economically distinctive. They wrote: "The upper class before the First World War was composed of house servants of the wealthy, Pullman porters, successful politicians, and a few business and professional men. Their common bond was social ritual and a concern with 'culture' and getting ahead. Family background, light skin-color, and length of residence in Chicago were important class attributes."[1] These works perpetuated a myth of halcyon days when Pullman porters ruled society, providing "leadership," and a messenger presided as the final arbiter over the delicate matters relating to social decorum. For the last three decades, popular sentiment has accepted a conceptualization of successive sets of monolithic leaderships with supposedly antithetical ideologies dominating civic affairs.

ESTABLISHING THE CHARACTER OF SOCIAL STRATIFICATION

In his classic 1940 study *Churches and Voluntary Associations in the Chicago Negro Community*, St. Clair Drake saw the international celebration of 1893 as accentuating the more salutary side of American race relations. He suggested the need to examine thoroughly the complex nature of the city's African American population, seeing the fair as significantly affecting black life externally, in race relations, and internally, in the quality of African American religious and associational life.[2] The extremely disparate nature of the interests among this expanding group of citizens produced further problems for an urbanizing group undergoing social change. While conventional *a priori* reasoning might have dictated analyzing the nature of a preconceived class system based on economic influences, Drake rejected its existence altogether during this era. He found neither a social grouping nor a system linked primarily to the means of accumulating wealth. Instead he uncovered a group differentiation that developed along cultural and social lines, producing a small *refined* element, an expansive segment of *respectables*, and the flotsam and jetsam of society who comprised the *riff-raff*.

Another University of Chicago student, Richard R. Wright, Jr., who in 1901 modeled his work on the pattern of Du Bois' recently published *The Philadelphia Negro* (1899), provided contemporary analysis of the city's African American community at the turn of the century, and, no doubt, influenced Drake's writings. Wright described "social grades" rather than socioeconomic class as the basis of stratification in a manner similar to Du Bois' influential analysis in *The Philadelphia Negro.*[3] Still another product of the university's famed "Chicago School of Sociology" provided an applicable conceptual apparatus for understanding stratification at the time of the fair. According to Hylan Lewis, a contemporary of Drake's who studied African Americans at mid-twentieth century in a Southern Piedmont community, the existence of a traditional class structure is never a given:

> If a class-organized society is one in which there is a well-defined system of ranking that distinguishes cohesive, self-conscious segments marked by differences in social honor and power, then Kent Negro society of today is not organized on a class basis. A clear-cut system of social ranking and basis of association or intimate access was not discovered. This does not mean that there is not a level of consciousness; it does not mean there is not a status pattern marked by different measures of prestige and privilege, despite the leveling tendency mentioned earlier. Rather, it suggests that numerically significant groups differentiated on a basis of intimate association or access are not present, and that the people themselves do not in behavior or verbalizations make references to or relate themselves to such prestige collectivities. . . . Insofar as there are status differences and insofar as the society is changing and becoming more differentiated, one might say that class is incipient, rather than full blown.[4]

Additional social science findings are relevant at this point, and especially for a historical study, from the discipline of history. Jackson Turner Main placed this issue of class structure in perspective when he posited that a full century before the fair, American seaboard society had "an embryonic class structure but it was potential only" because the basic unit of wealth, land, was equally distributed and "from the bottom to the top was but a short step."[5] Robert H. Wiebe encountered this problem of identifying class strata in his study of the roots of progressivism, explaining it as follows: "[I]n part, the new middle class was a class only by courtesy of the historian's afterthought."[6]

Still, the mass media provided further substantiation of Drake's contention. An 1896 *Chicago Daily News* article headlined "Colored Belles to Come: Chicago's African '400' Agog over Prospective Visit" reported that "the members of Chicago's Colored '400' are getting ready to entertain four young women who are recognized as the leaders of Colored society in the United States. These young women, who have long scoffed at the idea of the existence, among the representatives of their race, of 'society' in Chicago, have sent out an olive branch, and, to emphasize the acknowledgment of their error, will be here about the middle of May."[7] Although they were too polite to say so, these visiting maidens could not have found in existence in Chicago in 1896 the society to which they were accustomed in New Orleans, Washington, D.C., and Charleston. For host city Chicago, not until early in the next century would demographic increase and occupational differentiation produce a discernible socioeconomic change in previous sociocultural categories and result in clear-cut class distinctions.

Close scrutiny of contemporary sources clarified the levels of social status but required an elaboration at a particularistic level. African Americans in the professions of medicine, law, and journalism alone comprised the *refined* element of African American society at a time when mainstream American standards were being established. They also dominated black society in terms of status, but in absolute terms of their influence over all black society, their role was tenuous at best. Frazier wrote that "originally, the small group of Negroes who because of superior culture emerged from the mass of the population and constituted the upper class did not represent primarily the occupational differentiation of the population."[8] Infinitesimally small, they numbered about twenty among 6,480 persons in 1880, and perhaps fifty among 14,271 residents in 1890. Claiming group hegemony at the apex of a social pyramid reflective of Anglo-Saxon values, and needing constant legitimization from outside the African American masses, they headed Richard R. Wright's contemporary structure of extant "social grades" in Chicago. As they extolled their educational training, rigid moral codes, interest in the *beaux arts*, and close identification with the dominant WASP power structure, they assumed their right to pursue and share in the American Dream to the fullest. These were the Afro-Saxons recently referred to in scholarship.

In Du Bois' writings after the fair, the refined held the status he ascribed to a "Talented Tenth." As to African American Chicago possessing an aristocracy, or "400," that possibility depended on acceptance of probably little more than several dozen individuals as the equivalent of 400. Nonetheless, they did constitute a recognizable cultural and color elite. In the *Chicago Daily News* article "Colored Belles to Come," the young women are described as follows: "Miss Summerville is petite, plump, good-looking and shows little trace of the African . . . Miss Pinchback is tall and dignified and has frequently been mistaken for a white woman . . . Miss Griffin is an accomplished young woman of the Creole type. She has expressive eyes and is a clever conversationalist."[9] Erudite attorney Edward H. Wilson in 1909, responding to the question, "Are there signs of class distinction among Negroes?" observed: "There are gradually emerging classes among us. They not yet well-defined; social discipline and the acquirement of culture and wealth have not gone on long enough."[10]

COMPOSITION OF THE RANKS OF THE REFINED

While visible by the handful, the achievement of the refined element was nonetheless momentous for a group only a quarter century removed from slavery and quasi-freedom. Five physicians and a dentist were notable. Dr.

Daniel Hale Williams distinguished himself through his founding of the Provident Hospital in 1891, successful surgery on the human heart in 1893, service as chief surgeon at the Freedmen's Hospital in Washington, D.C., from 1893 and 1898, and founding efforts at more than forty African American hospitals throughout the nation. From his founding of Provident, a virtual crusade with national scope began to establish other black hospitals and nursing schools.[11] The child of free parents from Hollidaysburg, Pennsylvania, he was born in 1856 (or 1858). Following his apprenticeship under Wisconsin's renowned Surgeon General, Henry Palmer, Williams arrived in Chicago in fall 1880 to enroll at the rigorous medical program of the nationally regarded Chicago Medical College (now part of Northwestern University).[12] Upon completing his medical training, he received his M.D. in 1883. Moving freely in Chicago medical circles, he received an appointment as an attending physician at the Protestant Orphan Asylum and to the surgical staff at the South Side Dispensary. He later joined the Chicago Medical College as a clinical instructor. Further, the recognition he earned as a medical practitioner led to his membership on the Illinois State Board of Health, 1887-1891.[13] His discouragement with the dearth of training facilities and positions for other African Americans, especially nurses, motivated him to lead a group of African American Chicagoans in organizing the racially integrated Provident Hospital in 1891.

Dr. Charles Edwin Bentley was perhaps Williams's closest friend in the city. He, too, was born of free parents, but his birthplace was in the neighboring state of Ohio, in Cincinnati. After having shared their early adult years in Janesville in social and professional preparation, Bentley married their avuncular landlord's daughter, Traviata, and the newlyweds settled in Chicago shortly after Williams had arrived. Here, Bentley began an impressive career in dentistry after having graduated from the Chicago College of Dental Surgery (later the Loyola School of Dentistry) in 1887. He quickly developed a lucrative practice in the Loop built around a white clientele.

Dr. A. Wilberforce Williams, born in 1864, was a native of Monroe, Louisiana, who lived in Springfield, Missouri, and who reached Chicago in 1882 or 1883. Having graduated from Lincoln Institute in 1881 or 1882, he taught school but still dreamed of a career in medicine. He next entered Chicago Medical College, from which he graduated in 1884, and "soon became identified with Provident Hospital."[14] Dr. Austin Maurice Curtis, born in Raleigh in 1868, arrived in Chicago to attend Chicago Medical College, and completed his training in 1891. He held the position of attending surgeon at Provident in 1892 and four years later was on staff as an attending physician at the Cook County Hospital. He remained in the city until 1898, when he decided there were even greater career opportunities in Washington, D.C. Another colleague, Dr. George Cleveland Hall, arrived in the city late in the 1880s and started a practice in medicine by the time the fair's gates opened. A graduate of Eclectic Training at the downtown Bennett College, he supposedly lacked Williams's respectability as a practitioner because of the questionable rigor of Bennett's curriculum and competency of its staff. Despite Williams's apprehensions, Hall joined the staff of Provident and established a creditable medical record for himself as the new century dawned.

Beyond medicine, Fannie Barrier Williams exercised her prerogatives and entered the world of letters, becoming a journalist. She was born in Brockport, New York, in 1855 of free parents who themselves were the children of the freeborn. She lived her formative years in the less racially oppressive milieu of upper New York state. For a short while, hers was the town's only African American family. The doors of the schoolhouse were open to all children, so she attended the local school and later was graduated from the State Normal School in Brockport in 1870. Her full initiation into the world of racial proscription and intolerance came later as she embarked on southern teaching and travels.

However, she was never so shielded from racism or so oblivious to social realities that she could not fix conclusively the limits of her access to the American Dream. She was pragmatic as well as optimistic. As to her acknowledgment of that part of the nation's racial protocol that forbade marriage between the races, when she contemplated marriage it was to another African American. (In contrast, Frederick Douglass took as his second wife a Caucasian, Helen Pitts, who originated from nearby Honeoye in upstate New York.) So, Fannie Barrier married attorney S. Laing Williams in 1887 in Brockport and the couple moved to Chicago before the decade ended. Civically and socially prominent in Chicago, she and her husband founded the Prudence Crandall Club, which promoted the highest appreciation of Anglo-Saxon ideals and values among the few highly educated African Americans in Chicago. Once her activities and the nature of her cultural orientation gained the attention of the city's white women's elite, she was selected to join the exclusive Chicago Woman's Club in 1895, thus becoming the first and only African American member.[15] In the next century, she joined the Chicago Library Board as its first and only African American member for over a decade. Moreover, for the next half century, among the African American women of Chicago, only Williams gained entree into the upper levels of civic service dominated by polite white society.

Native-born Georgian S. [Samuel, although he preferred to use his initial only] Laing Williams spent his formative years before marriage to Fannie Barrier training for a legal career. After his graduation from the University of Michigan, he attended the Columbian Law School in Washington, D.C. (later George Washington Law School) and entered practice in Chicago. His intellectual interests as well as desire to expand the cultural scope and activities of other college-educated persons led to his co-founding of the Prudence Crandall Club in 1887. Williams also accepted an invitation to join the intellectually exclusive American Negro Academy in the late 1890s. This membership accorded him the opportunity to interact with the likes of Alexander

Crummell, W. E. B. Du Bois, and John Wesley Cromwell. Williams's reputation has suffered unfairly because of his later association with Booker T.
Washington. The portrait painted of him by his detractors is that of a syco-
phant, and a person without professional competence in his chosen field
of law.[16] Interestingly, the same charge grew about George Cleveland Hall's
skill after he developed a close association with Washington, opening the
door to speculation as to why twentieth-century scholars have accepted without investigation what appear to be *ad hominem* attacks without substance in
fact.

The rise of other African American lawyers merits mention. They included Lloyd Garrison Wheeler, Ferdinand L. Barnett, Edward H. Morris,
and Franklin P. Dennison. The latter four had vanguard status, ranking as
the first, third, fifth, and twelfth African Americans to succeed in passing
the Illinois bar. Lloyd Garrison Wheeler's birthplace was Ohio where his
family planted firm roots in abolitionism. Resentment of the Wheelers' efforts in behalf of aiding fugitive slaves forced them to flee to Canada, where
young Wheeler spent his adolescence and early adult years. Arriving in Chicago before the end of the Civil War, he quickly associated with the legend-
ary John Jones and became his partner shortly before the latter's death in
1879.

But previous to this financial union, Wheeler entered Reconstruction-
era politics in Arkansas, winning office and experiencing firsthand the difficulties of maintaining power in the South. His later close association with
Booker T. Washington was obviously influenced by their shared perception
of how best to achieve racial advancement in the peculiar venue of the
post-emancipation South. Back in Chicago, Wheeler soon achieved the same
prominence Jones held as merchant-tailor. Marriage to Jones's niece, popularly but incorrectly referred to as Jones's adopted daughter, Renae Petit, followed. Established financially by the 1890s, and known for his free spending
at a time when University of Chicago professor Thorstein Veblen was excoriating conspicuous consumption among persons of his class, Wheeler assumed
the mantle of "Ward McAllister (or social leader) of black Chicago." A devout
capitalist, he adopted the same economic mode of thought that mesmerized
the nation, and soon embraced Booker T. Washington as a friend. This piv-
otal part of their relationship evidently developed as a mutual sense of admiration grew once Washington spoke to the world's fair Congress on Labor in
1893.

Although he was born in Nashville, Ferdinand L. Barnett arrived in Chicago with his family in 1869 from Canada. Barnett's parents moved to Canada
after his father, a blacksmith, purchased his freedom and then married a free
woman of color. After completing grammar and high school in the city, he
attended Northwestern University in the northern suburb of Evanston. He
completed his studies in law and passed the bar in 1878. Out of a racial commitment to communicate and provide guidance to his race, he started Chicago's first black newspaper, the *Conservator*, in 1878. After four years, he

gave up active editorship of the paper and devoted his time entirely to law.[17] For a short period, he shared a law office with S. Laing Williams.

No ideologue, Barnett enjoyed a mixed relationship with what one historian has described as the militant wing of integrationism and racial chauvinism. Accordingly, his paper combined a racial appeal with a push for things American. Davis assessed Barnett in this manner: "The editor . . . was a force as a person—a reflection of what is referred to [as] personal journalism . . . Mr. Barnett . . . stated that the uplift and advancement of the Negro constituted a major feature of the paper's program."[18] When it came to segregated education, he was also recognized as an ardent supporter of placing the future of African American youngsters in the hands of teachers of their own group.[19] A person with civic concerns that positively affected the entirety of the small African American population, Barnett's social position was "associated with his position as a lawyer, and with the estimate and appraisal of his character as an educated person of culture and refinement. This was not only true of the community's conception of the editor, but, to a degree, the editor's notion of his mission was affected by this idea."[20]

Edward H. Morris arrived in the city from Cincinnati in 1868 as a youngster and enrolled at St. Patrick's Roman Catholic School in the downtown area. Seeking fame and fortune like many other young American men, he left the state and served in the Kentucky state legislature. Then, returning to Illinois, he subsequently was elected a member of the Illinois General Assembly between 1890 and 1892. His legal acumen earned him a reputation in the new century as dean of African American lawyers. Edward H. Wright was born in New York City, attended its public schools, and graduated from the City College of New York at the age of sixteen. He arrived in Chicago in 1888 and became the preeminent leader of early twentieth century black politics. Franklin P. Dennison distinguished himself in both law and the military, becoming a leader of the famed Eighth Illinois Regiment. Eager to join the ranks of this legal cadre was a thirty-year-old native Chicagoan named Ida Mae Platt. After nine years as a private secretary in an insurance office and currently serving as a stenographer in a law office, Platt was deeply engrossed in her law courses at the Chicago College of Law. Within a year of the fair she would complete her studies and earn the distinction of becoming the first African American female in Illinois to pass the bar.[21]

The spiritual leadership of black Chicago rested in the hands of learned clergy.[22] Ministers with college training pastored to the Christian faithful at three Baptist churches, Olivet, Bethesda, and Providence; three African Methodist Episcopal (A.M.E.) churches, Quinn, St. Stephen and Bethel; St. Thomas Episcopal Church; Grace Presbyterian Church; and St. Monica Catholic Church. (The one Catholic church was under the leadership of Father Augustin Tolton, the first African American priest in the nation.) From these nine churches, the clergy administered to the needs of religious African Americans in this Protestant-led city and influenced daily behavior immensely, so powerful was the church as a social agent.

At Olivet, the oldest African American church in the city, Rev. J. F. Thomas ministered to the needs of 2,000 parishioners in a new edifice at Dearborn and Twenty-sixth Street. Thomas was described as a "pulpit orator of much power." Bethesda was led by Reverend Dr. Birch, who was considered "one of the best educated ministers among the colored people." On the west side, Providence regularly received trained clergy called through the Wood River Baptist Association and screened at Olivet, the "Mother Church."

The A.M.E. Churches shared ministers from a national pool of educated clergy. Quinn Chapel changed pastors in May 1893 as Reverend Townsend, who received his degree from Oberlin College, replaced Rev. John T. Jenifer. Townsend's résumé included a mix of scholarly training, world travel, and political officeholding in Indiana. St. Stephen was the other major denominational institution serving African Americans on the city's near west side. Rev. D. P. Brown, the son of an A.M.E. bishop, was considered one of the ablest of the younger men of the church. Bethel was pastored by Dr. Graham, who was in his thirties and had been an ardent prohibitionist in Michigan.

Grace Presbyterian experienced an increase in membership under the leadership of its pastor, Lincoln University (Pennsylvania) graduate Rev. Moses H. Jackson. A Dr. Thompson, a graduate of St. Paul's College (New York), presided over St. Thomas Episcopal Church at which high church services were performed. The nation's first Catholic priest of African ancestry, Father Augustin Tolton, studied at St. Francis College (Illinois) and in Rome before he came to the city to head St. Monica's Catholic Church.[23]

However, even within occupational groupings, cultural interests differed because of a different view of the racial world. A physician such as Daniel Hale Williams, and his dentist friend, Charles Edwin Bentley, lived in a disparate world from that inhabited by an anonymous medical counterpart cited by E. Franklin Frazier. So, the account of the latter's informant of the city's black social makeup contrasted greatly with the picture of the city's culture and glamour imagined by Paul Lawrence Dunbar's friend, Eugenie Griffin, experienced by Dunbar himself, described by Gatewood in *Aristocrats of Color*, and, importantly, lived by the refined element.[24]

With a sense of personal dread, writer Ida B. Wells had to experience firsthand what writer Frederick Douglass assumed from decades of experience in the racially fluid North about the protocol of race relations as it was sometimes practiced for certain Afro-Saxons. In a world's fair experience at the Boston Oyster House, a popular white restaurant, she grew to appreciate that full privileges of worth, status, and service in America could extend to African Americans, if only to special ones. Although Wells was "cocked and primed for a fight if necessary," Douglass was relaxed and chided her about her apprehensions.[25] Based on her Brockport, New York, upbringing, writer Fannie Barrier Williams similarly made the same assumptions Douglass did about life in the upper North.

Length of residence in Chicago was designated by Drake and Cayton as an indication that one belonged to the world of the elite. A greater choice of residence was another option available to persons with ample resources. Many of the persons listed above chose to live outside the predominantly African American Dearborn Street corridor because of its shabbiness, poorly paved streets, and rising density of population. Notable were the S. Laing Williamses, who resided on 42nd Place off Grand Boulevard, a thoroughfare named appropriately for its actual appearance and on which some of the wealthier Anglo-Saxons, Irish, and German Jews of the city lived in magnificent mansions, and the Lloyd Garrison Wheelers, whose residence was located at 4344 South Langley Avenue. Overall, the worlds of the minuscule Afro-Saxon refined and the demographically preponderant respectables moved like two ships passing in a fog-laden night, often oblivious to one another and wishing to remain so to avoid the possibility of a collision.

OTHER SOCIAL GRADES

Of the three sociocultural clusters Drake described as comprising African American society during the 1890s, the respectables constituted the largest portion of the social arrangement. This group was composed of the solid working class element described in chapter 4, mainly domestic, service, and unskilled workers. The handful of part-time politicians and political appointees as well as barbers, restaurateurs, and saloonkeepers comprised the remainder. In 1885, the latter three categories numbered forty, fifteen, and twenty respectively. Eight years later, these businesses had grown considerably and were able to advertise world's fair entertainment and housing in impressive fashion. The *Indianapolis Freeman* reported that the number of saloons had increased fourfold, vacant lots stood ready for construction, and "several of our leading citizens have erected flat buildings for the exclusive use, if so desired, of Afro-Americans."[26] The wealth of saloonkeepers reached levels equal to or surpassing that of members of the refined cluster, or elite, with Andrew H. Scott, John Hunter, Frank G. Rollins, Emmanuel Jackson, and John Smith, respectively, being worth $350,000, $175,000, $90,000, $75,000, and $65,000.[27] At the time, physician Daniel Hale Williams, attorney Edward H. Wilson, and dentist Charles E. Bentley attained levels of wealth respectively of $150,000, $50,000, and $25,000.

The respectables best typified black Chicago. They were church affiliated, morally upright, but less culturally anchored in the dominant Anglo-Saxon world both because of less interest in that group and its high culture and because of a lack of socialization, or educational training, about its supposedly superior values. They felt comfort in their enjoyment of what St. Clair Drake referred to as an Afro-American subculture. Up-and-coming politician, soldier, and civic leader Robert R. Jackson epitomized this group. He was born in 1870 in Malta, Illinois; attended the public schools in Chicago before graduation in 1885; obtained a job in the Chicago Post Office as a clerk, and

15. The Cherry family of the host city's west side was typical of the "respectables" whose numbers dominated African American culture and society. Courtesy of the Cherry family.

rose to the rank of assistant superintendent at the Armour Station (by 1909); served with distinction in the Spanish American War; and was elected the second African American alderman to sit in the Chicago City Council in 1917.

Lettie Trent, a schoolteacher whose name would figure prominently in protest at the fair, represented Jackson's counterpart across the chasm of gender. Trent was one of perhaps a half dozen African American teachers in the city whose numbers reached thirteen by 1900.[28] Almost the entirety of Chicago's teaching corps of 5,100 in 1895, excluding its 300 college-trained teachers at the secondary level, had the reputation of being a mediocre mass of politically connected, high school–trained clericals.[29] Schoolteachers, therefore, lacked the professional status and liberal training in the 1890s necessary to be considered part of the refined cluster. Their earnings by 1900 ranged from $650 to $1,225 per year, further reflecting Chicago's shameful neglect of the educational process.

Although only limited documentation has been found to date of Trent's involvement in civic or community activities before 1891, by her demeanor and utterances she seemed to embody a rugged belief in her group's destiny as she defined it. She demonstrated an assertiveness in confrontational racial matters heretofore unseen until Ida B. Wells's arrival in 1894 as a permanent resident. In regard to unused training, both Wells and Fannie Barrier Williams had college training fully preparing them for their previous calling in teaching, but initially they used it in behalf of black southern youngsters, not those in Chicago.

Also representative of the respectable segment of the African American population was the Cherry family—father Wiley, mother Margaret, and daughters Mattie and Lovie, who arrived in Chicago from Colrain, North Carolina, in 1893. (Figure 15 shows this family, circa 1902.) Whether their coming to the "city of the big shoulders" was linked to the advent of the fair is unknown, but the spirit of the entrepreneur inspired Mr. Cherry in a city that catered to the independent-minded individual. Validating Isaac Harris's description of the mood of many African Americans, Wiley Cherry soon started a grocery, which within a short span of time had given way to a masonry and plastering business on Lake Street. Through the years, the Cherrys prospered, as evidenced by Cherry's ability to pay for his family's medical services with cash and at a private medical facility. His commitment to race pride led him and his second wife, Fannie, to choose Provident Hospital on the other side of town as the place for the birth of the newest addition to the family. Tragically, Mrs. Cherry died giving birth.

Earlier, after the birth of Wiley and Margaret Cherry's first son, Jim, in 1895, the family rented or owned a frame home at 442 South Western Avenue in a predominantly Italian neighborhood. Living on Western Avenue, the city's westernmost boundary until 1869, placed the Cherrys in the city's western division, or west side, which was home to 200,000 people in 1890, most of them newly arrived immigrants from southern and central Europe who were joining Germans and the Irish from previous decades, who in turn, were pressing on the heels of wealthier native white Americans. The Cherrys quickly affiliated with the expanding African American community found along a mixed residential and commercial corridor on either side of Lake Street, one-half mile to the north. The family's membership in the Original Providence Baptist Church (organized in 1863 as the city's third African American religious institution) followed. In fulfilling this confirmation of faith, they met a requisite for inclusion in the ranks of the respectables. Since the Cherry family never considered its prosperity as a private possession, steady contributions to Original Providence resulted in Wiley Cherry's name being placed on the cornerstone of a new church as a new century dawned. Households such as this one extolled the virtues of race consciousness, pride, and solidarity, and became receptive venues for a name uttered with regularity in following decades—Booker T. Washington.[30]

Drake's third segment, derisively labeled "riff-raff," did, in fact, constitute the black contingent of the nation's and city's *lumpenproletariat*, numbering perhaps 5,700 persons (25 percent) out of a total city population of 22,742 African Americans three years after the fair in 1896.[31] Only extensive extrapolation allows reaching a figure for the 1893 population. Because of the advent of the depression of 1893, which lasted for four years and increased the pool of unemployed, the 1896 total might be both ephemeral and inflated. Whatever its exact size, its existence confirmed the dread of Paul Lawrence Dunbar's mother in warning him of the pitfalls of journeying to a large city, in fact, a wicked city.

The physical dimensions of the "wicked city" stagger the imagination. Stretching from Van Buren or Harrison on the north to Twenty-second Street to the south, and from Michigan or Dearborn on the east to Clark or the meandering Chicago River on the west, it encompassed almost a full square mile of the city's south side heartland. In its southern extremities was the Levee red-light district. The African Americans who lived in this slum area were dwarfed by the foreign population, which represented Chicago's number-one social problem.[32] The small enclave dominated by African Americans took on the nickname of "Cheyenne" because of this section's resemblance to that wild city of the West. One guide to pleasure spots for the wicked recommended that "if this locality is visited at all, it should be in broad daylight and in good company. 'Cheyenne' might fitly be termed the Whitechapel of Chicago."[33]

Reflective of its proscribed status in the American economic order, the African American presence in police reports and in the prison population was disproportionately large.[34] Du Bois' description of its counterpart in Philadelphia is relevant because in their social genesis, both populations originated in the aftermath of economic isolation in the workplace and in the social disorganization inherent in the legacy of slavery. Both males and females engaged in economic crimes such as larceny, robbery, and burglary. Incidences of arrest for disorderly conduct were frequent. One female, "Big Mag," became the bane of police officers who dared to arrest her. Described as "nearly six feet in height, as straight as an arrow and of such marvelous strength that no officer on the force would take to arrest her singlehanded[,] she had a record with the pistol, too."[35]

PARALLEL, OVERLAPPING LEADERSHIPS:
CIVIC, COMMUNITY AND SOCIAL

A revisitation of the relevant contemporary documents led to resolution of a confusing perspective on the nature of black leadership at the end of the nineteenth century. As Spear formulated the guidelines for understanding the dynamics of life of Chicago's African Americans, persons of abolitionist backgrounds acting within an integrationist framework set the tone. Picturing a monolithic, linear leadership, his analysis was that "before 1900, the community was dominated by a small group of upper class Negroes, usually descendants of free Negroes and often of mixed stock, who had direct lines with the abolitionist movement. Concentrated in the service trades and the professions, they usually had economic ties with the white community and numbered in their associates white men of comparable position."[36]

The interrelationship between class, ideology, and occupation, therefore, was central to Spear's model as he identified the assimilationists that dominated African American society. Further, he described the post-Reconstruction generation of the 1880s and 1890s as being hostile to "any type of separate Negro institution [that] smacked of segregation and represented a compromise of principle." He continued, "At times, a Negro institution might be necessary as a temporary expedient, but it could never be regarded as a substitute for the ultimate goal of integration. Before 1900, most Chicago Negro leaders accepted these doctrines as articles of faith."[37] Then he concluded that "until after the turn of the century, [Afro-Saxons] formed a coherent elite group and set the tone of social, intellectual, and civic life of the Negro community."[38]

Significantly, extant data as presented in this world's fair study do not substantiate Spear's analysis. Acceptance of the purported hegemony of one leadership group adhering to one particular ideological strain eliminates the likelihood that any other had significant influence. Moreover, Spear's model excluded the possibility that before 1905, the purported date of black business establishment in Chicago's mature, urban, market economy, anyone other than ultra-assimilationists who depended on white clientele for business fit into that leadership mold.

Methodologically, Spear's circle of leadership depended on constructing a framework similar to that created by Hunter involving reputational recognition.[39] Spear evidently found recurring references to certain persons in newspapers and journals and built his pool with their discernibly high sociocultural status. This could not have constituted a listing by class, because the needed economic differentiation did not exist at that time. On the other hand, more extensive sources were overlooked, preventing him from compiling a longer list. As to his small pool, he listed a total of eighteen leaders for a population in 1900 of 30,000 people.[40] From his list, he excluded most ministers as well as all politicians and officers of military and fraternal organizations. Of the latter, Fannie Barrier Williams wrote that "50 percent of the best

men belonged to fraternal orders."[41] Importantly, at the time of the most intense protest against participation at the Colored American Day celebration
in August 1893, the clergy assumed a leadership role over what was perceived
as a major civic issue. Persons belonging to the civic leadership logically had
to conform to sociologist Floyd Hunter's definition of leaders. He postulated:
"Leaders are persons of power status. . . . They are persons of dominance,
prestige, and influence. They are, in part, decision makers for the entire community."

Further, the ideological model Spear constructed restricted his choices
as to who belonged to this civic leadership. Persons committed to self-determination, or separate development, could not qualify. In contrast, for this
period August Meier wrote of concomitant ideologies nationally of integration and separate development.[42] Historically, interest in the latter was all too
real in Chicago. In fact, no group-based, self-help belief system was ever anathema to assimilationists because of their willingness to employ any effective
tactics at almost any time to achieve their strategic end of advancing in American society. Whether one examines the lives of Lloyd Garrison Wheeler,
Ferdinand L. Barnett, or Drs. Charles E. Bentley and Daniel Hale Williams,
their actions in an urban, market setting rarely followed a distinctive path of
ideological consistency because they could not. Fighting racism in America
demanded that ethical and ideological relativism occupy essential places in
this group's struggle. Just as doctrinally correct Puritan New England accommodated itself to a changing reality when it formulated its Half Way Cov-
enant in 1660 to insure its spiritual survival, so black America has repeatedly
shown its talent for adaptation in its need to perpetuate racial advancement.

Clearly, the elite, or refined, or Talented Tenth, dominated the civic leadership because of its strategic positioning based on professional achievement
in either the black or the white world, or both. Occupationally, the professional cadre of black Chicago filled the ranks of the civic leadership. Physicians, dentists, attorneys, editors and journalists, ministers, military leaders,
and politicians (like State Representative John W. E. Thomas of Illinois Civil
Rights Act fame and state official Edward H. Wright) made up this pool. This
composition stood in stark contrast to a more inclusive grouping in Philadelphia, which included caterers, clerks, teachers, professional men, and small
merchants."[43]

The civic world of self-sacrifice, open to persons of abundant resources
and options, and the social sphere of personal enjoyment and aggrandize-
ment available to the ordinary citizenry, represented disparate spheres. The
Colored "400" sought respectability by demonstration of its sense of civic virtue and appreciation of what whites considered high cultural attainment.
Social skills related to recreation were of lower importance; cultural interests
counted more heavily. Gatewood described the characteristics of a "Negro
400," an aristocracy of color in which, as with Drake, the attainment and
method of attainment of wealth played no part in determining "standing."

Sophistication, acquisition of cultivated traits and preferences, and education represented the components of this "class." Significantly, when a host family offered appropriate lodgings to Frederick Douglass at the time he returned for the formal opening of the fair in spring 1893, it was the S. Laing Williamses who stood by their door, far from the Dearborn Corridor, to greet him. More often than not, dinner outside the Williamses' home meant that the Lloyd G. Wheelers were the host and hostess.[44]

Popular legend about the character of late nineteenth century life, the nature of which elevated members of the respectables such as Pullman porters into civic prominence and societal leadership, rested on misinformation, misunderstanding, and, finally, as if self-validation was not attainable, myth itself. The legitimization of the legend originated in the doctoral thesis of Frazier in 1929 which in turn heavily shaped the work of Drake and Cayton in 1945, and partially influenced Spear in 1967. In accordance with the protocol followed by students working under the auspices of the Chicago School within the department of sociology at the University of Chicago, Frazier undergirded his study of family life in Chicago by the mid-1920s with a historical sketch of early Chicago class formation. In the absence of a comprehensive history of black life since Du Sable and the 1830s, he relied on the unpublished manuscript of an anonymous physician to describe and analyze early twentieth century black society in order to build a foundation from which to explain the meaning of his study.

In perspective, the document and source that he chose proved flawed. Frazier's intriguing but confusing "unnamed physician" exhibited only a limited knowledge of the social structure, given his status as a self-described "interloper." At the time of his arrival in the city from the South in the 1890s, this social outsider encountered an expanding black population beginning to exhibit a dynamism just as impressive as the city's extravaganza of 1893. Frazier's elevation of this chronicler's recollections into fact accounts for the role assigned Pullman porters in the social structure in future years. While the "physician" perceived that "the leading business among the colored people was railroading," it was not.[45]

As the "unnamed physician" continued with his account of how the social structure evolved, he positioned headwaiters "at the top of society. . . . Next to the headwaiters were the porters and then came the barbers." His recollections also revealed a flaw related to his own frustration. "I have seen that whole thing change," he stated. "First there were four colored doctors. Very few colored people employed a colored physician, they didn't believe in it . . . (and) the home boys and girls outside of good times never stood out as leaders or people who accomplished anything." Revealingly, he proceeded, "There was great rivalry between the home people and the strangers."[46] As a stranger, he had evidently met with hostility upon his arrival. From his beginnings as a student and probably a waiter he then fell under the influence of the latter occupational group, adopting their view of society.

As to the notion that Pullman porters reigned as black society's ultimate social arbiters, it cannot be substantiated. Extant data clearly indicate the existence of a higher occupational grouping with access to a world of expansive social outlets unavailable to any other occupational categories. However, what also appears to be true is that the bulk of the African American population was probably totally unaware of and uncaring about the activities of a handful of refined families who felt comfortable practicing social distance within their race. The observation of a Pullman porter cited by Frazier, who said, "We handled more money than most of the colored people, and led all the social life," no doubt was accurate for most African Americans who knew of them and their social influence through their elaborate and sometimes elegant gatherings.

There is importance, nonetheless, in this account because it reveals the inner dynamics of the social sphere that existed simultaneously with the staid world of civic virtue inhabited by the refined element. In it, the physician speaks of "good times" and a social world dominated by Pullman porters and persons in close contact with wealthy whites. Social skills were important, and valet, porter, and waiter were transformed into the raconteur, the conversationalist, the hunter, and the "sporting man" at home in the South Dearborn Street Corridor. So, in the aftermath of the fair, and with social change apparent, the appearance of a new Ward McAllister from outside the ranks of the refined was not unexpected. Julius Avendorph, who was in local aristocrat Ferdinand W. Peck's employment, found his niche at this time and succeeded Lloyd Wheeler, described in 1893 as having "considerable money and [who] increases his opportunities as social dictator by liberal expenditure."[47] Indeed, Pullman porters or other occupational groups produced leaders, but only over their own social domain.

After 1893, Avendorph now stood as social leader over some major social functions, many featuring the same cuisines and wardrobe styles associated with higher-status whites. Two generations removed, Drake and Cayton explained the process in the twentieth century that allowed an Avendorph to reign: "The upper class admits to its circles many whose incomes are far less than theirs, but who possess other valued attributes, such as advanced education or high standards of public decorum."[48] Importantly, as Avendorph grew in popularity, he was always careful to avoid involvement in any of the issues of the day, such as the racial strategy that formed an integral part of the world of civic affairs.[49] In 1891, during the major civic dialogues about whether African Americans should found a black hospital and training school, his name was not mentioned.[50] When the influential white Unitarian minister the Rev. Celia Parker Woolley established the Frederick Douglass Center early in the new century to afford the refined element an opportunity to mingle with their white counterparts, the name of this social arbiter never appeared. What is even more conclusive, he never joined the aristocratic ranks of African Americans comprising one-half of the leadership of the Chicago branch of the National Association for the Advancement of Colored People (NAACP) when it began in 1910, as did S. Laing Williams, George Cleveland Hall, and Charles E. Bentley. Membership in the NAACP carried the ultimate status attached to Afro-Saxon arrival in the American mainstream and therefore represented a litmus test for leadership for generations of blacks.[51]

While Spear had contributed a model worthy of use, even with the possibility of future criticism, the civic leadership he described was a leadership that functioned across a chasm from the rest of African American society. Upper-status African Americans were literally separated from working class blacks through both social and physical distance. Understandably, in the absence of regular contact, neither group knew a great deal about the other or influenced the other. Rank and file citizens adhered to laws and rules passed at the behest of the city's white elite, not the black one.

Analysis conducted as part of and incorporated into this study indicated that rather than two successive leaderships existing along a linear or horizontal plane, yielding to change around 1905, as Spear contended in *Black Chicago*, a myriad of leaderships existed in parallel channels. They appeared vertically and simultaneously over these overlapping domains—civic matters, politics, social affairs, and community or neighborhood concerns.

Contemporarily, Harris's business directory showed a multiplicity of organizations and institutions functioning as early as 1885, thereby providing evidence of the existence of various leaderships. Wright's assessment from 1901 and Wilson's comments in 1909 on class formation also showed that a major chasm existed between their assessment of the nature of black society and that of Frazier. Moreover, the socially variegated Chicago described by Drake in *Churches and Voluntary Organizations*, written only a generation removed in time, supported this perception of multiple voices for various constituencies. In the aggregate, these data call into question any shift in the singular leaderships described by Spear.

Conceptually, sociologist Floyd Hunter's framework for a comparable African American community was applicable. That racial enclave contained "functional [sub]communities . . . [with] organization [representing] particular interests—especially its structure along lines of power."[52] African Americans in Chicago brought the same cultural baggage into the realm of social order that they did into the economic order, causing them to carve out their own niches and set their own protocol whenever possible along myriad lines of power. Less glamorous than the civic and social leaderships, the third and fourth types of parallel leadership existed alongside these other two, and focused on alleviating the more mundane problems of living in an urban setting. Neighborhood or community leadership developed to enable concerned citizens to achieve specific short-range goals that affected the quality of life for only a small segment of the community. In the Dearborn Street Corridor, one representative example occurred during the tenure of A.M.E. minister Reverdy A. Ransom, a Wilberforce University graduate. Arriving in Chicago immediately after the fair closed, Ransom assumed the role of neighborhood leader along the Dearborn Corridor as he successfully negotiated the paving of a hole-ridden roadway with the help of a wealthy and politically connected figure in the gambling underworld.[53] Later, a needed kindergarten for the Corridor which would have met the demands of working mothers for quality day care and educational training was almost blocked because of the issue of voluntary separation. Ida B. Wells-Barnett, now a permanent resident of the city and a voice for community improvement as well as civic betterment, provided the leadership required both to initiate the plan and see to its completion.[54] Lastly, engagement in partisan party politics provided an explanation sufficient unto itself as to leadership, followship, goals, activities, and purpose.

Part Three

AT THE FAIR

I was, as perhaps most people are, more impressed by the grounds and buildings themselves than by any of the exhibits. The picture of the Court of Honor, as I saw it on two evenings, encircled by the brilliantly lighted buildings, with the shining lagoon in the midst, the constantly changing electric fountains, the great search lights seeking out first one point and then another, the golden statue of Columbus standing guard over the whole, and the glimpses of the blue lake here and there between the majestic columns of the Peristyle, is one that will live long in my memory. I hope never to lose it. [But] the spot I visited oftenest at the fair was the Hampton Corner in the Liberal Arts Building.

—Correspondent, *Southern Workman and Hampton School Record*, September 1893

According to St. Clair Drake, "the great influx of Negroes coming to the World's Columbian Exposition served to introduce the Negro community of Chicago to Negroes in other areas, resulted in some persons staying in the city, and increased the interest in church and associational life. The trends originating during this period found their full expression in the [new century] which followed."[1] Beyond the social acquaintances forged at the fair and the individual and associational linkages being shaped, intellectually stimulating encounters at more than one hundred parliaments and congresses beckoned to diasporans. African Americans participated in many of the major intellectual and social phases of the fair's activities, and in one instance, using the Haytian Pavilion as their headquarters at the fair, they fashioned a presence rivaling those of other participating ethnic and racial groups. In 1,245 sessions featuring nearly 6,000 speakers in various congresses, namely, those on the Negro, on women, on labor, on Africa, and on religions, diasporans joined the ranks of the 700,000 persons who took part to the fullest degree possible. In two instances, this meant domination of their ideas over procedure and structure. Furthermore, as African Americans administered the special day fair officials assigned them, Colored American Day, they revealed the extent to which they had matured socially as a group since 1865 as they contested vociferously for cultural hegemony along ideological and social lines. At the exhibitions, diasporan and continental African progress was displayed. From African American to Caribbean to Brazilian to Liberian displays, the presence, spirit, and dynamic of the black world resonated. In regard to Jim Crow, African Americans prepared for the worst, but more often than not they encountered the best in American society.

James Weldon Johnson and Paul Lawrence Dunbar and Robert S. Abbott were there, and hundreds—probably thousands—of their racial kin joined them, experiencing exultation along with disappointments, enjoying themselves in every manner possible, benefiting from the event, and leaving their imprint on American society. Assuredly, in the most unequivocal of terms, there *was* a noticeable black presence at, matched by a fervent interest in, the World's Columbian Exposition of 1893.

6

"THEY MET AT THE FAIR": LINKAGES

> No one who has not seen it, can form any idea of the immensity and grandeur of the exposition; nor can I give any adequate description of it. It has been very fitly called "The White City," and one standing under the Peristyle and looking down the Court of Honor . . . might easily imagine himself in a fairy city.
>
> —James Weldon Johnson

LINKAGES

They met at the fair,[1] or if *they* did not actually meet, *they*—a simple, functional, but powerful pronoun conveying the variety inherent in animate and inanimate influences—surely could have. *They* were present in ideas, values, organizations, and people, of all classes, occupations, genders, and hues who were traversing the highways and byways of America to reach the Columbian Exposition's streets and promenades. Diasporans forged many lifetime as well as short-term friendships on and off the fairgrounds in Chicago in 1893. The list of African Americans who attended the fair in summer 1893 represented a virtual "who's who" of the movers and shakers in politics, business, civic life, culture, education, and entertainment of late nineteenth and early twentieth century America. And, of course, the rank and file from the dominant Protestant denominations came, as did a small number of Roman Catholics, members of sundry fraternal orders, and various service and community associations.

First and foremost, Frederick Douglass was there, continuing to serve as a fulcrum for both diasporan thought and action. He appeared to meet everyone, speak everywhere, and attempt to exert his influence over everything. As to Douglass's influence, he used it over matters in which most African Americans but only a few whites had an interest. Highly influential whites pursued potentially lucrative business deals in manufacturing and commerce, domestic and international. In this vein, the appearance of a fifty-nine-year-old Chicago domestic worker, Nancy Green, in her debut as Aunt Jemima, supreme salesperson of a relatively new brand of ready-made, self-rising flour products, mainly pancake mix, proved more congruent with the theme of the exposition. Hers was not just to be an affirmation of a negative racial stereotype;[2] hers was a promise to housewives of liberation in their kitchens, offering them more free time and admission into the modern world. To a nation accustomed to stereotypes, southern hospitality portrayed warmth, and the plantation cook represented the region's culinary expert.[3] While Douglass sought vindication for past wrongs in the seventeenth, eighteenth, and nineteenth centuries, monopoly capitalism searched for new markets in the twentieth century through use of a reassuring black face.

More importantly, the "New Negroes" of the 1890s attended the fair. As a generation defined by their detachment experientially from slavery, their youthful exuberance with their average thirty-odd years, fervent hope in the next century, and contributions to their group's accomplishments up to this date, 1893, they were impressive. Charles Edwin Bentley roamed the fairgrounds after methodically taking notes at the Congress on Dentistry as his profession's official observer. Journalist Ida B. Wells of Memphis and anti-lynching fame in western Europe took an early interest in African American involvement and contributed mightily to the publication and distribution of *The Reason Why the Colored American Is Not in the World's Columbian Exposition*. Her collaboration with Ferdinand L. Barnett on *The Reason Why* would lead to a friendship that bloomed into a love affair and successful marriage, along with a sustaining civic partnership. Hampton alumnus and current Chicagoan Charles Marshall welcomed Robert S. Abbott of Hampton Institute.[4] Marshall, future leader as colonel of the all-black Eighth Regiment of the Illinois National Guard of Spanish-American and First World War fame, bonded with Abbott in a friendship that contributed to the latter's permanent return to the city in 1897. Abbott sang with the Hampton Quartet and lost his heart to Chicago. Booker T. Washington of Tuskegee Institute spoke about the plight of southern labor.

Because of her popularity, elocutionist Hallie Q. Brown reigned as the queen of the recited and gesticulated word throughout the duration of the fair both on and off the grounds, and there were many other prominent African American women. Fannie Barrier Williams accepted two invitations and lectured at major congresses with her spouse, S. Laing Williams, listening supportively. Black feminist/womanist Anna Julia Cooper, who the previous year contributed *A Voice from the South, by a Black Woman of the South* to black womanist intellectual life and a sense of self-identity, came to the fair to speak at the Women's Congress, as did abolitionist Frances Ellen Watkins Harper. Traveling to join them at the Congress, Oberlin College–trained Fannie Jackson Coppin of Philadelphia's renowned Institute for Colored Youth arrived in Chicago with a commitment to share her wealth of experiences and insights. Mary Church Terrell, along with Wells, Harper, Cooper, and others, gathered and planned an agenda for their race.

Talented painter Henry O. Tanner exhibited "The First Lesson on the Bagpipe," inspired by a scene he had witnessed in Brittany. A native Philadelphian, Tanner was studying art in Paris, but had returned to America for an eighteen-month break. His representation earned him a top 40 award at the conclusion of the fair. Then it was back to Paris, although the painting appeared at the Cotton States' Exposition in Atlanta in 1895.[5] Iowa botanist George Washington Carver came to the fair and was so impressed with its scientific wonders that he felt compelled to return. His painting, "Yucca gloriosa," won an honorable mention in competition; but Carver's interest centered more on science. On the fairgrounds, he divided his time among the Art, Horticulture, and Science Buildings. Meanwhile, Louis B. Anderson crisscrossed the fairgrounds, fulfilling his journalistic duties in the world's fair Department of Publicity and Promotion, and probably thinking of a day when he might return to Chicago on a permanent basis. He would return shortly, begin and then complete law studies at the Kent College of Law, and enter the world of municipal power politics in the early twentieth century.

From the artistic circles of the nation, talent abounded. Musician Wendell Phillips Dabney, acclaimed as the world's greatest guitar player, was on the fairgrounds. With Frederick Douglass's approval, Will Marion Cook of New York City, along with Harry Thacker Burleigh and Prof. Maurice Arnold Strothotte from the National Conservatory of Music in New York joined other future composers and musicians and planned the cultural agenda to be unveiled on Colored American Day. Cook was about to begin a brilliant career as composer; his *Clorindy—The Origin of the Cakewalk* would appear on Broadway in 1898. He began a brief collaboration with Dunbar, whom he met at the fair, which resulted in Dunbar writing lyrics for *Clorindy*.[6]

From roots old and rural, jubilee singing reigned; from the newer and urban experiences, ragtime emerged to challenge that genre as the African American favorite. According to Reid Badger, Scott Joplin played his innovative ragtime outside the fairgrounds,[7] and maybe even found time to visit the Midway and listen to the syncopation of the Fon people's drumming. As for the advent of ragtime, Cook described it thus: "The public was tired of the sing-song, samey, monotonous, mother, sister, father sentimental songs. Ragtime offered unique rhythms, curious groupings of words and melodies which gave the zest of unexpectedness."[8] From South Carolina, over a score of jubilee singers performed at Festival Hall before a throng of 5,000 a month before the Colored American Day celebration. The *Chicago Herald* described the scene in this manner:

Two dozen colored jubilee singers from South Carolina drew just about twenty-four times as big a crowd into Festival Hall yesterday afternoon as did ever at one time Theodore Thomas and his late orchestra of 114. The singers brought their own orchestra, with several way-down-south fiddlers and a double bass that rasped like a Kansas cyclone. There wasn't a soggy melody in the entire programme, and from top to bottom the houseful of people applauded each number to an encore. . . . [The singers were physically diverse.] Some were tall and some otherwise, with fat ones

always next to lean, men and women. The selections were characteristic camp meeting and plantation ballads, queer of dialect and jamful of jumpy music.[9]

The blues had met white Chicago in a linkage that would extend throughout
the entirety of the twentieth century.

Frederick Douglass and the budding poet laureate of Afro-America,
Paul Lawrence Dunbar of Dayton, met at the fair, much to posterity's benefit.
Douglass subsequently hired Dunbar as his assistant at the Haytian Pavilion.
The former personified the spirit that the latter immortalized for the ages.
James Weldon Johnson of Atlanta University also met Dunbar, initiating a
friendship that lasted until the latter's early death.[10] The black world's laure-
ate was productive, too, presenting "Oak and Ivy" to the world and finding the
inspiration for "Lyrics of the Lowly."

The religious leadership and their respective flocks were at the fair. Included among the former was Episcopal Bishop Alexander Crummell, the
foremost intellect among diasporans. His presence was felt through his in-
sightful thought. African American Catholics appeared in small numbers but
were heartened by the recent ordination of two diasporan priests, Fathers Augustin Tolton of Chicago and Charles R. Uncles of Baltimore. A.M.E. church
bishops Henry McNeal Turner and Henry Arnett were there also. The masterful tandem of father and son from the world of religious imagery, both the
aural and the visual, A.M.E. Bishop Benjamin T. Tanner of Philadelphia and
his Paris-based painter son, Henry Ossawa Turner, toured the fairgrounds as
confident participants in the exposition as speaker and exhibitor. With their
familial affinity known to all,[11] this sight must have produced a salutory effect
on all African Americans within their presence.

African Americans arrived in Chicago individually, in families, and as
members of organizations. The most notable organizations were the nation's Masonic orders, which claimed late eighteenth century origins with the
founding of the African Grand Lodge No. 459 under Prince Hall's leadership.
Several orders appeared in Chicago at the time of the fair along with the
Knights of Pythias and other groups committed to fraternalism. The Most
Worshipful Grand Lodge and Appendant Orders, State of Illinois Jurisdiction, exerted itself as a locally based group to serve as world's fair headquarters. Early in January 1893, the organization publicized its intention to serve
as a clearinghouse for Masons seeking housing, transportation guides, church
referrals, entertainment, and other sundry services.[12] More importantly for
organizational unity, it called for an assembly of all Masons to engage as "de-
liberative bodies for conference, fellowships, mutual understanding, and consideration of such subjects and plans (of a non-legislative nature) whereby a
more perfect and harmonious Masonic Union may be consummated in the
future."[13]

Acutely aware of the significance of the world's fair as an event of global
importance, Chicago attorney John G. Jones chose 1893 as the year to orga-

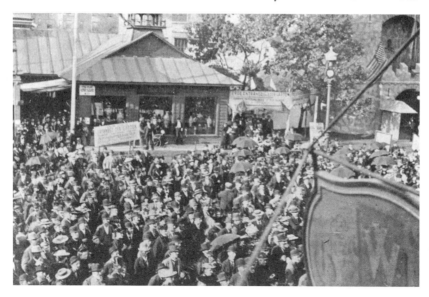

16. A scattering of African Americans can be seen among fairgoers watching the spectacle of lion taming. Courtesy of the Chicago Public Library.

17. A group of Nubians who arrived in Chicago as part of the Egyptian contingent on the Midway. Courtesy of the Chicago Public Library.

18. A group of "Boushareens" at the fair, another part of the Egyptian contingent.
Courtesy of the Chicago Public Library.

nize another branch of Freemasonry, the Ancient Arabic Nobles of the Mystic
Shrine. Challenged in August as to the nature of his authority "to organize an
imperial council of Colored Masons of the Mystic Shrine in this country,"
Jones, as Imperial Potentate, claimed the same sources of English and French
Freemasonry as white Americans, further affirming an Arabian connection as
of June 1, 1893.[14]

That the Masons came, saw, and conquered host city Chicago was well
documented in newspaper coverage of this period and event.[15] The Grand
Chapter of the Holy Royal Arch Masons of Illinois and Iowa, and the Grand
Commandery of Illinois and Iowa Knights Templar, concluded a joint convention in mid-August after having used the fair as their backdrop. The baton
then was transferred to the Corinthian, St. George and Godfrey Command-
eries Knight Templars, who met, drilled, dined and feasted exhaustively.

Furthermore, persons wishing to meet authentic Africa could. One recently married couple arranged a camel ride for the bride and experienced
the flavor of Egypt on the Midway. For those who wanted to see the famed
African animals, a lion taming exhibit was held (see fig. 16). Significantly,
Africans from Dahomey, Nubia, the Sudan, and Algeria had the opportunity
if they desired to became loosely associated with persons of West African de-

scent, especially those who sought a positive racial affinity. (See figs. 17 and 18.)

Varying ideas, values, mores and even musical techniques and concepts among differing social segments of the African American population also met at the fair, and their convergence affected the state of their relations among those involved. Lastly, the interests and agendas of white and black converged, and the status of relations nationally was changed permanently.

OUTSIDE THE FAIRGROUNDS, ALONG DEARBORN STREET

The excitement and bonding found in activities on the fairgrounds and stimulating discussions in the meetings held in the Art Palace did not end at the fairgrounds' perimeter, nor did the activities held at the downtown Art Institute. They resumed or were replicated in the geographical and cultural core of the Chicago African American community. Parallel activities ran continuously in Chicago's African American churches throughout the duration of the fair in contradistinction to the usual Sunday ceremonies that marked so much of the rural and small-town southern experience. Emotive expression yielded to the cerebral serenity of northern, cosmopolitan African American church life. This shift in emphasis at first seemed aimed at the usual, celebrating the greatness of God and the influence of the church's commitment to the Creator. Significantly, it sought to purify the soul while it also elevated the diasporans' intellectual and cultural appreciation to include upper and middle class, mainstream America's values found in higher education and the *beaux arts*. Churches continued their tradition of providing not only a salutary venue, but also ambience, status, and an audience for diasporan events and cultural development.

The locus for this extension of the fair was the Dearborn Street Corridor, an expanding diasporan racial enclave in close proximity to the fair. It anchored an expanding community extending from Twenty-second Street southward to Thirty-fifth, and from Wentworth Avenue on the west to State Street on the east that was home to about one fourth of the city's diasporans, the bulk of its churches, and black-operated Provident Hospital. Its impressive growth meant that building a successful commercial strip along State Street, one block east of Dearborn Street, entered the realm of the probable as African Americans expanded their economic options. By streetcar, elevated, or carriage, this community sat about five miles north of Jackson Park and two miles south of the heart of the central business district.

Newspaper accounts highlighted Bethel A.M.E. as the source of most of these fair-related activities, with collateral events taking place at Quinn Chapel A.M.E., Olivet Baptist, and Grace Presbyterian. One might surmise that the dynamic presence of the African Methodist Episcopal Church leadership at the fair as well as the location, capacity, pastorship, and prominence of Bethel itself explained the latter's importance in the summer of 1893.

Bethel had moved by 1890 to the heart of the Black Belt, at Thirtieth and Dearborn. Here, it was situated in a better residential neighborhood, among a host of respectables and the refined, and surrounded by high-status whites to the south and east. The structure that housed it was described in the *Chicago Tribune* as "a handsome church edifice."[16] Its seating capacity must also have been larger than most other diasporan churches, given the fact that several were in the process of moving into larger quarters or would in the near future.[17] The thirty-two-year-old Rev. D. A. Graham assumed the mantle of leadership in the spring of 1892, succeeding Rev. George W. Gaines. The dynamic leadership of this youthful minister resulted in expanding church membership and a retirement of the church's debt by 1893. As the city's third A.M.E. Church, it fit both into the prominent role held by Methodism locally and African Methodism nationally.

Unlike earlier nineteenth century frontier Methodism with its emphasis on emotional evangelism, late nineteenth century urban Methodism took a deliberately staid tone. Intellectual, cultural, and social activities revolved around an attempt at behavioral and, thereby, status transformation. With meetings held in houses of worship, sacred music assumed a special role, although it never dominated. The choice of "Nearer, My God, to Thee," heard so frequently, nonetheless made it a standard. The secular choices, though, reflected the congregation's and pastor's appreciation of the operatic and the classical. Using the instruments, voices, and selections associated with these genres, concert performances consummated a summer of cultural elevation. Violins and pianos proved the instruments of choice while coloratura and mezzo sopranos joined contraltos to provide range to selections for female artists, euphoniously counterbalancing baritones and tenors. Well-known performers of operatic pieces, with experience in major operatic venues, such as Mmes. Maria Selika, Deseria Plato, Maggie Porter-Cole, and Sissieretta Jones, appeared before appreciative church throngs. Concert stage artists included well-known baritone Harry Burleigh and tenor Sidney Woodward from the National Conservatory of Music. Will Marion Cook and Joseph Douglass (grandson of the Great Sage) delighted audiences with their virtuoso violin performances.

Musical selections tendered included the "German Conqueror's March"; "From Crag to Sea"; "A Friar of Arder's Grave"; Arditi's "Magnetic Waltz"; and excerpts from *Il Trovatore, Romeo and Juliet,* and *The Merchant of Venice.* Popular songs of the day leaned toward the melancholy and serious, epitomized by "O, Promise Me" and "Out in the Deep." Elocution and recitation had their place as Ohio's Hallie Q. Brown, Boston's Ednorah Nahar, and Henrietta Vinton Davis enthralled listeners with their masterful blend of word and gesticulation.

The choice of music revealed another dimension of black cultural transformation underway since the Emancipation. When the fund-raising committee of the Masonic Orphans' and Old Folks' Home, located at the south

19. This portrait of mezzo-soprano Flora Batson appeared on a flyer for a benefit concert in February 1893 that illustrated the wide spectrum of cultural interests as well as the charitable concerns of Chicago's African Americans. Courtesy of the Jones family.

end of the Dearborn Corridor at Thirty-sixth and Armour streets, planned its first major benefit to aid its building fund, it decided on a venue and program appropriate for eclectic musical tastes. African American mezzo soprano Flora Batson, billed as the "Queen of Song," had top billing at the Central Music Hall in downtown Chicago on February 15, 1893, and the program (fig. 19) included two of the city's aspiring sopranos and two of its tenors and was intended to appeal to the socially rising. Miss Octavia Lucas, whose lineage included forebears from the Emerald Isle, rendered her portion of the evening's entertainment in Irish dialect.

As a civic venture, it was consistent with the emerging character of the respectables as they grew to appreciate various genres of music previously assumed too aesthetically advanced for their class and race. Revealingly, Ferdinand L. Barnett's name appeared as the only recognizable member of the refined among its board of directors. In reality, it was reflective of the respectables' ability to appreciate the most exemplary kind of American culture in the *beaux arts* while transcending the worst features of American racism. An examination of the promotional flyer shows no attempt to disguise the singer's racial features or to cast aspersions on the African physiognomy as it extols Batson's artistic abilities.

Thus, the plethora of summer concerts were noticeable for their depth of variety, artistic quality, strong popular support, and racially uplifting emphases. On July 25, 1893, the *Indianapolis Freeman* reported that Rachel Walker of Cleveland, a "soprano of enormous sweetness, the acknowledged prima donna of her state" would perform in a "concert of unusual magnitude" at Bethel. Joining Miss Walker on the stage were "Miss Edith D. Bushee of Aurora, Illinois, contralto and whistler, who, in company with Prof. W. A. McCormack of Riverside, Illinois, the world's famous whistler, have won laurels everywhere they have appeared." Miss Valetta L. Winslow, a former Chicagoan, returned from San Francisco "where she is the declared delsartist of the state" to perform and visit the fair.[18] On Tuesday evening, August 8, 1893, a special Emancipation Concert was held, again at Bethel, which featured singers, elocutionists, whistlers, violinists and dramatic actors who delighted a capacity crowd. This was followed by another large event at Bethel on Thursday, August 17.

More cerebral activities occurred at the regular Thursday night meetings of Bethel A.M.E.'s Payne Literary Society. Topics included "Social Distinction," "The Past, Present and Future of the Negro," and "Bravery of the Colored Soldiers in the Wars of the Republic." At the same time, Quinn Chapel's Quinoniam Lyceum League provided nourishment for the mind by presenting such leading political and reform figures as former Virginia congressman John Mercer Langston, Frederick Douglass, and Ida B. Wells, speaking on issues of national importance.

Club activities, both civic and social, grew. The Albion Tourgée Club for men was joined after the fair by the Ida B. Wells Club for women and young maidens. Overall, activities along the Dearborn Street Corridor expanded the fair's many salutary influences and engendered a greater sense of community among black Chicagoans.

Old settlers, newcomers, and visitors interacted collegially, which boded well for the future of this group in this enclave.[19] Population growth would be spurred by an internal migration occurring far in advance of the Great Migration accelerated by labor opportunities during World War I. Benefitting the fair's host city, both Robert S. Abbott and Ida B. Wells returned to Chicago as permanent residents, as did other less well known individuals who helped Chicago's climb to prominence in the twentieth century.

DIASPORAN AND CONTINENTAL AFRICAN EXHIBITS

The second crucial matter African Americans debated once Congress authorized the exposition was how they would exhibit their accomplishments and other items demonstrating their progress since the Emancipation. Optimistic because of all that they had accomplished in the twenty-eight years since Appomattox, they shelved rancor and used a reservoir of good will to present separate exhibits that would allow maximum exposure of their race's advancement. The proposed Negro Exhibit which had been discussed since 1890 failed to materialize, due in part to a shortage of funds from Congress as well as to an absence of a concerted African American movement to formalize just what shape that exhibit would assume. It was a matter, though, that refused to fade away, because some of those who were disappointed in 1893 set to work immediately to guarantee that the next national or regional fair of note would have a prominent Negro exhibit.[20] That place was Atlanta, where the Cotton States' Exposition was to be held in 1895.

To one segment of African Americans, the important link in racial affirmation in 1893 was their being seen, or visually appreciated, in a major capacity before themselves, white Americans, and the world. A national Negro exhibit would have accomplished this end, but in its absence the bitter taste left some to lament during the fair and even years afterward. Thomas J. Bell of Hartford, Connecticut, an alumnus of Atlanta University, represented his alma mater's exhibit at Chicago. While proud of the university's presentations, he lamented his race's inability to mount a major exhibit that stood proudly alone for the world to see. As he surveyed the grandeur of the fairgrounds, he noted that "so far as the colored people are concerned, the Fair is a failure. They are not represented here at all, only in so far as their representation comes in through the exhibit of the Nation. They have no individual exhibit as a race. But on account of the position the Negro held thirty years ago, and for the good of those who would deny that they belong to the Nation, and declare that 'a Nigger can't learn nothing,' it would have been well if they had made a special effort to get up an exhibit."[21]

Nonetheless, there were exhibits that were assembled in Chicago, and they varied greatly in purpose. Visually, the black race had a presence both on and off the fairgrounds, thanks to the black women of New York State, three of the major educational institutions of the South—Atlanta University, Hampton Institute, and Wilberforce University—and the nations, colonies, and peoples of Liberia, South Africa, Egypt, Dahomey, Algeria, Jamaica, Curaçao, Hayti, and Brazil.

First, as a result of the determination of Joan Imogene Howard, the black women of New York State contributed the largest exhibit mounted under African American auspices at the fair. As the only African American manager on the twenty-one-member New York Board of Women Managers, Howard had worked hard to collect the materials on display in the Women's Building, and to encourage the women of her race to participate in this endeavor. She did not fear that a separate exhibit would lead to the slighting of African American accomplishments. On the contrary, "when it was suggested by the executive committee that the Afro-American exhibit should be made by itself in order to give it a larger scope, urged by some members of her committee who claimed to see the advantage to such a division, she went to work earnestly to collect an exhibit that might show to some degree on what lines progress [was] being made."[22]

The finished product validated the faith New Yorkers had placed in Howard and her herculean efforts. It contained the literary works of black abolitionist Lydia Maria Child, gathered in their near entirety, which were part of "the only collection ever made of the literature of New York colored women. It shows that they have written books, and it contains stories, biographies, poems, and sonnets. Among the authors are graduates of the University of the City of New York. The first example of book illustration by a colored woman is shown, as are samples of bookbinding. Specimens of commercial typewriter work by a colored woman employed as a bookkeeper and collector in New York City, and of legal typewriting by a colored woman who is court stenographer in the County Court of Saratoga County, are among the exhibits." Edmonia Lewis's statuette "Hiawatha" was placed on display. Other items included various forms of embroidery, from the ecclesiastical to the personal, gold and silver jewelry made in West Africa, paintings, and a patented kitchen invention that combined the features of a pastry fork and a whipper. In total it comprised 65 different categories of women's creative productions ranging from the fine arts to the liberal arts to manufactures to horticulture.

As a statement of women's accomplishments, the Empire State exhibit shone for the entire race. *The New York Times* hailed as "creditable" the finished product.[23] The official *Report of the Board of General Managers of the Exhibit of the State of New York at the World's Columbian Exposition* declared that Howard had "accomplished her task as only a woman with remarkable energy and executive ability could."[24] Overall, what these women had presented compared favorably to what the white women displayed in the Women's Building, but could not be compared to what the white men displayed in a world they dominated through arms, technology, machines, and wealth. Unfortunately, the standard of the fair was set by the male-dominated imperialist nations of Western Europe at a time when they were at the apex of their national development.

There were also separate representations of women's achievement that appeared throughout the fairgrounds. Philadelphian Gertrude Mossell reported that the "City of Brotherly Love" prepared a women's exhibit.[25] One Cincinnati female native, Adina White, an artisan who worked in wood, carved an "elaborate cherry table" for display at the fair after it left its exhibition spot in downtown Cincinnati.[26] Mount Hermon Female Seminary, founded in Mississippi in 1875 with the aim of "elevation and education of the Negro race," either prepared a small exhibit or contributed money to the state's display.[27]

Second, in higher learning, Hampton Institute mounted a major offering in the Liberal Arts Building with dozens of other educational institutions. Its staffer was Cora M. Folsom, who arrived on time in April, only to find that operations for setting up the display lagged behind schedule. Once the exhibit was up, the woodwork caught the eye of most visitors. She quickly learned that "the Hampton exhibit is . . . doing the work for which it was undertaken." That meant simply that the Caucasian world could no longer deny nonwhite creativity, craftsmanship, and endeavor. The work was so impressive that "it is hard to make people believe that all this . . . are all products of Negro or Indian labor." Student-produced clothing was also displayed, including "dresses, suits, underwear and fancy work." Folsom confided that our "one weak point is our technical work. We are surrounded with work from the best schools and ours cannot stand the comparison."

The work of the Hampton students was "systematically arranged in what is known as a Prentiss frame—a large 40 inch book of wooden leaves." Photographs allowed visitors to see another part of Hampton also. The purpose of the exhibit bore fruit when a group of white men happened by and after initial disbelief, acknowledged its quality. Folsom described their revelation: "[They] went out convinced that Negroes and Indians are good for something, though they would have been condemned to dire punishment before they would have believed anyone who tried to tell them. A great many people express the same idea, though generally with less force or profanity." Encountering a group of the African American elite added to Folsom's satisfaction about the work that she was doing in hosting for Hampton. "I have met some very superior Negroes here," she wrote, "and they [were] all pleased that Hampton is making so good a showing for their race."[28]

Hundreds of visitors passed through the section that housed the Hampton exhibit and expressed amazement and satisfaction at seeing the progress made by African American students and their Native American colleagues. C. H. Stokes wrote to Hampton about an encounter he had had at the exhibit: "A few days ago there was a gentleman quietly looking through our work [who] startled a company of whites with the question, 'Have you ever been to Hampton?' When the reply was negative, the gentleman told them that 'you should do so at the first opportunity.'"[29]

Hampton, of course, was not the sole representative of African Americans in higher learning. Folsom reported that "Atlanta and Wilberforce are here, but their exhibits are small and not so conspicuous, though they are in some details superior to ours."[30] Wilberforce University's academic contribution to the fair comprised two large books filled with examples of its students' academic work. In rhetoric, grammar, logic, and mathematics, the students demonstrated their capacity to perform at a high level. The small display, next to Oberlin University's, paled in comparison, but the spirit behind it did not. Wilberforce also sent taxidermy specimens and samples of needlework and woodcraft.[31] In recognition of its participation, Wilberforce earned a Columbian Medal and Diploma for its presentations.

In the estimation of the disconsolate Thomas J. Bell, official representative of Atlanta University at the exposition, Atlanta University showed up "better than any others, what is being done for the race and what the race is doing for itself." Atlanta University occupied three hundred feet of floor space and four hundred of wall space in its enclosure in Section K South Gallery in the Liberal Arts Building. Photographs of the faculty, student body, and physical plant were visually arranged to impress any observer of Atlanta's efforts. Then, specimens of the students' work in academics, nursing, home economics, and the crafts were shown. Bell adopted a different tone altogether and talked of success as he wrote that "the friends of colored people and those interested in Southern education often remark, 'This [Atlanta University] exhibit and that of Hampton are enough to convince the most skeptical, that the colored people of the South are people capable of learning just as other people are.'"[32] During a decade when W. E. B. Du Bois had his academic credentials from Fisk challenged by Harvard, the salutary influence of the exhibits brought only incremental affirmation of black accomplishment.

Third, the international contingent of exhibitors contained small displays from the Old and New Worlds. While they were diminutive in size, to one resident of Yazoo City, Mississippi, their very presence made the contribution of African Americans seem even smaller. With a supranational perspective on the place of blacks, he shared his views that were a mixture of global racial pride and national racial disillusionment with the *Indianapolis Freeman*: "I was struck with wonder when, on a careful examination of the home and foreign departments at the World's Fair to find every nation possessing ability enough to represent save the American Negro. Hayti the pygmy government her representative; even Egypt from the time of the Ptolemies is represented by its own nativity."[33] His discontent stemmed from there being neither a national Negro exhibit assembled for display nor an African American named to the exposition's National Board of Commissioners.

Without a doubt, what appeared in the international exhibits showed a black presence, but only in a limited or subservient capacity, given the control over agricultural and mineral resources that the European imperial states maintained. Nonetheless, they did capture the imagination and the moment. The exhibit of the independent African state of Liberia was situated on the north side of the Agricultural Building instead of the massive Manufactures Building as part of an overflow of international exhibits. According to a reporter from the racially friendly journal *The Independent*, "Far-off Liberia, a country from which the hasty observer would assert we could learn nothing, makes a really excellent exhibit." Aiding the cause of his nation is an "intelligent looking young Liberian, whose skin by no means betokens his nationality, and whose English is as faultless as that of those with whom he converses. He rather opens the eyes of his hearers as to the intelligence of the better class of his countrymen."[34]

American overenthusiasm and biases aside, Liberia was neither ignored nor treated unfairly at the fair. Liberia was honored with its own day at the fair, July 26, on which the nation celebrated the forty-seventh anniversary of its independence. It had as its official representative Commissioner Alfred Bennedict King, who was born in the United States but resettled in Liberia with his parents when he was seven. A member of the Liberian Senate, King initially proved a credit to his country because it was through his efforts that the exhibit for the exposition was assembled. While in Chicago, he was frequently seen about the fairgrounds, and gave many talks about his country. At one such lecture, sponsored by the world's fair agricultural department, he was able to extol Liberia's forest products and speculate about the possibility that cotton might one day become a premier crop.

The Liberian exhibit displayed the nation's agricultural potential as seen in its rubber, palm oil and kernels, cocoa, ivory, beautiful native woods, cam, curios, and animal skins, along with a new coffee strain from a new species of the plant, called *Coffea liberica*. It was purportedly stronger than any other coffee variety around and was intended for blending with weaker strains. A rare albino hippopotamus was also on display. Manufactures of the Mandingo people were featured as an example of indigenous products used internally. Representations of indigenous housing, composed of palm leaf and bamboo, and of European-style housing helped complete the story the nation wished to portray. Most disturbing to visitors were relics of the slave trade that robbed Africa of its human wealth.[35]

From the southern extreme of the continent, South Africa was represented by the women of Cape Coast Colony and the men of Zululand who appeared in Chicago in the disparate capacities of combat soldier and industrial worker. The women's colonial exhibit featured the wares and handicrafts of the women of Cape Coast Colony and included ostrich feathers that were prized for their beauty and stuffed birds with exquisite plumage.

Some Zulu men worked as reenactors at a replay of the Defense of Rourke's Drift, in which the British Army proved its mettle and emerged victorious against the army of Zulu Chief Cetawayo. This battle followed the massacre of British troops who were outfought at the Battle of Isandhlwana in 1877. The military confrontation was presented off the fairgrounds to the west where many military reenactments took place in accordance with the martial spirit of the decade and tertiary feature of the fair. First, technological advancement was served; then, the intellect was satiated through classical music, the congresses, and the physical layout of the fairgrounds. However, the Midway Plaisance and the outer, western fringes of the fairgrounds provided another set of venues to please the human palate for excitement, sexuality, and violence.

The Anglo-Zulu conflict took place at the Military Tournament at Tatterhall's on the anniversary of Queen Victoria's birth. At least two hundred Zulu warriors[36] would charge the British garrison, exchanging their assegai stabbing spears for British bullets in repeated charges into the British line. As over fifteen hundred spectators watched the spectacle, the cries of battle and the dying permeated the air in what was "the first attempt made at the tournament to show the way in which real battles are fought."[37]

At the Mines and Mining Building in Chicago, Zulu men reproduced the actual refining process that brings forth diamonds in South Africa. Other Zulu worked as guards at the exhibit, which was enclosed behind iron gates and plate glass.[38] In a process involving the actual thing, diamond ore was loaded into carts and dumped into a chute which led to a gigantic crushing machine. Water was pulsated through the mix and workers sorted through the hard pebbles for rough diamonds, which were cut and polished. What made the exhibit all the more spectacular was the value associated with this economic activity. Diamonds worth more than one million dollars were to be processed at the fair.

While the exhibit clearly demonstrated the power and wealth of the British Empire juxtaposed with the subservience of the Africans, the latter confirming the colonial subject's manifest inferiority under Darwinian rules of intercultural contact, the reaction to the Zulu conformed to a peculiar attitude prevalent at the fair. Racism did not preclude appreciation for the military and human abilities of the vanquished as they defended their way of life. The physical characteristics of the Zulu did not escape the probing eyes of the reporters, who described them as "powerful chaps" and persons "of giant build" as well as "ugly black devils."[39]

Dahomey was represented by 100 of its citizens who presented indigenous dances, music, carving, cooking, and other cultural activities. Their presence has received such contemporary and historical coverage that it is also discussed separately in chapter 8. Egypt displayed its wares and culture on the Midway Plaisance and seemed to dominate the entertainment specter with a replica of its imposing pyramids, the sensuous dancing of "Little Egypt," and torturous camel rides. Algeria was next to Egypt on the Midway and presented dancers, swordsmen, and some of its indigenous crafts.

If Hayti was so well known to African Americans through Douglass's service to that republic, and, before him, Toussaint's heroic exploits against white domination, what about the other nations and colonies with African-based populations that brought exhibits to the fairgrounds? From the Caribbean, independent Hayti, Dutch-controlled Curaçao, British-controlled Jamaica, and Spanish Cuba exhibited. Hayti had made its presence felt at its pavilion; its significance is covered in chapter 9. The island of Curaçao, the largest island of the Netherland Antilles chain located 60 miles north of Venezuela, showed its wares to the world in a space located close to the Liberian exhibit in the Agricultural Building. It included two human figures, a black man and a black woman, to represent its population. Various agricultural products were arrayed: fruits and jams, peanuts, licorice, and seeds. In addition, products from the sea shared space with handmade items such as baskets, fans, and jewelry. Jamaica also exhibited in the Agricultural Building and presented similar offerings.

Cuba, "the Pearl of the Antilles," represented an interesting case because it existed both in the black reflective mind and the current consciousness. Cuba harbored the last slave port of the famed *Amistad* and it was the place to which slave holders threatened deportation if African slaves resisted plantation discipline. According to John Hope Franklin, before the Spanish American war five years hence, African Americans already recognized a kinship with the Cuban people "whom they regarded as blacks and mulattoes."[40] During the revolts of 1848-1851 and 1868-1878, the news of the heroism of the blacks in the "patriot" armies that brought the abolition of slavery and the promise of political reform had spread, so the next upheaval in 1895 was expected.[41] Some contemporary African Americans also knew of the insurgency of mulatto general Antonio Maceo and his military compatriot of unmixed blood, Quintin Bandera, "the Black Thunderbolt."[42] Furthermore, in 1890, New Yorkers witnessed the establishment of a school solely for Afro-Cubans by revolutionary leader Jose Marti and others.[43]

Cuba, most importantly at the fair, was a reflection of the American investment in the island, by 1890, of more than $50 million in plantations and sugar refineries.[44] She displayed sugar, the mainstay of her colonial economy, along with her tobacco delight of the Western world, the "Havana" cigar. With the economic depression of 1893 in the United States, a ripple effect resulted in the disappearance of U.S. sugar subsidies. This caused economic instability and the deterioration hastened the military insurgency in 1895 by Cuban insurgents. White and black, peasant and middle class, they united against the Spanish and Cuban economic elite that exploited the human and natural resources of the island.

From South America, British Guiana had a large exhibit of agricultural products, including sugar and molasses, bird feathers, highly polished woods, and a virtual "pyramid of gold."[45] Brazil paraded its ships at the October 1892 naval extravaganza in New York harbor and made itself conspicuous to white Americans because of its sailors of mixed blood. In addition, this giant of a nation built a pavilion near Turkey and Venezuela and about 600 feet west of Hayti. Here it showed its wares to the world and, at its separate music hall on the Midway, it played the syncretic music reflective of its Afro-Portuguese culture.

Fourth, there were other exhibits guaranteed to cause dismay among African Americans. If the gentleman from Yazoo City, Mississippi, who agonized over the absence of a Negro exhibit saw his native state's exhibit, he experienced even greater consternation. In the age of industry, white Mississippi revealed its lack of economic development with an agricultural exhibit fixed in time. King Cotton still dictated the mode of economic production. One history of the fair described it thus:

> A unique feature of the exhibit, and one that attracted thousands of visitors, was the design of a cotton plantation, with an old cabin near in which could be seen the figure of a typical "Aunt Dinah" busily engaged in filling her basket with the fluffy article. Other pictures of southern life were represented, among them being a Tougaloo plantation. . .[46]

Louisiana continued this pattern by having reenactors of the slavery days sell miniature cotton balls. In addition, dressed in checkered bandanas and starched aprons, Creole waitresses served opossum stew, red beans and rice, and gumbo in the Louisiana State Building. Here, the manipulation of racial images reigned in an obvious attempt to legitimize a racist social order in the eyes of white Northerners and foreign visitors.

THE SPECTER OF JIM CROW AT WHITE CITY

A sense of fair play met and apparently neutralized some of the most invidious features of racial discrimination at the Columbian World's Exposition in 1893. Several factors contributed to this momentary improvement in race relations. America lacked a caste system to subordinate the will and behavior of African Americans completely and managed only a jerry-built protocol that failed in its consistency. Fairgoers arriving in Chicago expected to interact under a northern racial protocol that relied near totally on physical distance, partially on social distance, and completely on numerical insignificance of the African American population to maintain racial equilibrium. For example, when the black Masons invited fellow African Americans to the city for the fair, they warned them of Jim-Crowism in housing. Moreover, they offered to provide referrals to available housing. A brochure read: "Understanding quite well the annoyance our people is usually subjected to in securing accommodations in public places, especially when all accommodations are in great demand, manufactured excuses are usually made for not granting such when a colored lady or gentleman make application to be accommodated. In order to protect any and all of our people from such annoyance special arrangements have been made. . . . ."[47]

Before Booker T. Washington could announce to the South in 1895 that both races could function separately as fingers on one hand in social matters and united in matters of mutual importance, African Americans nationally experienced the imposition of racial *place* in occupational, political, social, recreational, cultural, and religious spheres. Chicago in 1893 proved no exception. However, convenient excuses were concocted to avoid equality of choice and opportunity.

As the *Chicago Inter Ocean* opposed segregation or involuntary separation, the purportedly liberal newspaper published the following racial schematic in August 1893: "There is little or no tendency toward social admixture of the races in Chicago. White and colored prefer to associate with those like themselves. No sensible white person feels aggrieved when he rides from Van Buren street to the Fair grounds, or from State street to Garfield park on a seat shared by a decent colored person. No one with good sense will hold that he has been introduced into Negro society by reason of having sat next or near to a Negro during the delivery of a sermon or the acting of a play. At the close of the sermon or play white and colored will return to their respective homes, careless or forgetful of their recent proximity."[48]

The most egregious reported incident on the fairgrounds occurred in complete variance to northern protocol. Miss Mary Britton of Lexington, Kentucky, was refused service in the Kentucky State Building on the fairgrounds. Assuming she could participate freely at an international event taking place in a metropolis of the upper North, she instead experienced humiliation. Adding to her discomfort came a rebuke from a black newspaper, the *Indianapolis Freeman*. Perhaps it was her "hankering after the sensational that

20. An African American couple is seen strolling past the Kentucky Building; they might just be citizens of that Commonwealth. Courtesy of the Chicago Historical Society.

prompted her to experiment, or that she was laboring under the seductive influence of the lake breezes from the state of Michigan and wandered up to the 'Blue Grass' building ignorantly," chided the paper.[49] The Indiana paper's insensitivity aside, figure 20 shows African Americans walking past this structure in utter disregard of any invisible line of Jim Crow, so Britton's misfortune seemed to have been unexpected.

The absence of other reported incidents of discrimination revealed neither an open society nor a blackout on negative news coverage. More likely, what was experienced was a deferral by African Americans to *place*, or a reluctance to report what was a daily occurrence in most parts of the country. According to Rudwick and Meier, "it is doubtful whether Negro visitors experienced discrimination at the restaurants and amusements on the exposition grounds." After surveying newspapers of the period, they found note of only Mary Britton's encounter.[50] Importantly, complaints openly criticizing the fair's management persisted, but not complaints about restaurants or places of public accommodation on the fairgrounds.

The proactive character of African American protest before and during the fair could very well have played a significant part in curbing any egregious displays of racism. The noted pamphlet highlighting injustices, *The Reason Why the Colored American Is Not in the World's Columbian Exposition*, opened up a channel between the races, allowing a constructive discourse that is relevant a century later. At the same time, the pamphlet carried the threat of an international exposé of America's festering racial sores. Yet on another level, it heightened the African American consciousness to the need to challenge the racial status quo, overall spurring a positive impulse toward improving the milieu of 1893 in Chicago.

Meanwhile, on the periphery of the fairgrounds, Ida B. Wells did recall years later that she and Frederick Douglass encountered a situation that challenged her assumptions about northern race protocol. While Douglass attempted to allay his southern guest's apprehension about the availability of service at a restaurant, white waitpersons purposely delayed serving the party. Then, a supervisor recognized Douglass as a family hero from the era of abolitionism, apologized, and immediately ordered that the two be served.[51] A conversation ensued between Douglass and the white man with the latter acting as though the slight had not occurred, or at least could be forgiven. In general, Jim Crow tendencies appeared to have been minimized for at least one summer's duration in America.

As to the historical significance of African American involvement at the fair over time, it did leave in its wake permanent organizational and processional consequences. A recent study by two academics in the field of journalism explored "the strategy, group alignments, and mentoring relationships that were nurtured by African Americans as they experienced the exposition" and established the influential nature of these factors.[52] Organizational and associational life among African American women nationally received a boost when Hallie Q. Brown helped establish the Colored Women's League, a women's group in D.C., in 1894. Further spurred by a vile letter defiling the moral character of black women in 1895, the National Federation of Colored Women's Clubs was formed, which merged the following year into the National Association of Colored Women's Clubs. Locally, after fourteen months of racial wrangling, Fannie Barrier Williams was inducted into the membership of the Chicago Women's Club in 1895 as its first black member. Overall, the black presence at "White City" had been beneficial to African Americans as they passed another milepost on their way to racial realization.

7

THE SCOPE OF INVOLVEMENT

If the love of humanity more than the love of races and sex shall pulsate throughout all the grand results that shall issue to the world from this parliament of women, women of African descent in the United States will for the first time begin to feel the sweet release from the blighting thrall of prejudice.

—Fannie Barrier Williams, "The Intellectual Progress of the Colored Women of the United States since the Emancipation Proclamation," May 1893

Today is Colored American Day at The Fair, and arrangements have been made to observe it in a manner that will reflect the highest credit upon the race. Excursions have been coming in all week, bringing colored people from all over the country. It is estimated that there will be at least 50,000 colored people present.

—*Chicago Inter Ocean*, August 25, 1893

Along with satisfying the aesthetic and corporeal wants and cravings of fairgoers, the planners of the fair set as a primary goal the nurturing of their intellectual needs. Accordingly, they scheduled more than one hundred meetings and conferences, referred to as congresses and parliaments, to deal with the weightier issues of the day. In these, diasporans also participated as lecturers, willing to face complex issues involving interracial and gender-based relations, civil and political rights, and economic exploitation. As to their overall importance, the conferences themselves represented a venue from which to communicate the interests of one-half the Earth's population.

CONGRESSES AND PARLIAMENTS

Between May 15 and May 22, 1893, the World's Congress of Representative Women met. Along with the white world's female luminaries—Addams, Lott, Anthony, Palmer, Stanton, Couzins, Hooker, and scores of others of European renown as well as those of little celebrity—six black women shone also. Two presented major addresses and four provided commentaries. The address delivered by petite, thirty-eight-year-old Fannie Barrier Williams of Chicago stands as the most notable, although a lecture and certain words of sixty-eight-year-old teacher, abolitionist, and novelist Frances Watkins Harper on May 20, 1893, fresh on the heels of her publication of *Iola Leroy*, have provided some black feminist theorists with an ideal for their intellectual tradition.[1] Nonetheless, when the prepared statements of the women are taken holistically, all six made outstanding contributions.

Williams's lecture, entitled "The Intellectual Progress of the Colored Women of the United States since the Emancipation Proclamation," took place on May 18, and was followed by short discussions by Washington, D.C.'s Anna Julia Cooper and Philadelphia's Fannie Jackson Coppin. In a carefully crafted address of approximately 5,500 words, Williams analyzed the exploited status of African American women within the American political economy, their victimization by white leadership, the cruel and enduring legacy of slavery, the hypocrisy of white liberals on the issue of social equality, and, most important for blacks' ears to hear, their achievements despite seemingly insurmountable odds along with recognition of the indomitability of black women as they protected and enhanced their virtue and sense of womanhood.

Williams's lecture perfectly fit the times, the place, and the audience. Assuming that her oral presentation matched the intellectual depth of the record, the quality of her upbringing in upper New York state, and her deportment, it can be surmised that she delivered an objective, courageous, and substantive discourse. Whether she was also poignant is conjectural. She exhibited prescience, and also the ability to place the contemporary status of African American women in perspective in terms of both the significance of this event and their role in it. Williams declared: "The Negro people of America have reached a distinctly new era in their career so quickly that the American mind has scarcely had time to recognize the fact, and adjust itself to the new requirements of the people in all things that pertain to citizenship."[2] In the age of Darwinism, she spoke of progress achieved despite adversity and without outside assistance:

> There is no wish to overstate the obstacles to colored women or to picture their status as hopeless. There is no disposition to take our place in this Congress as faultfinders or suppliants for mercy. As women of common country, with common interests, and a destiny that will certainly bring us closer to each other, we come to this altar with our contribution of hopefulness as well as with our complaints.[3]

With power brokers within both the white feminist and domestic circles present, Williams sought an aural receptivity that had the potential to bring about change.

Deferential but not obsequious to white progressives of the abolitionist stripe, she awarded plaudits and yet maintained the importance of recognition by the nation of the special obstacles placed in the path of diasporan women. In a manner reminiscent of Douglass, with his constant references throughout the summer to a white tardiness in extending justice to its fellow citizens, Williams began:

> Less than thirty years ago the term progress as applied to colored women of African descent in the United States would have been an anomaly. The recognition of that term to-day as appropriate is a fact full of interesting significance. That the discussion of progressive womanhood in this great assemblage of the representative women of the world is considered incomplete without some account of the colored women's status is a most noteworthy evidence that we have not failed to impress ourselves on the higher scale of American life.

She continued with this pronunciamento of inherent and damning truth: "[But] less is known of our women than of any other class of Americans."[4] The reasons were obvious, but Williams reiterated them to an audience that must have felt shame for its past and current treatment of its fellow citizens, especially its women.

As to the issue over which white America most suffered amnesia—slavery—Williams lamented:

> [At the advent of the Emancipation], yet it must be counted as one of the most wonderful things in human history how promptly and eagerly these suddenly liberated women tried to lay hold upon all that there is in human excellence. There is a touching pathos in the eagerness of these millions of new home-makers to taste the blessedness of intelligent womanhood. . . .
>
> While I duly appreciate the offensiveness of all references to American slavery, it is unavoidable to charge to that system every moral imperfection that mars the character of the colored woman. The whole life and power of slavery depended upon an enforced degradation of everything human in the slaves. The slave code recognized only animal distinctions between the sexes, and ruthlessly ignored those ordinary separations that belong to the social state.
>
> It is a great wonder that two centuries of such demoralization did not work a complete extinction of all the moral instincts. But the recuperative power of these women to regain their moral instincts and to establish a respectable relationship to American womanhood is among the earlier evidence of their moral ability to rise above their conditions.[5]

Williams clearly enunciated that from this sordid systemic base, African American women had to fight for their virtue physically, their moral reputations verbally, the opportunity to work competitively, and the right to manage their households autonomously in the same manner as white women. On the related issue of social equality, she lambasted whites for using it as a shibboleth to justify discrimination and exclusion, saying, "It will soon appear to those who are not hopelessly monomaniacs on the subject that the colored people are in no way responsible for the social equality nonsense."[6] Yet, as an optimist, Williams claimed that the important strides made by diasporan women in education and religion resulted in a betterment of the entire African American condition.

As a humanist and racial tactician, Williams advised against the harboring of any hatred against whites on the part of African Americans but never deviated from her strong tone of demanding justice and equal economic opportunity. Moreover, unlike Fannie Jackson Coppin, who would laud upper class whites while condemning the white middle and working classes,[7] Williams recognized where the locus of power lay and attacked it:

> Not long ago I presented the case of a bright young woman to a well-known bank president of Chicago, who was in need of a thoroughly competent stenographer and typewriter. The president was fully satisfied with the young woman as exceptionally qualified for the position, and manifested much pleasure in commending her to the directors for appointment, and at the same time disclaimed that there could be any opposition on account of the slight tinge of African blood that identified her as a colored woman. Yet, when the matter was brought before the directors for action, these mighty men of money and business, these men whose prominence in all great things of the city would seem to lift them above all narrowness and foolishness, scented the African taint, and at once bravely came to the rescue of the bank and society by dashing the hopes of this capable yet helpless young woman. No other question but that of color determined the action of these men, many of them foremost members of the humane society and heavy contributors to foreign missions and church extension work.[8]

To Williams, the deliberate and systematized exclusion of African American women from opportunities in the workplace at a time when it was touting its economic vitality ranked beyond contradiction as hypocrisy.

At the end of the session, an invited guest but an uninvited speaker who was seated on the podium rose upon special invitation to address the assemblage. By his presence, demeanor, and message, the individual had to be the Sage of Anacostia, whose ubiquitous appearances became an integral part of fair activities. Douglass's stature loomed so large that he was the only man to speak after the opening session and before the General Congress of the woman's conclave.

The response of Douglass validated women's demands and clearly stamped them as appropriate for the nation. Douglass's words carried such weight that a portion of his remarks has to be included. He proudly concluded: "I have heard tonight what I rarely expected to live to hear. I have heard refined, educated colored ladies addressing—and addressing successfully—one of the most intelligent white audiences that I have ever looked upon. It is the new thing under the sun, and my heart is too full to speak; my mind is too much illuminated with hope and with expectation for the race in seeing this sign. . . . Fifty years ago and more I was alone in the wilderness. . . . [Tonight I know that is no longer true] . . . A new heaven is dawning upon us, and a new earth is ours, in which the discrimination against men and women on account of color and sex is passing away . . . the grand spirit which has proceeded from this platform will live in your memory and work in your lives always."[9] Douglass had begun to realize that the Colored American was indeed in the World's Columbian Exposition.

A century after her triumph, Williams became the target of a criticism inexplicably contradicted by historical records and reasoning, as she was criti-cized both for timidity and for approaching white racial liberal Albion W. Tourgée to help refine her presentation with additional data about progress in the South.[10] Nevertheless, couched in eloquence that is apparent one hundred years after its utterance, the presentation helped build what has become an intellectual tradition of black feminism/womanism.

Four other women who sounded the same call for dignity, respect, opportunity and the elevation of humanity followed her. They could never be labeled militant, for they were more conciliatory than anything else. Yet in the nuances of their moderate intellectual to metaphysical tones, they exuded the forcefulness that announced the emergence of a "New Negro" to whose ranks they belonged because of generational mindset, experience, and age. They had made this day possible.

Thirty-five-year-old Anna Julia Cooper, who headed the highly successful M Street School in the nation's capital, spoke briefly in about 1,500 words, one quarter of the number Williams had used. "Let woman's claim be as broad in the concrete as the abstract," she majestically intoned. "We take our stand on the solidarity of humanity, the oneness of life, and the unnaturalness and injustice of all special favoritisms, whether of sex, race, country, or condition."[11] She also glorified in the black woman's ability to maintain her virtue in a manner no American white woman could ever conceive. In hidden, heartfelt pain she spoke: "Yet all through the darkest period of the colored woman's oppression in this country her yet unwritten history is full of heroic struggle, a struggle against fearful and overwhelming odds, that often ended in a horrible death, to maintain and protect that which woman holds dearer than life. The painful, patient, and silent toil of mothers to gain a fee simple title to the bodies of their daughters, the despairing fight, as of an entrapped tigress, to keep hallowed their own persons, would furnish material for epics."[12] Fannie Jackson Coppin then moved to the rostrum, speaking only 570 words. She lauded the best white people who had protected blacks, but reserved her most eloquent praise for the Almighty.

Alabama's Sarah J. Early presented an address of just under 2,000 words on "Organized Efforts of the Colored Women of the South to Improve Their Conditions," describing self-improvement measures of southern blacks to an audience that was not altogether convinced of their abilities. Seeking to strike a responsive chord, she laid claim to strong African American support for abstinence, education, and material accumulation, citing the $263 million in real estate that blacks controlled. Early was followed by Hallie Q. Brown, who had completed her tenure as Dean of Female Students at Tuskegee. Her presentation equaled Early's in length and, as might have been expected, was filled with praise for the Institute's achievements. Since the assemblage valued home production, she took the occasion to proudly call attention to her dress, which had been sewn by Tuskegee students. She then recited a poem dedicated to the bravery of Civil War troops, provided some commentary on the indispensable service rendered by the Freedmen's Bureau to the South, and lauded black female authors of such literary works as A Voice from the South and Iola Leroy.

Frances Harper spoke two days later at a session devoted to the civil and political status of women. Eloquent in the space of a little less than 2,000 words, she talked of the advent of a new time. While Harper could tell women at the fair that change was in the air and that they should envision themselves as being "on the threshold of [a new] women's era," actualization of that belief proved to be generations away in an uncertain future. Interestingly enough, her support for a restricted suffrage for both men and women with moral and education tests seemed to obviate a brilliant exposition of the positive role which women were playing even without the franchise.[13] Since educational opportunities still eluded so many African Americans in the South, the implementation of an educational test would surely fall disproportionately on blacks. To Harper's credit, she dismissed any challenge to enfranchisement diminishing domestic stability by stating that "the result will not be to make the home less happy, but society more holy."[14] There can be no doubt that Harper's words carried immense power, but what other black women talked about and acted upon at the fair ranked just as important to black women's advancement. Just as surely, they contributed to racial advancement in general by redefining the image of African American women and reaffirming their intelligence, morality, economic value, and domestic creativity. Throughout the fairgrounds they accorded themselves as molders of a new African American identity with a destiny they planned to help shape.

Ida B. Wells did not speak at the conference,[15] probably because of her scheduled anti-lynching lecture tour in Great Britain, which kept her out of the country until after the opening of the fair. As soon as she returned from England, however, she headed for Chicago where she would speak frequently and fervently on various topics. In her multifaceted pursuits, Wells proved herself the equal of any feminist of the day, with views crossing the intellectual spectrum from emigration to culture to labor exploitation. Within a month of her return, Wells had her first opportunity to participate at the fair, both at the Haytian Pavilion and at the Congress on the Negro.

On June 26, 1893, what was described as the Congress on the Negro convened for a three-day session that focused on African American advancement and an elimination of oppressive conditions in the South. More accurately, this purported Congress was the annual conclave of the three-year-old Colored Men's National Protective Association. The attraction of the fair convinced its leadership to hold its convention in Chicago instead of St. Louis as originally planned. Initially organized in the Windy City in 1891, evidently as an alternative to T. Thomas Fortune's declining Afro-American Council, which was organized in Chicago in 1890, the Protective Association aimed to fight against southern outrages such as lynchings, peonage, and disfranchisement. The agenda of this year's fair focused on revitalizing the organizational structure of the Association through constitutional changes.

The Association was truly national in membership; representatives arrived from every state in the Union. Chicagoans were present but in comparatively small numbers, interspersed as they were among 300 delegates. Being the hosts, they asserted themselves fully, with attorney Edward H. Morris temporarily presiding over the conference. He balanced complaints about his heavy-handed decisions from the chair with his smiles and wit which allowed "management of some of the refractory brothers."[16] As for his important, initial contribution to the conference, Morris set the tone as he said, "We are here to try and hasten the time when all over the land the humblest, the poorest, the blackest citizen will not be obliged to beg and plead for the thing which he has the right to demand—ordinary justice and common fair play."[17]

For the naive who thought that all was right in the world, the appearance of the mayor of Chicago, the Hon. Carter G. Harrison, corrected that misperception. As he welcomed the delegates, the mayor resorted to a combination of stock political antics mixed with southern paternalism to deliver a most unusual address. The liberal former Kentuckian quickly reminded the delegates that they were wise to remain ambivalent about the nation's abilities to keep its promises of equal protection and opportunity for all as it worked its way to a color-blind solution to national problems. The mayor's paternalism emerged as he talked of faithful African Americans in his home state who still referred to him as "Massa Cartah." He continued with appropriate references to African American women. "I am one who thinks the nut-brown skin capable of higher beauty than that of the Caucasian skin," the *Chicago Evening Post* reported, whimsically noting that the mayor could not resist such insensitive remarks since "the influence of the blarney stone soon asserted itself." Harrison continued, "I have seen black men whose forms were as handsome as an Apollo of ebony. But there is a prejudice against you. It will take time to eradicate it. Don't try to do it in a day. Don't try to break down such prejudices. Live with them with honest earnest conduct."[18] Since no Chicago politician could conclude a meeting without self-congratulation, the mayor's peroration included references to the political progress he had engineered through his African American appointments. Most notably they included police and fire departments' hirees along with a second female employed in the Chicago Public Library.

The "grand old man," the walking Colored Rock of Gibraltar, acted to neutralize the Blarney Stone. More importantly, the presence of Frederick Douglass at its opening session legitimized the organization's existence and program. When word spread that he would attend the meeting, even whites came to hear the American legend speak. Douglass entered the hall and initially sat inconspicuously in the rear, but as soon as the conveners noted his presence they immediately asked that he speak from the podium. Douglass's speaking routinely meant he would challenge the perennial Caucasian obsession with the "Negro Problem." Douglass tore at the heart of the Anglo-Saxon's fixation on blaming the victim. "The black man was not a problem. He was a man. There was nothing problematic about the Negro. The Negro was all right," declared Douglass, "whose great head of white hair was very conspicuous among the darker heads of his brethren."[19] He concluded with a challenge to America to live up to its promise of opportunity for all as embodied in the Constitution and Declaration of Independence.

After being named temporary secretary, attorney Edward H. Wright read a paper entitled, "The Immigration of the Negro to Africa." Acknowledging the many obstacles to enjoying full citizenship in America, Wright still argued that the most logical option for diasporans lay in forgoing emigration to Africa. The spirit of Tubman and Truth lived as Ida B. Wells spoke forcefully about protecting the basic rights of citizenship. It continued as Lettie Trent called for a boycott of the fair because of repeated racial slights extending back to 1891. Her militant tone disturbed so many present that they shouted her down.

After three days of deliberations, the most salient results of the meetings were a commitment to return home and spread the word among local citizenry about the merits of the Association, and to vote on the constitution. A call to all African American organizations to support the next year's conference brought immediate support, as did condemnation of Colored American Day as a move to separate the races. As the organization addressed its national commitment, it devised an inclusive organizational structure that included an Iowan, George E. Taylor, as president, with a Louisianan, an Arkansan, a South Carolinian, a Mississippian, and Ida B. Wells as vice presidents. Also, Wells and Lettie Trent served on a Ladies Auxiliary Board of Directors. Chicagoans Edward H. Morris and Edward H. Wright joined the National Executive Committee and the Committee to Address National Issues on Race, respectively.

In addition to the interests African Americans had in attaining their full rights as citizens, education seemed indispensable in its own right. A special session on education for African American youth convened in the Art Palace downtown on August 2, 1893. The American Educational Association

for the Advancement of Colored Youth met as the formal sponsor while prin-
cipals, teachers, students, and college presidents discussed the best methods
of improving academic conditions for African American youngsters. A virtual
who's who of education attended the conference; the *Indianapolis Freeman*
headline, "Art Palace Crowded with the Intellectual Elite of the Race," rang
with the sound of truth.

With confidence in the promise that education offered their race in the
twentieth century, Prof. J. M. Gregory of Howard University, the organization's president, called the meeting to order. Recitation of who attended
and belonged, in and of itself, would merit mention only if the listing were
smaller. It was, in fact, long and impressive.[20] Expectedly, Frederick Douglass
headed the list. All the universities, colleges, high schools, and academies
serving African American youth sent representatives. Almost miraculously in
the thirty years since bondage, the enrollment of African American youngsters in educational institutions in the year of the fair had reached a level of
1,352,352 pupils attending 25,530 schools.[21]

Next, the Congress on Labor be-gan its proceedings on August 28, 1893
against a backdrop of national depression and widespread unemployment.
Throughout Chicago, from the south side to the lakefront and downtown, the
specter of the unemployed, overwhelmingly white, appeared so real as to re-
quire its being hidden. Nonetheless, labor riots provided daily fare for the
city's newspapers, which denounced the unemployed as ingrates, communists, and in general deserving of their plight.

The Congress's relevance was manifest in the economic conditions of the
day and in the very existence of the fair. The famed Henry George, apostle of
the single tax and author of *Progress and Poverty*, spoke, as did other labor
organizers, theorists, and agitators. Booker T. Washington from Tuskegee Institute was there to speak on "The Progress of Negroes and Free Laborers." It
was a presentation typical of Washington when away from the South—assertive, honest, and forthright—very different from his southern voice of concili-
ation and compromise.

In his stirring introduction of Washington, Frederick Douglass recalled
how he once responded to Harriet Beecher Stowe's inquiry about the future
independence of the freedmen: "The only way in which the Negro could be
lifted from the level of common farm-hand was to give him a knowledge of
the handicrafts, making him a blacksmith, machinist, brickmaker or what not,
so long as he was not confined to field labor." The "grand old man" then
presented Washington as someone who was conquering the white prejudices
of the South through essential regional planning and increased production.
"Today the bricks, wagons, buggies and tinware manufactured by the scholars
of the Tuskegee Institute are in demand all over the state," boasted Douglass,
as he motioned Washington to the podium.[22]

Washington minced no words as he flailed the South's outmoded, oppressive labor system. But, in what was becoming the typical Washington style, he both extolled the virtues and criticized the deficiencies of black labor. He lambasted the crop lien and mortgage system in minute detail as being no more than modern slavery and the perpetrators as mortgage sharks. Specifically, the Tuskegeean lamented:

> It is safe to say that of the colored farmers of the black belt of the South three-fourths are today in debt for supplies to raise last year's crop; and it is safe to say four-fifths are in debt for supplies furnished to make the present crop, and those four-fifths live in small one-room cabins. This system affects the black man not only industrially but morally as well.
>
> It is claimed that the Negro as a free laborer is not a success. . . . The returns of the Agricultural Department [indicate the contrary and] throughout the South there are now nearly 8,000,000 acres cultivated by Negroes as renters or owners.

He added that educational methods addressing the problem of eliminating the mentality of dependency represented the solution for that region's ills.[23] Nevertheless, he also placed part of the blame for the southern African American's plight on his own ignorance. A thorough Social Darwinist, Washington, like the so-called ultra-assimilationists, sincerely believed in maximizing one's efforts to succeed in a competitive world. Washington's experiences convinced him that his fellow blacks could succeed if they adopted new attitudes, especially as to their need to *will* themselves as they worked themselves out of their predicament.[24] Beyond new habits involving morality, health, and thrift, he sought to create a new world and succeeded in the area surrounding the town of Tuskegee.

Ida B. Wells elaborated further about how indebtedness led on a downward path to peonage. As Frederick Douglass vacated the chair in deference to Henry Demarest Lloyd, he reiterated his hostility to the sharecropping system and the use of scrip in place of legal currency. The plight of the northern African American working man and woman, excluded by custom and relegated through connivance to the domestic and service trades, received no hearing. With the bulk of the African American population located in the South, Douglass could easily overlook black Northerners in his introductory remarks, saying, "Poverty in tenement houses in the city is nothing to the poverty of the colored farm tenant in the South." Of course, the reality of northern life stood in stark contrast.

The Parliament of Religions, the fair's most anticipated convocation, began on September 11, 1893. This monument to religious tolerance was preceded and followed by a series of small denominational congresses extending from Sunday, August 27, 1893, to Sunday, October 15, 1893, which allowed the fullest inclusivity possible. A delegation of Colored American Catholics even met as part of the Columbian Catholic Congress, giving them "a spotlight never dreamed of."[25] Headed by Chicago's Rev. Augustin Tolton and by Father Charles R. Uncles, they discussed the benefits of membership in their universal church and the encouragements evident in the rising recognition accorded African American Catholics.[26] For the larger conclave, Christians were joined by Hindus, Jews, Muslims, Bahai, Taoists, and many other religions.

African American Protestant involvement was significant. Bishop Benjamin Arnett of the A.M.E. church spoke on "Christianity and the Negro" and Fannie Barrier Williams spoke on "What Can Religion Further Do to Advance the Condition of the American Negro?" With deep compassion Williams called on her African American brethren among the clergy to make religion a force for good. With equal fervor, she challenged America's white leadership to live up to the American Creed and extend opportunities and amenities of full citizenship to its Colored citizens. "In nothing do the American people contradict the spirit of their institutions, the high sentiments of their civilization, and the maxims of their religion," she intoned, "as they do in practically denying to our colored men and women the full rights of life, liberty and the pursuit of happiness." Religion was not to remain static in its theological mode, but must become activist in working to "unite, and not to separate, men and women according to the superficial differences of racial lines."[27]

COLORED AMERICAN DAY

A scrupulous overview of the disparate activities of the fair in which African Americanas participated indicated that Colored American Day was perhaps of tertiary importance among all the hustle and bustle on and off the fairgrounds. Ranking ahead of this solitary day's limited activities was the eight-day Congress on Africa, which had concluded triumphantly several days earlier. Haytian Day and the daily activities at the Haytian Pavilion also ranked higher in importance. Yet Colored American Day earned unwarranted recognition because of the controversy surrounding it contemporarily and the interest it garnered subsequently through a misreading of the past. The *Inter Ocean*, filled with pride because of the conduct of its African American friends in holding substantive discussions during the Congress on Africa, chided that the group had a racial obligation to insure that Colored American Day maintain a comparable level of decorum, and to "make it a day that will give other visitors as good an impression of the colored race as did the discussion and the attendance at the African congress last week."[28] The Congress on Africa probably represented the pinnacle of African American and continental dialogue as well as interracial contact for the nineteenth century. Its importance was immense, and it will be discussed in chapter 10.

As for Colored American Day, Frederick Douglass's involvement in planning the celebration pleased the *Inter Ocean* immensely. From the moment he assumed the presidency of the committee planning the event, he began to envision it as a springboard from which to expose a standing criticism of the nation's treachery toward African Americans and to present a living exhibition of black accomplishment before an international audience. Douglass knew that his acceptance of the position and association with the event opened him to criticism of accepting the half loaf when ideological consistency required rejection of a dubious honor. Nonetheless, the opportunity to demonstrate race achievement proved too attractive to dismiss. Nearly four decades later, Dr. M. A. Majors of Chicago, who had served as one of several vice presidents on the committee, fondly reflected on the event as a shining moment for his race. Majors's reflections in 1929 on the eve of planning the 1933 world's fair provided a contrasting version to the tone of earlier African American denunciations of their near total exclusion that spurred this study.

In one sense, Colored American Day promised to be a festivity in which African Americans consummated their newly acquired absorption of high culture. Their mastery of European musical and literary endeavors could surely impress the white friends of the race who might spread the word that a "New Negro had evolved," one far removed mentally from his or her servile days in intellectual and physical shackles.

As expected, formidable opposition appeared. Ida B. Wells, who described herself retrospectively as a "hothead" on the issue, and Lettie Trent, who locally urged a boycott of activities associated with the fair, personified how intense the thought, rhetoric, and actions of assertive young African Americans could become. Wells refused to treat the special day as anything other than an insult. She assessed it as an attempt to relegate African Americans to a separate and inferior status that accentuated subordination. Her mind filled with the racial stereotypes of minstrelsy, cakewalking, and watermelon contests whenever she imagined what the day would bring.

As a middle-aged James Weldon Johnson was to describe minstrelsy, it "was, on the whole, a caricature of Negro life, and it fixed . . . the tradition of the Negro as only an irresponsible, happy-go-lucky, wide-grinning, loud-laughing, shuffling, banjo-playing, singing, dancing sort of being."[29] Chicago's Quinn Chapel A.M.E. minister, the Rev. John T. Jenifer, despised the rising popularity of the cakewalk and feared its possible appearance as part of the world's fair activities. Lecturing in 1892 before a multitude of eager listeners assembled at the church, Jenifer said that "there are two ways in which a race may become distinguished. First, through its intelligence, its industry, progress and God-fearing good citizenship; second, through its ignorance, depravity, indolence, and antagonism to the genius of good government and the spirit of progress. I am pained to notice [from] the newspapers that some of our people are becoming distinguished by the latter method." As to the cakewalk, he singled out this dance craze as a form of "race luggage" better left behind: "We must abandon all these grotesque features that serve to remind others of our former degraded condition in life, and cherish the best that is at our command. We are in the midst of a journey from a past condition to a better [one]. Improvement has been made, but 'race luggage' still hampers some of us, holding back the entire race." The impending fair offered both an opportunity to demonstrate advancement and a pitfall to confirm backwardness, and a curious America would ask which it was to be.[30]

Ministers at several Chicago churches also agreed that the special day posed a major threat to their race's image. At Olivet Baptist, the mother church of the city's Baptists, Dr. J. F. Thomas condemned the event. At Quinn Chapel, Dr. G. C. Boot, who replaced Jenifer, along with his fellow A.M.E. colleague, Dr. D. A. Graham at Bethel, opposed it. The same situation held true at St. Stephen on the city's west side. Rev. J. E. Thompson of St. Thomas Episcopal "did not see the fitness of it." As their congregations listened, the clergy preached the rightness of a boycott.[31] To provide an alternative activity for Chicagoans and visitors, they scheduled a massive picnic for the following day, far from the fairgrounds in a public park.

So, the refined element legitimately feared that Colored American Day might just as easily deteriorate into a "Jubilee Day," during which the most objectionable features of black folk culture and expression in the eyes of the elite might be exposed to white view. This last factor explained why the chasm between the elite and respectables continued to widen. The latter could never fathom the depth of in-group resentment on the part of these parvenu African American racial leaders toward what they saw in their own eyes as worthy and legitimate cultural expressions. And, after all, had not the respectables embraced European aesthetics as part of their holistic appreciation of culture from around the entire rim of the Atlantic Complex, both in the spheres of the *beaux arts* and in African-influenced indigenous forms?

During a period of ever increasing racial conflict in the South, where the bulk of the African American population lived, some advocates of African emigration could only approach the event with great caution. Not only were its conveners Afro-Saxons who extolled the virtues of everything European, but the president of the day was none other than the ultra-assimilationist Frederick Douglass, one of the most vocal enemies of emigration. However, to Bishop Henry McNeal Turner initially, the event still held promise. He reached a conclusion that paralleled that of the integrationists, in that recognition of his group in a black-run activity extolling racial achievements represented a fine opportunity to convince both whites and blacks alike of African American attainment. His position shifted as the clamor for a boycott gained momentum.

In the same manner that the event conveyed an ideological signal, it also held importance along social lines, among the various "social grades" comprising black Chicago. Within both the elite and the respectables, sizeable segments existed who shared misgivings about as well as confidence in the celebration. To many, however, the one outstanding point appeared to be that whatever was done in the name of the race had to be equally redemptive and enhancing of its reputation. At the same time, there were many citizens who were indifferent to whatever was done in the name of the race, and no appeal for a boycott was needed to keep them away.

Friday, August 25, 1893 was a historic day as African Americans gained the recognition they sought to present their story to the world. Important whites attended, pleasing Frederick Douglass and others greatly. Their presence confirmed the arrival of blacks as equals in American society, if only for several hours on one afternoon. Isabella Beecher Hooker, sister to Harriet Beecher Stowe and Rev. Henry Beecher, accompanied Douglass to the stage to the thunderous applause of the 2,500 persons who filled Festival Hall. At her side were her two nieces, daughters of the Beecher who commanded the first black regiment in Civil War South Carolina. Hooker embodied the abolitionist spirit that historian James M. McPherson described as still vital in liberal circles in the nation.

Assimilationists were not the only African Americans who needed the affirmation brought by the presence of elite whites. Other integrationists seemed to believe white involvement confirmed the humanity of blacks in a white-dominated world. The attendance of approximately 800 whites, one-third of the assemblage, further attested to the possibility of racial harmony. Phoebe Couzins, who had befriended African American interests during the pre-fair period as a member of the Board of Lady Managers, attended. So did Baltimore Catholic priest the Rev. John R. Slattery, who shared his plans for building a $300,000 facility to train African Americans for the priesthood.

However, some prominent African Americans failed to appear, among them the featured opera singer, coloratura soprano Sissieretta Jones, known as the Black Patti. Even though Jones's manager, Major James B. Pond, had accepted a deposit, the contractual failure of those in charge of the musical program to make one timely payment led to a cancellation on her part.[32] There was heavy propaganda from opponents of the event, led by Ida B. Wells, who had contacted the singer to try to dissuade her from appearing, but financial considerations outweighed ideology. Ironically, Madame Jones had appeared the previous year at Madison Square Garden in an event advertised as a "Jubilee Spectacular and Cake-Walk."[33]

Ida B. Wells stayed away, but retroactively reversed her assessment both of the propriety of staging the celebration and of its value to racial progress. Originally motivated by a whimsical impulse, it appeared she responded to favorable white newspaper accounts about the event, especially in the *Inter Ocean*, by later seeking out Douglass at the Haytian Pavilion. There, she apologized to the "grand old man" for placing her youthful exuberance before the qualities of racial leadership he had displayed in deciding to participate. A.M.E. Bishops Arnett and Turner absented themselves while two of the committee's vice presidents also avoided it. Former U.S. Representative John Mercer Langston skipped the event, having previously urged Chicago audiences that they should follow his lead.

In looking at Colored American Day itself, dividing the program into four constituent parts provides better understanding of the proceedings. First and foremost, the oratory of Frederick Douglass dominated, and subsequently served as the standard for any evaluation. Short addresses by whites comprised another portion. Musical selections of a classical nature represented a third part. Lastly, musical selections and recitations from established and rising African Americans provided entertainment and enlightenment as part of a fourth section. Each had significance by itself, both contemporarily and today.

Douglass's speech evoked great emotion and mesmerized an audience of the faithful. "Shaking his white mane and trembling with the vehemence of his eloquence the old man for more than half an hour held 2,500 persons under a spell," the *Chicago Tribune* reported (see Appendix I).[34] By delivering a message of defiance in the face of increasing American racism and violence, and of African American resilience and progress only one quarter of a century after two centuries of abject subordination, he accomplished his goal of winning racial redemption. In addition, Douglass denied the existence of a "Negro problem": "There is, in fact, no such problem. The real problem has been given a false name. It is called Negro for a purpose. It has substituted Negro for nation, because the one is despised and hated, and the other is loved and honored. The true problem is a National problem."[35] Further, "the problem is whether the American people have honesty enough, loyalty enough, honor enough, patriotism enough to live up to their own Constitution. . . . We intend that the American people shall learn of the brotherhood of man and the fellowship of God from our presence among them." In the climax of his speech, he demanded that the measuring rod of African American progress be one that was rooted on the American, rather than the African, continent. "Measure the Negro. But not by the standard of the splendid civilization of the Caucasian. Bend down and measure him—measure him—from the depths out of which he has risen."[36]

The speech sounded the same themes that Douglass had enunciated during the fair's inaugural ceremonies and in the pamphlet, *The Reason Why the Colored American Is Not in the World's Columbian Exposition*. While the presentation did not epitomize originality, Douglass's rhetorical tour de force amplified its impact. Even at age seventy-five, Douglass's well-contrived gesticulations mixed with tonal variations and speeds made him a rhetorical force for the ages. As to the utterances of whites, they were far more important for their having been articulated than for their content.

Young composer Will Marion Cook of New York at age twenty-two deserved credit for having arranged the musical program, which featured both classical pieces and presentations from the African American idiom, including musical selections by mezzo soprano Mme. Deseria Plato (Mrs. Boardley) of New York and tenors Harry Thacker Burleigh from the National Conservatory of Music in New York and Sidney Woodward of Boston. Prof. Maurice Arnold Strothotte from the National Conservatory of Music in New York provided piano accompaniment for all of the performers. Last, Douglass's grandson, violinist Joseph Douglass, played several classical pieces.

Contemporary newspaper sketches depicting scenes on Colored American Day at the fair, all courtesy of the Chicago Public Library. This page: 21. A well-dressed crowd assembles outside the building. Opposite page, from top to bottom: 22. Frederick Douglass. 23. Nationally known elocutionist Hallie Q. Brown, reciting "The Black Regiment" in honor of fallen heroes in the struggle to defeat slavery. 24. Celebrated baritone Harry T. Burleigh of the New York Conservatory of Music. 25. Classical violinist Joseph Douglass, grandson of Frederick Douglass.

Madame Plato, a substitute for Sissieretta Jones, sang "Lieti Signor" from *The Huguenots*. Plato was reported to have previously performed arias from *Il Trovatore* at the Union Square Theater in New York and was lauded by African Americans for being the nation's only Creole mezzo soprano. However, music professor John Graziano contends that Violetta's arias in *Il Trovatore* fall into the musical domain of the soprano, and therefore out of Plato's range, which extended from high D to low B.[37] Nonetheless, on the fairgrounds, her performance was well received, and in response to a call for an encore, she pleased the assemblage with "Nearer, My God, to Thee." Burleigh and Woodward both sang selections from Will Marion Cook's uncompleted opera, *Uncle Tom's Cabin*, and Woodward added an aria by Verdi, possibly from *Aida*. Woodward's vocal abilities were impressive; the *Tribune* reported that "he sang . . . in a tenor that for smoothness and purity of tone has rarely been equaled at the exposition."[38] Accordingly, several calls for an encore also followed his rendition.

This musical fare would have been a delight to the classically appreciative ear, and that would have included persons without elite status who were accustomed to the classics after being exposed to many performances within the sanctuaries of the Dearborn Street Corridor churches. No doubt, though, to many of the rank and file it proved as unappealing as it did to the disinterested whites on the fairgrounds who refused to support Theodore Thomas's classical concerts. They favored Sousa marches and popular tunes of the day, and the tastes of the African American rank and file probably followed suit. In the end, perhaps what mattered most was the satisfaction that Douglass and the white and black elites enjoyed.

The concert and literary portion also featured the Fisk Jubilee Singers with their specialty, the songs of slavery. Renowned elocutionist Hallie Q. Brown from Tuskegee Institute and Wilberforce College displayed her skills as she read "The Black Regiment." This recitation of black valor under fire in the first war of African liberation, the American Civil War, thrilled the audience. Paul Lawrence Dunbar read an original poem, "The Colored American" as well as his soon to be famous "Oak and Ivy." Overall, the success of Colored American Day rested primarily with effective presentations of the audible word—whether spoken or sung—along with the musical chord.

As to a substantive influence of this event over African American life and race relations, the record is mute. In the absence of Gilmore's Band, the white musical group authorized by the fair to start the ceremonies with the "The Star-Spangled Banner," the participants improvised their own commencement proceedings. However, the racist climate that excluded black musicians within the city from practicing their skills openly was simply highlighted by Gilmore's unexplained nonparticipation, owing possibly to nonpayment of promised monies.

The white press presented the celebration as a triumph for African Americans, especially insofar as they showed decorum in their dress and demeanor.

The *Chicago Herald* commented that the "better type of Colored people" were present, represented by schoolteachers and ministers. The tone of the *Tribune's* reporting indicated satisfaction with the appearance both of "prominent colored men" on the stage and the socially prominent Beecher family. The *Inter Ocean* gave the event page-one, column-one treatment, with the headline "HONOR TO THEIR RACE: Colored American Day at the Exposition a Success." Aware of dissent in black ranks, the newspaper aired the facts as they existed and immediately legitimized the staging of the event with its opening paragraph: "Colored American day at The Fair, and the dignified manner of its observance, did honor to the race. Even in the face of opposition in their own ranks, with which those in charge had to contend, the celebration was everything that grand old statesman and sage, Frederick Douglass, had hoped for."[39] Accompanying sketches (see figs. 21-25) presented African Americans in a very positive light.

At an event which ultra-assimilationists knew must be pleasing to white eyes and ears, the black press also carried immense weight. The *Cleveland Gazette* disappointingly characterized the festivity as "a farce."[40] The *Indianapolis Freeman*, trying to sound like the voice of Chicago—recently labeled the "Windy City"—first mistakenly reported that it would not take place, and then assessed it, with the exception of the oratorical and musical portions, as a great failure. It was relatively enthusiastic about the oratorical portion, which featured Douglass, and the music. Its assessment of failure finally relied on low attendance figures at the event as well as on the fairgrounds. In its conclusion, the *Freeman* stated, "'the Negro Jubilee Day' has gone glimmering."

In reality, because of its ephemeral nature, being entertainment, this single day's activities did not amount to more than much ado about nothing. The complexity and multifaceted character of African American and continental African involvement throughout the duration of the fair and in other venues and events could obscure it, and did so rather easily. Overall, Colored American Day brought no redemption to African Americans for past sufferings, it established no new dialogue with whites in the present, and it resulted in no ameliorative framework for the future, as the Congress on Africa seems to have done.

Part Four

"ALL THE WORLD IS HERE!"

It represented an unassailable verity. That is how Harvard University Professor Frederick Ward Putnam interpreted the frequently repeated refrain echoed on the fairgrounds, "All the World Is Here!" Accordingly, the respected academician posed this question to readers of a magnificent photographic treatment of the various ethnic and racial groups that populated the exposition site: "What other combination of words could have expressed the truth so effectively as these five monosyllables?"[1] Frederick Perry Noble of the Newberry Library of Chicago, who conceived of having the Congress on Africa, the fourth in a series of international conferences on that continent's future, proudly wrote in a similar vein:

> Man and woman; Negro and white; Christianity and Islam; Africa, America, Europe and Oceania; North and South; high and low; rich and poor; Austria, Angola, Belgium and Congo, Denmark, England, Egypt . . . ; artists, authors, editors, divines, diplomatists, educators, explorers, jurists, legislators, physicians, missionaries, rulers and statesmen, scholars, scientists, former slaves and former slave-holders, ex-Confederates and Union veterans — in short, THE WORLD — made the Chicago Congress on Africa a senate of representative men and races, and the world's supreme court of deliberation on its once-lost continent.[2]

There were a myriad of other interpretations of the meaning of the Congress. Frederick Douglass's utterances carried almost Olympian importance, as did scientific findings printed a generation later by anthropologist Melville Herskovits. When Bishop Henry McNeal Turner spoke, the earth quaked. As a reporter for the *Chicago Herald* recounted, when Bishop Turner made his remarks on the African origin of humankind before a packed audience at the Congress on Africa, there were "looks of amazement, shudders and then a few smiles, followed by applause from some of the colored people."[3] The anonymous white reporter considered the remarks "sensational," but similar assertions were commonplace among persons of African descent during the Gilded Age. They were spoken earnestly, whether people wanted to hear them or not, or whether they believed them or not. Significantly, Turner's remarks, in the main, fit the mold of this conference, where most speakers repeatedly extolled the virtues of things black, both on the African continent and among its children scattered abroad.

The World's Columbian Exposition became the occasion at which bonds of racial fraternity could be reinforced by blacks from all around the United States. Racial consciousness and group solidarity were raised, both as questions and as components deemed essential for group survival in racist America of the Social Darwinian era. Four events in particular—Colored American Day, the Congress on Africa, the World's Congress of Representative Women, and the World Parliament of Religions—provided the appropriate settings for strengthening of the bonds of racial identity. The presence of the Fon people of the West African state of Dahomey at the fair revealed several perspectives on the tenuous character of the diasporan-continental African link during the age of Western European hegemony. The visitors at Dahomey Village on the Midway represented one reality, positive to themselves, but negative to some in the western world who desired to see them in a depreciatory light. An elitist, Francophone Hayti and its Afro-Saxon spokesman, Frederick Douglass, wished to project a new reality and image to the Western world, so they ignored the Fon at their pavilion on the fairgrounds. Since the Fon and all other continental Africans served as an embarrassment to Afro-Saxon claims to being the embodiment of the best of the western European and West African worlds, they and their interests were rendered invisible at the Art Palace along the shores of Lake Michigan in Chicago's downtown. The reality of culture in continental Africa took a back seat to the dream of an independent, Pan-African world led by the New World Africans of the Diaspora.

As significant as the Congress on Africa seemed as a defining moment in history on this first day, it was destined to be, like so many things at the fair, to be one spectacular event, one sensational episode, among many. At the Haytian Pavilion, the Liberian exhibit in the Agriculture Building, the Dahomey Village, the Caribbean island exhibits from Dutch Curaçao, Spanish Cuba, and British Jamaica, and the Cape Coast exhibit at the Woman's Building, the planned diversity of global culture also attracted fairgoers.

8

CONTINENTAL AFRICA AT THE FAIR: DAHOMEY VILLAGE

We had anticipated an hour or two with the inhabitants of Dahomey, but owing to the . . . cool weather the Dahomey tribe had folded up their tents and silently stolen away.

— James F. Alston, A.M.E. Church

In photography, history lives like a corpse in the grave, awaiting resurrection.

— John Durham Peters, "Beauty's Veils"

Sounds which address the ear are lost and die
In one short hour; but that which strikes the eye
Dwells long with the mind; the faithful sight
Engraves the knowledge with a beam of light.

— Horace, Ars Poetica,
cited in *Portrait Types of the Midway*

To Frederick Ward Putnam, Harvard anthropology professor and chief of ethnology at the exposition, the element that made the fair vibrate was life, as humanized through the foreign contingents from non-Western areas of the world. The disparate peoples of Asia, Europe, and North and South America arrived. And from continental Africa came Nubians, Zulu, Algerians, "Boushareens," and "Dahomeans." Impressive and awe-inspiring structures and waterworks, such as the massive Manufacturing Building with a capacity of 100,000 people, the 1,500-ton, 265-foot Ferris Wheel with its 1,440 seats, the Woman's Building, and the lagoons and canals, paled in comparison to the vitality manifested in the very presence of the world's diverse peoples. The media that captured these disparate images of life in their fullest vibrancy were photography, illustration, and the printed word.

In an occurrence of great importance in the history of the African Diaspora and American racial imaging, the arrival and seasonal stay in America
for five months, beginning in May 1893, of more than one hundred Fon[1]
men, women, and children—all subjects of Behanzin, King of Abomey, also
known to outsiders as Dahomey, hence its inhabitants became *the Dahomeans* in the American media—evolved to represent quintessentially both the
primary, contemporary image of continental sub-Saharan Africa at the fair
and the basis of a propagandistic myth which has endured for a century. Set-
tling in for the summer in larger numbers than their continental counterparts
found within the Algerian and Egyptian contingents, who also resided in en-
campments on the Midway, the Fon immediately became a media sensation.
Subsequent myth and reality surrounding the Fon people of Dahomey unfolded as part of a multifaceted saga of an enduring and successful propaganda effort aimed at reinforcing a racial hierarchy of white supremacy counterpoised against the self-actualization of a proud, foreign people who had a
mixed influence on white and black Americans.

Obviously no one at the fair, including diasporans such as African Methodist Episcopal (A.M.E.) church observer James F. Alston, with his dilettan-
tish preoccupation with Africa, or Frederick Douglass, with his open sentiment of cultural revulsion and dissociation, fully understood the intricacies of
Fon life as it was lived on the continent of Africa or in Dahomey Village,
located along the Midway Plaisance. What those familiar with white midwestern and national folkways, whether friend or racist critic, would have
thought, for example, about Fon dance and its accompanying music, is hard
to imagine. More substantive differences in physiognomy, social organization, language, dress, and religion proved unfathomable, for the most part.
The fairgoers' puzzlement was replicated, of course, if they visited the enclo-
sures of the Eskimo (or, as they were called in 1893, Eskimaux), the Samoans,
the Native Americans, the Turks, and the other foreign groups. One thing was
certain: a lack of understanding by members of one society did not prove a
lack of substance in the attitudes, views, and behavior of those in another.

As to the importance of the Midway Plaisance as a door to the world,
contemporarily, *Frank Leslie's Illustrated Weekly* saw in the spatial purity of
the White City something lacking in interest for the ordinary white fairgoer,
so the Midway offered a vitality in its diversity. "To the layman not interested
in the arts and sciences it will remain *the great attraction* of the fair. One
leaves it with a delightful feeling of having seen the one spot on the globe
which gives in a very comprehensive way an idea of the world's nationalities
with their various customs and manners in surprising detail [emphasis add-
ed]."[2] In fact, many ordinary fairgoers exhibited disinterest in the activities
inside the fairgrounds, such as the performances of Chicago's splendid sym-
phony orchestra led by Theodore Thomas.[3] Sousa's march music as well as
saloon and beer garden music, and maybe Scott Joplin's syncopation, were

A PRIVILEGED RACE.

ANABEL.— Just look at those African women! I should think they'd hate to go out with such scanty clothing.
MADGE.— Well, you know, people with their complexions don't tan easily.

26. Courtesy of the Chicago Public Library.

the substitutes which whetted and then satiated the public's appetite. Much to their chagrin, the fair's managers were forced to adjust to the public's taste and reduce both performances and fees.

Any racially motivated attempt to disparage non-Western groups would have enjoyed some success in its own right, based on documented, ingrained native white responses to darker skinned strangers. Whether Sioux, Samoan, or Fon, these visitors to Chicago appeared repugnant to persons subscribing to either the national norm of acceptable physical appearance and beauty or the popular racist notions of the decade. Moreover, rank and file white Americans, intimately attuned to their economic needs for uncontested land, religious well-being as proselytizers of the Truth, the legacy of a divinely sanctioned Manifest Destiny, and experience with subjection of the militarily and politically impotent, needed no nudges from the intellectual and pseudoscientific suppositions of Social Darwinian doctrine to convince them as to what perspective they should bring with them to Chicago. But if they had doubts or curiosity, racially biased guideposts abounded. Harvard University displayed its concept of the perfect human physique at the fair, showing a youthful Caucasian couple with measurements and a physiognomy gleaned from data collected from university students in the East. A pale complexion, aquiline nose, thin lips, and muscular definition for the male, and an hourglass figure for the female, set the standards for humankind. Once dressed, the female would wear the requisite corset to produce an ample to buxom bosom matched by broad hips, set off by a small waist.[4] When these physical attributes are compared to the depiction from *World's Fair Puck* in figure 26 of a discerning, or perhaps vacuous, set of Caucasian observers, exclaiming their disdain for Fon females on the fairgrounds, the ultimate in Victorian standards becomes manifest.

In contrast, fair management's aim to let fairgoers decide whether the African and other non-Nordic types, bereft of the civilizing tendencies of an Anglo-Saxon culture, had made progress of the type exemplified by the peoples of northwestern Europe since Christopher Columbus' monumental voyage in 1492, fell short of this goal in light of the condemnatory treatment the Fon have received in lay and scholarly literature. One such contemporary commentary reported that "if contrasts teach lessons, then such spectacles as are depicted (such as the Fon Village) . . . must have leavened the multitudes with a great many seeds of knowledge."[5] Another view commonly held was that "the visitor who passe[d] along Midway Plaisance [was] entertained by seeing people and customs . . . [and] the student of the races of mankind [had] ample opportunities in a stroll along this wonderful street, where he [could] examine and criticize without fear or favor."[6] One succinct description announced that the visiting inhabitants of this Dahomey Village were transported to the fair primarily "to illustrate the customs of their country." Once here, they were expected to "sing their war songs, give exhibitions of their methods of fighting, which is one of their chief occupations, and show a number of their artisans at work." Clearly, the intent of the fair's promoters of the Midway attractions was aimed at simultaneously turning a profit and presenting the world in all its diversity, based on actual observation and interaction. But if the expectations of *Harper's Weekly* materialized, a sense of global fraternity might also emerge.[7]

COUNTERVAILING INFLUENCES

As these West Africans settled in their summer village, two countervailing influences developed that shaped the public's image of just who the Fon were, what they represented, and their place in contemporary life and for posterity. First, of course, the Fon people as a portion of global humanity imposed an

27. Courtesy of the Chicago Public Library.

undeniable human presence at the fair and represented a reality that could never totally be denied. Journalistic references confirmed this acceptance despite the manipulative molding of images, both contemporarily and posthumously, to depict the Fon as savages, barbarians, or cannibals. To be sure, white fairgoers' perception of the Fon could be accurately described as convoluted. But the Fon were popular—defined to mean attractive, appealing to, and commanding interest in the eyes of many fairgoers—the latter, no doubt, gaping in curiosity and awkward amusement at a representative group from a nonindustrial, non-Christian society during the era of Social Darwinism. Nonetheless, these Fon of Dahomey managed to become real, living persons as they were personalized by the very use of their names in the newspapers. All of a sudden, Chicagoans were introduced on a personal level to Butagalon, Amessang, Sosolangago, Ipoke, Umbibi, Cogabi, Aballo, and Adajemus, rather than the impersonal *the Dahomeans*.[8]

Journalist and author Teresa Dean, in one of her frequent visits to the world of the Africans, found herself and a colleague in the strange position of cuddling a frightened Fon child, with all parties enjoying the moment. She was disposed to write, "The babies in this village and the other villages and the world are all alike. When they are not old enough to talk they might as well belong to one race. There's no difference in baby natures."[9] An account of children in the *Chicago Inter Ocean* gave a view of life that exposed bias at its worst and showed the transcendent core inkling of humanity at its highest: "The Dahoman baby dressed in a white cotton bag, ran about and kept his ugly mother chasing him. Once he found a white baby in the crowd and expressed great curiosity at the sight. He was going to hug him, but the white mother thought that she had seen enough of Dahomey and left hurriedly."[10] And when those babies grow into adults who comprise family units, they resemble the small group posed in figure 27, apparently observing us as we view the image.

Novelist Julian Hawthorne observed: "As time passes on, people are able to visit the Fair and begin to pick up an acquaintance among the strangers. We shake hands with the Soudanese, and ask them how mother is; we walk arm-in-arm with the Moslem, poke the Dahomeyans in the ribs. . . . "[11] While their presence was made possible solely by manipulative whites, if anyone deigned to look at the fair through the eyes of these transatlantic visitors, it must have seemed a strange and exotic place. Teresa Dean observed the following encounter between Nordic and African:

> The Nubian's face lighted up, and he said something which signified "Yes," and that he understood now. The other woman had been laughing during this time, whether at his decorated hair, queer costume, or what she considered his stupidity, she did not say. The Nubian looked at her and evidently decided her smiles, whatever they were for, were not complimentary to him. He turned to the woman who had questioned him, and said: "You nice. She"—with a disdainful wave of the hand—"no good."[12]

Mrs. Mark Stevens, the wife of a Michigan state official, also wrote of her observations in Chicago in *Six Months at the World's Fair*. Regarding the Fon of Dahomey, she showed great amazement as she shared her revelations:

Toward the end of the Fair one native only had succeeded in stringing a few English words together, while the rest had learned none; neither had they ambition to ac-quire our language. Their delight at the thought of returning home one burly savage expressed as follows: "Tar Ra-bum-de-day. Checog likey. No." And spreading out his arms he yelled: "Home, glady, glady."[13]

Lastly, as to the significance of having their images preserved for posterity through the wonder of nineteenth century photography, "the person whose photographed image comes into the world has been singled out as worthy of some attention," wrote Max Kozloff in *Photography and Fascination.* "Clearly the photo zone testifies limitlessly to [elections to a different status], grave or slight, evident or obscure as they may be. And they tend to set into motion a curiosity of which photographers or those who abet their work are well aware. For the moment, at least, the others are like us, they're not an issue. The ones framed in the photograph are. To examine their appearances is also to be teased by them."[14]

The media produced the second major countervailing influence on the presence of the Fon, exploiting that presence to create a second reality. This feat was accomplished adroitly through newspaper articles featuring illustra-tive sketches and the popular photographic souvenir books published about the fair that were the delight of Victorian tea tables and parlor conversation. Newspaper accounts, based on impressionistic ignorance of the Fon and con-taining sensationalistic suppositions about what these visitors thought and felt, attempted to feed the insatiable appetite of a news-hungry American public. The influence of yellow journalism induced a growing readership to accept nonsense over knowledge, and racist prattle over intelligent understanding.

Further, the plethora of souvenir guidebooks and books about the fair, which publishing companies distributed widely between 1893 and 1895, has negatively influenced ostensibly objective scholarship on the event over the last three decades. The intrinsic intrusiveness of photography was trans-formed into voyeurism and denigration. Kozloff stated: "At the vernacular core of photographic culture is a supreme tactlessness, an inquiring, very of-ten prying gaze, from which no action, in theory, can be averted."[15] While many twentieth-century historians of the fair have relied on these newspapers and photographic guidebooks as documents, they portray a one-sided reality, showing the Fon as objects of ridicule and scorn, rather than subjects of ob-jective inquiry, or even popular curiosity, as the academic organizers of the fair envisioned them.[16]

In counterpoise, another set of references to the Fon existed, scattered in articles and books about the fair. Hawthorne's *Humors of the Fair,* Dean's *White City Chips,* and Stevens's *Six Months at the Fair* carry too much infor-mation on the Fon for them to have been as despised as some recent histori-ans claim. A love affair with the grotesque notwithstanding, the inordinate amount of attention they received is inexplicable except on the level of an eclectic interest, all too human, born of curiosity, fascination, appeal, and possibly grudging respect.

28. Courtesy of the Chicago Public Library.

Frederick Douglass, America's best known victim of its slave system, provided one key to understanding some American journalistic negativity toward the Fon in the famed pamphlet, *The Reason Why the Colored American Is Not in the World's Columbian Exposition.*[17] Planted deep, or perhaps not so deep, in the nation's psyche lay its reluctance to reconcile itself with its past transgressions against African humanity. The Fon's arrival came slightly three decades after the end of the South's involvement in *illegal* Atlantic slave trading, only nine decades after the suppression of the *legal* international slave trade, and a scant twenty-eight years after slavery as an institution in America had been militarily crushed and constitutionally halted. Their presence stood as a grim reminder of the imperfection of the nation during a time of American self-adulation and anticipated international recognition of American technological genius. Similarly, diasporans, whether elite or rank and file, persistently reminded Anglo-Saxons of a past imperfect. The response of white America to them continued as it had for more than two and one-half centuries through ridicule, satire, and caricature. African American and African females were transformed either into promiscuous vixens or menacing Amazons, conveniently counterpoised negatively when held up to the projected chasteness and beauty of Victorian ladies of Anglo-Saxon lineage. During this heyday of Social Darwinian hierarchical positioning, the aversion to dark skins,[18] the scant clothing of the rain forest, and the partially exposed breasts of Fon females marked these continental Africans as inferior culturally. Not surprisingly, on the Midway Plaisance, African American and African males were relegated through imagery, respectively, to becoming vacuous, obsequious "Georges" with whiskbrooms in Pullman cars, and savage warriors with spears and clubs, lacking human compassion.

The influence of newspaper illustrations approximating caricatures, in a day when photographs were not commonplace in daily newspapers, combined with the appearance of such photographic collections accompanied by racist commentaries as *Midway Types: A Book of Illustrated Lessons about the People of the Midway Plaisance, and Oriental and Occidental[,] Northern and Southern Portrait[,] Types of the Midway Plaisance: A Collection of Photography of Individual Types of Various Nations from All Parts of the World Who Represent, in the Department of Ethnography, the Manners, Customs, Dress, Regions, Music and Other Distinctive Traits and Peculiarities of Their Race[,] with Interesting and Instructive Descriptions Accompanying Each Portrait*, better known as *Portrait Types of the Midway Plaisance*, to guarantee the castigation of the Fon, other continental Africans, Native Americans, and a host of other foreign visitors from Europe and Asia. This deliberately contrived mix of images and words created a propaganda apparatus that bolstered Nordic race ideology.[19] Such reportorial opinions and commentaries presented a negativity so prevalent and so strong that it affected the perception not only of whites but even of the diasporan-continental connection. One egregious example appeared in a purportedly racially liberal newspaper, the *Chicago Inter Ocean*. Its reporter, obviously seeking to present a pejorative description of a racial encounter, wrote pithily: "Each Dahoman is an ugly-looking creature."[20] Strangely enough, newspapers displayed a gender preference in their *ad hominem* attacks; Fon women were universally vilified, while men at times were referred to in salutary terms. One reporter described the men as "tall and well shaped" while one book's author saw them as effeminate.[21] As propaganda to bolster white claims to racial superiority, the commentaries served to convince fairgoers of what they might have missed at first observation, and, aided by racist narratives, how they were supposed to think when confronting the image of any exotic visitor. The unmeasurables, what effect they did have, are unknown and have yet to be considered historically.

Beyond the effects of propaganda, what the unprejudiced eye saw was "the art of recollection[, photography as it] revealed correspondences that would otherwise remain obscure and hidden."[22] Without commentary or titles, the photograph was open to interpretation. With commentary, the photograph was relegated to the genre of storytelling.[23] Viewers buying photographic souvenir books without commentaries benefitted, therefore, by being able to intelligently form their own opinions. On the other hand, newspaper readers could not escape such manipulation. Twelve reproductions of original photographs, showing the Fon in natural, formal, and staged poses, are included in this study and allow the viewer to form his or her opinion as to what elements in photographic documentation record beauty, savagery, courage, cowardice, exuberance, confidence, and fierceness. As always with artistic reproduction, beauty and acceptability are in the eyes of the beholder. However, "much that is convivial or festive or imposing in photographed behavior remains what it is, but one still has this submarine aspect of the picture: people disporting themselves apparently for our inspection. . . . What went on in the subject's mind, what rights and integrity were considered proper to the individual, these have no obvious continuity with the attitude of the viewer. Frequently the interests served are indeed contradictory to each other."[24] By way of modification, these photographs are presented without the original obnoxious captions. For purposes of comparison and to insure objectivity, the full text of these captions is included in Appendix III.

Francis Bruguiere, the noted French photographer, declared: "The documentary value of the photograph is immense, as is universally acknowledged: about such a self-evident value it is unnecessary to speak, seeing that there already exists so much underlining of the obvious."[25] What the amateur and professional photographer accomplished in 1893 reigns as indispensable to historical research and human understanding; the interpretative version of the truth that the photographs contained in and of themselves, without the aid of narrative captions, warrants a thorough examination. At a time when pictures were taken for their own sake, rather than toward any artistic end,[26] a realism born of purity of purpose reveals a glimpse of humanity invaluable over time. As a matter of indisputable fact, the Fon appeared as all too human, cultural differences notwithstanding.

Examining the photographs at the end of the twentieth century surely precludes any claim to unbiased historical-mindedness. As one imagines what the eyes and mind of the late nineteenth century perceived in these images, a

29. Courtesy of the Chicago Public Library.

30. Courtesy of the Chicago Public Library.

century's gap and the present-day appreciation of the humanity and value of the world's peoples make it virtually impossible to know if the captions denigrating the Fon did in actuality reflect the feelings of elite, middle class, and working class whites at the fair and at home. In today's global community, the commentaries represent an embarrassment to all and are obviously deserving of the summary repudiation they receive. But the focus here is, of course, 1893.

In figure 29, nine Fon males march to participate in one of the many daily parades held on the fairgrounds. They exude confidence as they stroll, probably singing in their native tongue of their homes, personal triumphs, and national glory. In figure 30, their gait is similar, but their facial features are somewhat obscured in photographic reproduction. The image of the white males in figure 29, watching intently, and especially of the man in the white suit, who walks alongside as the Fon march to the fairgrounds, encourages inquiry. This photograph, and the one shown in figure 30, were reproduced without commentary in a souvenir book. Perhaps the interested facial expressions of the three white men in the first photograph mean something, perhaps they do not. Do their faces display scorn, or just plain curiosity? Are they evincing a level of riveting interest that indicates that they will follow "these sturdy fellows" closely?

Over the last three decades, historians and analysts of the fair have tended to single out the Fon as the *most* African and non-Western of the scores of visiting foreign groups. Queries as to why they came and under what circumstances they were supposedly perceived further contributed to the recent interest and mystique surrounding their presence. Without a doubt, their appearance on the Midway served the dual purposes of presenting the exotic to the Western world as entertainment and illuminating the cultural differences between the supposedly backward societies of the world and the advanced nations of the Nordic sphere. Unfortunately, whether a group or exhibit enjoyed the sponsorship of Harvard University's anthropology department under Professor Putnam's auspices, or arrived under impresario Sol Bloom's direction, the question of their very *being* invariably focused on the pejorative.

THE FON AS SELF-PERCEIVED: RETROSPECTIVE HISTORICAL APPLICATION

Originating in a society described by anthropologist Melville J. Herskovits as a civilization, one would commonly expect civil behavior on the part of the Fon, both within their ranks and in their dealings with the many diverse peoples at the exposition. Among the Fon, respect for the rules of communal living was practiced; they were a well-organized society. A sense of social distinction was also noticeable as one observer wrote, "Presumably, they have among them people of low degree and those of high degree. The latter were stalking the grounds with most discontented expressions."[27] The village leader was described by Bancroft as a "king, a coal-black potentate, sleepy and fat, with a thick, bushy beard and head and jaws like a bull-dog. All day long he sits dozing with half-closed eyes and changeless expression of face."[28] Figures 34, 35, and 38 show the elderly leader, who in his appearance bears little resemblance to this view of him. It is probably the village leader who is being carried by subordinates in figure 31.[29]

But who were these foreign visitors, as examined through the prism of scholarship? The Fon were, first and foremost, members of a highly central-ized nation whose most prominent attributes were valor and military skill, hard work, family loyalty, obedience to state leadership, and discipline. Mel-ville J. Herskovits lived among the Fon in Dahomey and found "a ready response to discipline, and above all in the acceptance of the stricture that the path to ultimate satisfaction [lay] in constant application to the task at hand. For the Fon . . . exhibit[ed] a capacity for hard work that [stood] in striking contrast to the [European] stereotype of the tropical [African]."[30] An-other anthropologist, W. J. Argyle, in writing of the complexity of this society, maintained that they also socialized their children with a sense of a national past.[31]

Importantly, what the Fon thought of themselves stands as a partial mea-surement of how they were also going to be perceived. What they had to over-come were views such as those held by Susan B. Anthony, who visited Da-homey Village and observed: "I wonder if humanity sprang from such as this? It seems pretty low down, doesn't it? But I don't think Adam knew much more than this."[32] That they were not universally despised and rejected bears tes-timony to the strength of their being—resoluteness in carriage, disarming smiles, cheerfulness despite a longing for home, confidence in belonging to a self-defining group. In this case, the photographs reflected an obvious pride in group and collective belonging. If one were to deduce the meaning of Fon activities as they were observed at the fair by examining all pertinent docu-mentation, the starting point would not be the souvenir books, or the univer-sally insulting, sometimes satirical, but usually sardonic *Puck*. The meaning of life for the Fon began with their existence in their natural venue as Hersko-vits observed them in his classic study of this African kingdom.

Any objection to the thirty-eight-year interval between the Fon's sojourn to the United States in 1893 and Herskovits's field trip to West Africa in 1931 seems less formidable as impediments to understanding the Fon if one ac-cepts Herskovits's contention that the Fon way of life he observed remained virtually untouched after the time of the fall of Dahomey state under King Behanzin in 1894. Any subsequent change in cultural patterns was super-ficial. Dov Ronen observed that the initiation of French imperial rule in 1894 failed to transform Fon society because it lacked a base of legitimacy. The French successfully removed King Behanzin from his throne, but "the nomi-nation of a new king while the old king was still alive was an act contrary to the custom of succession, although the choice of the new king was support-

31. Courtesy of the Chicago Public Library.

32. Courtesy of the Chicago Public Library.

ed or suggested by Behanzin himself and made, according to custom, from among the founder's family."[33]

Last, this absence of change over time did not imply that Fon society was stagnant. Rather, Fon society was able to withstand French influences over that period and grow, but always in accordance with indigenous standards. This left the anthropologist free to observe the culture and people as they would have existed at the time of the fair.[34]

On a site measuring 150 by 195 feet, American carpenters and Fon craftsmen reconstructed a village of three thatch structures (as shown in figs. 31 and 32) both to provide the exotic to fairgoers as a moneymaking event and to represent the African's place in the modern world, a world dominated by Anglo-Saxon technology. Africa, in all its variety, met America in its equal diversity. In its physical location, Dahomey Village was not physically isolated, as one recent fair history contended in its provocative conceptualization; it was situated approximately 800 feet west of the mammoth Ferris Wheel, and next door to Austrian Village and other European exhibits.[35] And spatial positioning was more than a case of a classic turn-of-the-century racism involving white and black. North Africans from Algeria and Egypt, Zulu from southern Africa, and Sudanese all walked the fairgrounds. The Egyptian contingent featured the admixture of modern Egypt with very dark to cream-colored hues, with fully Negroid to "Hamitic" to Caucasian typologies present.

What was observable in the behavior of the Fon, and in the images conveyed by exhibits, according to Robert W. Rydell, was constantly misinterpreted, especially when viewed, as James Gilbert put it, by "tourists [who] were as varied as the exhibits themselves."[36] Constant references to their "dancing and drumming" were absolutely correct, but the reasons for this activity were never understood. They were equated by Frederick Douglass with "barbaric rites" when Douglass wished to elevate the status of diasporan Africans on August 25, 1893, at Colored American Day at the expense of their continental counterparts.[37] What he and countless others saw were, in fact, either social dancing or ancestral rites;[38] possibly some of the dancing was a kind of "thanks-offering" for a safe journey from West Africa across the same Atlantic Ocean over which so many relatives had sailed, never to return home. For these agriculturists, being in Chicago during the harvest months of June and July might have induced them to dance as they would have done at home in appreciation of life and agricultural abundance.

As soon as the Fon landed and began playing their music, newspapers lambasted this new sound, one that many whites linked to southern plantation music.[39] One visitor with a self-described "discerning ear" found the music at Dahomey cacophonous and distasteful. "The natives danced to a noisy confusion they called music but better likened to the rattle and noise made by a party of boys with tin pails, pans and sticks."[40] Similar criticisms would be made among whites of "Coon songs" by the century's end.[41]

The THEODORE THOMAS of DAHOMY

33. Courtesy of the Chicago Public Library.

Nonetheless, the exuberant dancing accompanying the music attracted attention in its strangeness to Western eyes. Reporters recounted this experience repeatedly. One account in *The New York Times* read: "They indefatigably perform the most amusing evolutions on a platform erected at the center of what I am informed and believe are wattled huts. They execute it with the greatest enjoyment and pantomime of song and dance, to an accompaniment of crude drumming and tambourines and their own crooning and characteristic singing."[42] Yet, given the popularity of the diasporan Africans' cakewalk in Anglo-Saxon society during the 1890s, total disdain as a widely endorsed sentiment seems unlikely. This appeared especially so since the intricacies and precision of these exotic rituals mesmerized so many of these fairgoers. The *Chicago Daily Herald* recounted at least one white youth who became so enthralled with the rhythmic dancing that he imitated it in his suburban neighborhood, much to the chagrin of his parents.[43] Importantly, what seemed to influence an impressionable youngster at an emotional level left an even more indelible mark on the refined Anglo-Saxon landscape at the cerebral and aesthetic levels. Over time, this acculturation would prove itself irresistible as Africa overwhelmed America. So, the world's fairs of the nineteenth century became venues for a new vista of musical expression. In fact, "composers and scholars in Europe and America, hearing the music of other cultures for the first time, became increasingly interested in them."[44]

Beyond the molders of Western musical tastes, ordinary folk took notice. Locally, the *Chicago Tribune* reported, "men and women appeared in breechclouts and loose tunics of yellow, blue, and white cloth of a light texture. Of all the strange people on the Plaisance none have such startling music or what is allowed to pass as music. The Dahomans seem to have just a bare idea of harmony and a rudimentary knowledge of instruments. Skins stretched over empty kegs, hollow tree trunks, and wicker work furnish them with drums, while the horns of animals with but a single tone are the only wind instruments used."[45] Visitors to the fair observed that the music of the Fon was played on several basic instruments, which were the drum, the gong, and the rattle. Stringed instruments were a rarity; a zither-like device was used on occasion, and one newspaper reported that a Fon who was acting as the Village's gatekeeper "was sit[ting] and strum[ming] a rude little harp."[46] The rhythmic beat was syncopated, "divided so that an element of two beats alternates with one of three, to make a 7/4 measure, there being an interval between the double and triple figure and between each total unit and the next," this being something totally foreign to the Western ear, and considered cacophonous since early contact with the music of African slaves. "The need of setting and maintaining a basic beat [was] of the greatest of all types of Fon music, since no song [could] be carried without such an accompaniment. So deeply [was] this configuration of melody plus rhythm lodged in Fon musical patterns that a person singing a song without accompaniment [would] accompany himself by clicking the finger-nails of the thumb and second finger in the proper rhythm."[47]

Also contemporarily, Bancroft wrote in his *Book of the Fair*:

> The instruments are as grotesque as the performers, and some of them are fearfully and wonderfully made. The best is a stringed instrument, resembling somewhat the zither seen in the Tyrol, but of ruder workmanship. There is an orchestra of drums and bells, with a single flute, a rattle, and an ivory horn of the most primitive pattern. The last is used for giving signals by the warrior who keeps guard over the village, and is similar in shape to the brazen war trumpets used by the ancient Kelts . . . There are other horns of wood; with stones shaken in a bag of skin, producing sounds like the hissing of serpents, and vessels and disks of copper clashed together like cymbals. The singing is much better than the instrumentation, for the Dahomeans have a certain knowledge of harmony, and their dances are accompanied with choral song as well as the beat of drum.
>
> The drum beat opens the performance with gentle, rhythmic tapping of drums, rapidly increasing in tone. Then another drum is heard, and presently the clashing of a cymbal, the sound gradually gaining in volume until all the musicians are hard at work. As the concert opens, the men and women crouching in the center of the floor, some 30 in number, are aroused from sleep or stupor, and rising to their feet, begin to beat time to the music. When all are ready the war-dance or march begins at a signal from their leader. Forward and backward passes this motley crew, brandishing war-clubs and grinning as only Dahomeans can grin. Louder and yet more loud grow the beating of a drum, the blast of horn, and the clash of a cymbal. Then the posturing begins; but in this there is nothing of the graceful or sensuous; simply a contortion and quivering of limb and body, with a swing of weapons as though nothing would more delight than to kill and destroy.[48]

Music critic Henry E. Krehbiel was enthralled by the music of the Fon. Noted for his work on American folksongs, especially the origins and meanings of African-based melodies, he presented a paper at the Congress on Music on this topic.[49] For days at a time, he sat diligently at the village recording what he heard:

> I listened repeatedly during several days to the singing of a Dahoman minstrel who was certainly the gentlest and least assertive person in the village, if not in the entire fair. All day long he sat beside his little hut, a spear thrust in the ground by his side, and sang little descending melodies in a faint high voice. . . . To his gentle singing he strummed an unvarying accompaniment upon a tiny harp. This instrument, primitive in construction (like the ancient Egyptian harps it lacked a pole to resist the tension of the strings), was yet considerably developed from an artistic point of view. It was about two and a half feet high and had eight strings accurately tuned according to the diatonic major system, but omitting the fourth tone. With his right hand he played over and over again a descending passage of dotted crotchets and quavers in thirds; with his left hand he syncopated ingeniously on the highest two strings.
>
> A more striking demonstration of the musical capacity of the Dahomans was made in the war-dances which they performed several times every forenoon and afternoon. These dances were accompanied by choral song and the rhythmical and harmonious beating of drums and bells, the song being in unison. The harmony was a tonic major triad broken up rhythmically in a most intricate and amazingly ingenious manner. The instruments were tuned with excellent justness. The fundamental tone came from a drum made of a hollowed log about three feet long with a single head, played by one who seemed to be the leader of the band, though there was no giving of signals. This drum was beaten with the palms of the hands. A variety of smaller drums, some with one, some with two heads, were beaten variously with sticks and fingers. The bells, four in number, were of iron and were held mouth upward and struck with sticks. The players showed the most remarkable rhythmical sense and skills that ever came under my notice. . . . The fundamental effect was a combination of double and triple time, the former kept by the singers, the latter by the drummers.[50]

Future diasporan composer Will Marion Cook also sat outside Dahomey Village, listening to and learning how the intricate musical patterns of West Africa unfolded. He was embarking on a career which one day would find him widely recognized as the leading "orchestral contributor to early syncopated music."[51] The popular and talented vaudevillian team of Bert Williams and George Walker listened too, and within a decade had written and produced a Broadway musical entitled *In Dahomey*, based very loosely on their encounters with these Fon visitors.[52] Unfortunately, it represented just another piece of minstrelsy belittling West African life and culture.

Meanwhile, artisans among the Fon practiced their craft production of plastic items at the fair as they would have at home. A blacksmith kept a forge operating with bellows made of goat skin.[53] Artisans whose materials at home included bronze and silver carved solely in wood in Chicago.[54] Any items that caught fairgoers' eyes were quickly sold by this market-oriented group which engaged in extensive commercial operations in West Africa, activities facilitated by their currency of cowrie shells. The alacrity with which the Fon acclimated to American capitalism and linguistic use of "monee" and "nickel" shows the pace at which cultural adaptation occurred.[55]

Economic organization in Dahomey at this time was based on diverse pecuniary activities involving agricultural production and commerce. Property ownership encompassed private, communal, and royal claims. Thus, for individual men and women, property ownership was common and valued. Notwithstanding accounts in the Chicago newspapers, slovenliness and primitive attitudes toward acquisition were unfounded.[56] Perhaps the observation of novelist William Dean Howells's traveler from Altruria applied to the Fon also. He had assessed the foreign contingents to be as much the profit-seekers as their American hosts. "One must be aware that the citizens of the Plaisance are not there for their health, as the Americans quaintly say, but for the money there is in it," he remarked.[57]

Not to be overlooked among the many features of this marvelous event, the fair exuded a deep sense of admiration for the martial spirit of the age. From the construction of a mock battleship, the U.S.S. *Illinois,* cemented into the lake at its edge, with its full complement of active-duty sailors and real guns, to the world's largest cannon from the Krupp works of Germany, militaristic ardor abounded. Marching cadets from West Point, Zulu warriors brought to Chicago to stage reenactments of their victory over the British square in South Africa, and Buffalo Bill's Wild West Show replete with Indians and soldiers thrilled the crowds and satiated their appetites for violence and manly confrontation. In the ranks of the Egyptian entourage, "Nubians . . . with their sword dances and mimic contests with long-bladed weapons, revive[d] memories of the campaign undertaken for the relief of General [Charles "Chinese"] Gordon, a large contingent came from Khartoum or its vicinity, and within the walls of Cairo Street is one who performs a warlike dance in which the long Egyptian gun, often leveled at the soldiers of the British Army, is handled with telling effect."[58] In such a heavily soldierly setting, the presence of the Fon at the fair was a *natural.*

One souvenir book contained this commentary: "Perched upon the gates of the village are sentinels in full war regalia, bearing spears that glisten above the heads of visitors. Many of the natives still have their hair closely shaven, a punishment inflicted as a penalty for being captured in battle."[59] As to their military prowess, these Fon, who were supposedly active-duty combatants,[60] served a military state that was unsuccessfully concluding a war against French imperialism. Beginning in 1892, under the leadership of their king, Behanzin, the Fon people of Dahomey fought the French throughout that rain forest kingdom both to maintain Fon independence and to gain access to legal commercial intercourse throughout the rain forest and down to the Guinea coast. Abomey, the capital of the Fon state, fell to French arms in late 1892; hostilities persisted until 1894 in other parts of the kingdom. In a few areas, resistance continued until 1911. By the time the Fon at the fair returned home in 1894 after their sojourns in Chicago and, later, San Francisco, Behanzin would have been deposed and their homeland titularly turned into a French protectorate.

Further, at an exposition devoted as much to the martial as to the scien-

34. Courtesy of the Chicago Public Library.

35. Courtesy of the Chicago Historical Society.

36. Courtesy of the Chicago Public Library.

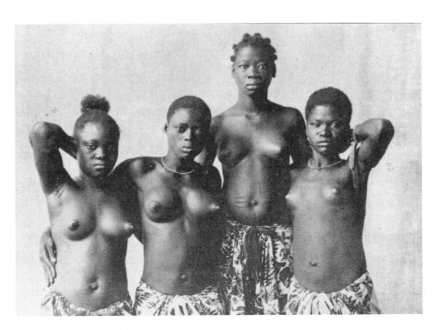

37. Courtesy of the Chicago Historical Society.

tific, the intellectual, and the materialistic, the sight of Fon warriors, especially with their "Amazonian" counterparts, evidently enthralled fairgoers. Figures 34 and 35 show the same group, while 36 and 37 are actually the same photograph, modified for different audiences. The upraised weapons on display in figure 34 are meant to indicate fierceness. Some of the Fon in fact appear bored, some are cooperative; all exhibit a confidence that precludes any acceptance of racial submissiveness. The females, eleven in number—comprising two youngsters, five young maidens, and four matrons—were photographed with their breasts uncovered, no doubt because the photographer was not satisfied with just the image of formidable combatants. The four maidens shown in figures 36 and 37 were probably induced to pose together for purposes of image manipulation. The latter image appeared in only two sets of photograph books, probably because it was deemed too offensive for Victorian eyes. Oddly, 35 and 37 are artistically real, because they show the Fon as they actually saw themselves, free from inhibitions about the human body. Figures 34 and 36, with their painted-on clothing, on the other hand, are artificial and exploitative. Overall, this temporal aversion to the natural served to stultify photographer, publisher, and viewer, while remaining consistent with Victorian convention.

In a blow to gender limitations, visitors attracted to the Midway were encouraged to see "the Amazons who fight the battles of King Behanzin."[61] In all probability, these "Amazons" lacked military prowess altogether, being the wives, daughters, and daughters-in-law of the village or compound leader, mistakenly referred to as a king. The famed female warriors of Dahomey were considered the king's wives, and would not have left Dahomey to journey to the United States under any circumstances.[62] Illustrative of the influence of the Fon on American thinking, one local newspaper wit saw fit to tweak the nose of a feminist leader, Susan B. Anthony, by running a headline that read: "EQUAL RIGHTS HERE: Susan B. Anthony Finds the Long Sought Purpose at Last—DOWN IN DAHOMEY VILLAGE, The Dear Old Lady Sees the Girls That Bear Arms and Says Our Girls Could Fight Too."[63]

Overall, Fon women bore the brunt of intense ridicule for being "a savage looking lot of females, muscular in appearance, and not particularly attractive."[64] Upon their arrival in Chicago, *The New York Times* ridiculed them in this manner: "The Dahomey gentleman, (or perhaps it is a lady, for the distinction is not obvious). . . . "[65] Fairgoers were stunned by the facial scarring on some of the younger women in Dahomey Village. One young lady was described as having "deep scars in her ebony cheeks." When other observers commented on the physical appearance of the women, in particular their facial cuts, they were unaware that in Fon culture facial scars represented signs of familial linkage and personal beauty.[66] The teeth of the Fon women were another story; one newspaper described them as white and beautiful enough to be the envy of the Caucasian women of America.[67]

Racism and sexism aside, the various groups arriving in the city for the fair were quite different from what Americans expected, and their manners, of

38. Courtesy of the Chicago Public Library.

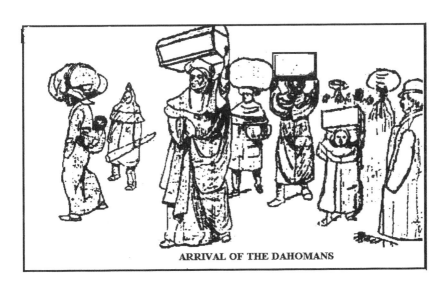

ARRIVAL OF THE DAHOMANS

39. Courtesy of the Chicago Public Library.

necessity, would have raised the level of curiosity of the bewildered. When the Fon arrived in Chicago in the spring of 1893, there was a reference to their shaved heads. In contrast, a series of photographs taken during the summer and in the fall show that their hair had grown back to its full length. The people of this compound, all members of an extended family, had suffered a recent family loss through death in New York, and shaved off their hair, it being the custom for the family of the deceased to perform in this manner as a sign of respect.[68]

Quite notably, the dress of the Africans and their hosts differed—with the summer heat of Chicago making fairgoers uncomfortable in their attire but leaving the Africans unaffected. But when the Fon first arrived, in the midst of a cold spell, they were both photographed and sketched (as shown in figs. 38 and 39) after being forced to don blankets and other heavy garb to compensate for the temperature drop. One woman in the front row is bored, possibly with Chicago, and probably wants to return home—*gladly*. Some persons appear to enjoy the camera, filled with a sense of personal contentment, vitality, or exuberance, while others cooperate as a matter of courtesy. Participating in frequent parades the Fon are shown in a variety of clothing of their choice.

In an early acknowledgment of the cultural relativism of twentieth century pluralism, other customs deemed barbarous by western European standards found the *Chicago Inter Ocean* asking "if they were any more cruel than the sacrifice of the Druids?"[69] The repetitious telling of wild tales about the Fon being cannibals and engaging in human sacrifice lent them credence in the minds of some whites. In reality, the stories were false.[70] Moreover, the hosts' attitude of moral superiority and tolerance failed to measure up, given the ritualistic American lynchings of African Americans and ethnic cleansing of the Western landscape of Native Americans.

Significantly, evidence of the Fon's cooperation with foreign peoples was common. When they left home, they were probably curious about what they would encounter in a new world. However, many Fon had already encountered Europeans along with other African groups because of their extensive commercial and military activities. Three, in fact, had mastered French.[71] When the fair managers sponsored international swimming and canoe contests late in the summer, the Fon joined the competitions and emerged victorious in both events. Cheered on by hundreds of whites as men with black, brown, yellow, and white skins competed, the fair showed a salutary side of humankind worth noting. Further belying the racist claim of social isolation, July Fourth celebrations on the fairgrounds included the Fon.[72] When the international ball was held, the Fon also participated.[73]

Religion formed another element of the Fon culture that perplexed Americans. In attempting the difficult at best, a *Tribune* reporter wrote: "Several fetichers are also in the party to attend to the spiritual wants of the Dahomans, who believe in a Supreme Deity, but worship minor ones, such as a snake god and tree gods, under an impression that the Supreme Being has no time to consider such humble mortals as themselves, where lack of Phariseeism is said to be one of the redeeming traits of these people."[74] Herskovits found that the Supreme Creator, Nana-Buluku, along with the Sky pantheon of Mawu (female and represented by the moon) and Lisa (male and represented by the sun), sometimes referred to as Mawu-Lisa, were anything but transcendent, their being immanent.[75]

As in most groups, elaboration on the meaning of religion often related to social status, so perhaps the reporter heard what he reported but asked the wrong set of informants. Herskovits explained that "in a culture as highly organized as that of Dahomey, where the economic surplus has made possible a resulting social leisure for ruling and priestly classes, there was no lack of opportunity for the development of a complex philosophy of the Universe. The upper-class Dahomean does not need to restrict himself to describing concrete instances when discussing the larger concepts underlying his everyday religious practice; he is not at a loss when questions of the nature of the world as a whole, or abstract principles such as justice, or destiny, or accident are asked. As in every civilization, the less sophisticated person is perplexed when confronted with such problems, but the mature Dahomean with intellectual curiosity is able to analyze these difficult concepts with an assurance that bespeaks long and considered speculation."[76] Ultimate understanding of Fon religion rested on dealing "with numerous deities and forces, which, differing in their nature and powers, are thought of as playing on the destiny of mankind as a whole, and, in a particularized sense, on the destiny of every individual."[77]

Herskovits also found a sophistication in Fon narratives about the nature of the world and the individual's role in it. One result of his 1931 field work was, finally, the publication in 1958 of narratives which "left no doubt at the time of their telling [of a] a mature and subtle art form." As if explaining the Fons' stoic expression which masked an incredulity as to the exoticism of the Caucasian on the fairgrounds six decades previously, Herskovits talked of how in West Africa "we came to know individual Dahomeans, without their solid traditional defenses against those in authority, or the stranger. They reacted to our evident interest, and often delight, with initial wariness and even with troubled astonishment that a white outsider should get a point of satirical allusion. But in time this changed."[78]

Social organization in Dahomey revolved around the immediate family and extended families which comprised the patrilineal sib (clan). Each of the former two was led by a sib chief who exercised authority by virtue of his age and blood line. Next in authority came elderly women. They lived in compounds that formed the bases of the village and town system. No doubt this arrangement was replicated at Dahomey Village. At the head of this social hierarchy of sibs was the king of Dahomey, who, at the time of the fair, was heading into a French-imposed exile signaling an end to Fon independence for a generation.

THE FON AS PERCEIVED BY AFRICAN AMERICANS

In all probability, while the Fon were in the city, their presence proved edifying for a number of the people they did encounter. Significantly, the relevance of contemporary black nationalist discourse on emigration to an African homeland rested on the strength of this pertinent issue. The possibility that a bridge existed between the Fon and other continental Africans and the Africans of the Diaspora, about 1440-1888, becomes a more pertinent question to be explored than the matter of continental African physical repugnance (or appeal) to whites on which some recent fair histories have concentrated.

Perception of the Fon among the diasporans in America differed by social grades. Frederick Douglass and members of the black elite saw little physical attractiveness and quite a bit of cultural backwardness in the Fon. The Sage of Anacostia described the Fon in a defamatory manner on at least two public occasions while seeking possible strategic control over the African American image in the American popular mind. He was not, however, reluctant to visit Dahomey Village, and did so on several occasions, once on July 4, 1893 with Stephen A. Douglas, Jr., as his guest. Befitting Douglass's status among diasporans, the Fon found a seat of honor for him.[79]

The reasons for Douglass's criticism of the Fon might be surmised to rest with a combination of the influence of his mixed ancestry, which produced a sense of duality, his need to position the Colored American image of the 1890s separate from the negative image of Africans held by many white Americans nationally, and his personal abhorrence of them based on his appreciation of things Western, such as classical music. Douglass's anti-African bias manifested itself as he shaped the ambience both at the Haytian Pavilion where he reigned as that black nation's official representative and at the Colored American Day celebration held on August 25, 1893. For other members of the elite, it could be assumed that the higher the level of acculturation by diasporans into the WASP mainstream, the lower their appreciation of things purely African.[80] Unfortunately for them, as mentioned previously, whites were apt to relegate all diasporans into a common pool on which they heaped collective scorn. According to Putnam, "The Negro types at the Fair—Soudanese, Dahomeyans, Nubians and the Congo people—represented very fairly the barbarous or half civilized state of a people who are a numerous and rapidly increasing class of American citizens. . . . Perhaps one of the most striking lessons which the Columbian Exposition taught was the fact that African slavery in America had not, after all, been an unmixed evil, for of a truth, the advanced social condition of the American Africans over that of their barbarous countrymen is most encouraging and wonderful."[81]

The missionary effort of the dominant Protestant denominations within universal Christendom, A.M.E. and Baptist churches, also assumed an air of cultural superiority as it aimed to elevate the pagan. Even current African emigrationist leader Bishop Henry McNeal Turner, and past African emigrationist spokesperson Episcopalian Father Alexander Crummell, both civilizationists (as Wilson Moses described this group, which legitimized itself in the eyes of white American Christendom as it saved its heathen brethren in Africa), agreed that the Africans were in need of transformation. By the time of the fair, Crummell, while seeing beauty in Africans physically, saw no hope in redeeming them short of uplifting them spiritually to bring social change into their societies.[82] This included new modes of dress, a change in marriage practices, political reorganization, other modifications in behavior to conform to Western standards, and, of course, conversion to Protestant Christianity.

Ida B. Wells's views represented another strain of thought among the elite that bespoke of understanding the worth of continental Africans. Wells, along with many other persons, knew that the Africans of the Diaspora remained under the same Anglo-Saxon scrutiny as did the Fon, the Nubians, the Bushareens, and the Algerians. It was left to Herskovits, however, to place the problem in its fullest perspective:

> Unfortunately, the native cultures of West Africa have far too often been written of in a deprecatory tone, so that the "savage" African background has become stereotyped in references to the ancestral traditions of the Negro peoples of the Americas to a degree that it has attained almost universal currency in the United States, at least, and is today accepted by Negroes no less than by whites. But a consideration of this Fon culture, with its excellence in technology and art, its complex political and social structure, its profoundly integrated world-view and its mythology rich in elaborate conceptualization, may prove of help toward a truer and more realistic view of how far removed from the popular is the actuality of the cultural heritage of the New World Negro.[83]

James F. Alston, the A.M.E. Church member whose account of the fair appeared in the pages of the *A.M E. Church Review,* was determined to come to Chicago, attend the fair, see the world appear before both his feet and his eyes, and importantly, to spend time with the representatives of the Fon people of Dahomey. Disappointment awaited him, though, because by the time he arrived in the city, the pleasant and comfortable warmth of the midwestern summer had given way to the uncertainty of a Chicago autumn. Strong winds and a chilling nippiness filled the air. Unaccustomed to this rude treatment from Nature, the Fon left their village on the Midway Plaisance and headed for the San Francisco Midwinter Exposition before Alston could meet them.[84]

Alston's attempt to reconnect with authentic Africa, the West Africa of his forebears, proved unsuccessful and would grow to symbolize the tenuousness of the continental-diasporan link. Of course, the strong, positive interest evinced by Alston, who apparently belonged to the middling class of respectable churchgoers, should not be construed to be anomalous. The popularity of emigrationist rhetoric throughout the nation rendered it and the support it garnered a force that assimilationists felt uneasy challenging. Membership in Bishop Turner's denomination placed Alston in a position to seek diasporan-continental common origins.

James T. Campbell's work on this contradiction "between racial affinity and cultural distinctiveness, between a reverence for Africa's past and a commitment to western-style progress" is explored fully in *Songs of Zion: The African Methodist Church in the United States and South Africa.* Turner personified the contradiction, but he was not alone. What Alston sought in the way of a genuine homecoming is conjectural. As Campbell wrote of Turner, "for all his emphasis on race pride and 'consanguinity,' he never articulated a vision of black genius, which would become a hallmark of twentieth-century black nationalist ideology. And for all his postulations on the wonders of African civilization, he continued to see Africa through a distinctly American lens. . . . One searches Turner's writings in vain for any suggestion that African culture was legitimate or worthy of preservation in its own right."[85]

The impression that African Americans at the mass level had of the fair is basically undocumented but not necessarily unknown. Nate Shaw, the New South's Everyman, offered another source of insight into the thinking of rank and file diasporans. Shaw recalled youthful memories that were explanatory rather than condemnatory.[86] His recollections of images of Africa seem to convey an air of interest in group origins balanced by a hope of redemption at some future date. Just like the gentleman shown in the Frontispiece, his seems to be a world of more self-confidence than outsiders have been willing to admit. A paucity of documentation has hampered interpretation throughout this century, but an absence of specifics should not preclude an attempt at historical reconstruction.[87] Barring a self-hatred that has yet to be proven empirically, but was widely accepted by the last two generations of Americans, self-loathing seemed unlikely. On the other hand, the rejection of many urban, northern churchgoing diasporans of an emotional self-expression during church services surely implies that the expressive dancing and drumming of the Fon might have been distasteful to them.[88]

At a time and place when within its ranks the identity of America's African citizenry was being debated and their relationship to the continent and culture of Africa seemed problematic to a substantial number, the presence of these proud, statuesque West Africans heightened inherent contradictions of race and nationality. Importantly, their lives did not represent lives filled with contradiction, for the Fon knew who and what they were. On this question of blood linkage, metaphorically, Crummell grew to ignore a bridge, Frederick Douglass burnt his bridge, Edward W. Blyden reinforced its basic construction, and Alston saw fit to survey its utility in his journey.

Certain New World blacks wanted a bridge to close a gap with their racial counterparts from the Old World as much as certain whites sought to maintain a gap of physical and social distance between the races. The presence of continental Africans at the fair, particularly the Fon, probably satisfied neither group fully. With the supposed offensiveness of the Fon not so well established that it could dissuade some whites from taking an interest in persons from halfway around the globe, a number of observers saw the Fon and others as different, but interesting and human, after all. As to diasporans, an appreciation for the aesthetic creativity of the Fon through their music and dancing, if not for their social organization and folkways, might represent a reasonable expectation for the times and circumstances. In summary, the Fon collectively paraded through the fairgrounds, individually competed in sporting events, socially interacted with strangers with sometimes sanguine results, and, overall and with no evidence to the contrary, more likely than not in reality left an indelible, and, in a few instances, a positive, imprint on the fair and its visitors.

9

ON THE FAIRGROUNDS: THE HAYTIAN PAVILION

Considering what the environments of Haiti were ninety years ago; considering the antecedents of her people, both at home and in Africa; considering their ignorance, their weakness, their want of military training . . . the achievement of their independence, is one of the most remarkable . . . events in the history of mankind.
— Frederick Douglass, 1893

The Haitian building was the chosen spot, for representative Negroes of the country who visited the fair were to be found along with Haitians and citizens of other foreign countries.
— Ida B. Wells

If there was anywhere on the fairgrounds that diasporans could familially call home and meet, it was the Haytian Pavilion, where the inscription "1492 Republique 1893 Haitienne 1804" epitomized black independence and sustained triumph. According to Ida B. Wells, "Haiti's building was one of the gems of the World's Fair."[1] Hayti's exalted presence in the diasporan consciousness rested on its near-century's-long independence from external white domination. This factor was equally special to the consciousness of the ruling elite and the farming inhabitants of the western portion of Hispaniola. At a time when Social Darwinism bespoke a superiority manifested through materialistic might in the Western mind, historic Hayti had proven to the New World African the accuracy of Lockeian philosophy as Right had beaten Might; the power of sustaining belief in the biblical prototype of David besting Goliath; the possibility of racial triumph as Africa conquered Europe and black overcame white. The French, with 30,000 veteran troops under Le Clerc, succumbed to Haytian forces under Toussaint in a struggle that has alternately inspired and intimidated different segments of the U.S. population since the early 1800s.

In addition, the Haytian Pavilion held the distinction of being the first national structure to be opened on the fairgrounds. Comments made in the opening days described it as a "fine headquarters" and "one of the prettiest structures in the foreign section."[2] While destined to be one of the three smallest pavilions built, its distinction of being completed and dedicated early added to its luster. Although Douglass was quoted as saying that "they were ready to give us possession before we were ready to accept it,"[3] yet in its early completion it carried a tone of the providential, coinciding as it did with the eighty-ninth anniversary of Haytian independence. Haytian coffee was the official beverage of welcome, a selection that was quite agreeable to teetotaler Douglass.[4]

The Haytian Pavilion proudly stood in the northwest section of the fairgrounds where the Latin American nations were showing their wares and culture to a world slowly coming under the scrutiny of its avaricious, industrializing neighbor to the north. In this vein, a Pan-American Congress convened in 1890 to promote U.S. economic interests throughout the New World. In its economic dimension, the exposition allowed the wealthier nations of the northern hemisphere to demonstrate the full range of their material advancement, while at the same time allowing the undeveloped areas to expose themselves unwittingly for future exploitation in the spirit of the Congress of Berlin (held in 1884-1885 to facilitate the economic exploitation of Africa). Predictably, in this climate when the Haytian Pavilion was opened, the fair's Director-General welcomed its actions as having shown "a sagacity . . . full of promise for the future . . . as she [prepared] . . . an object lesson, teaching the abundance and variety of her natural resources that [were] only waiting development." Further, Hayti had the sympathy and support of many for "her aspirations for industrial growth and intellectual development."[5]

It should have been a place to get a unique glimpse of the multifaceted black world, a taste of transplanted, mixed Africa, with a French overlay, removed one century in time, but not totally in culture, from Africa. It was one place, above all, where recognizable pride in color of skin existed for the mass of African Americans. As former Haytian minister John Mercer Langston, himself a quadroon, wrote after the fair: "It is hardly necessary to state here that the inhabitants of Haiti, so far as the Haitians themselves are concerned, are chiefly black people. They are of delicate and refined physical as well as mental make; not ashamed of their complexion, nor apprehensive of their equal ability with any other class of people."[6] And although not completely under the influence of the Fon of Dahomey, whose numbers had filled the revolutionary ranks of the peasant army that won liberation, Hayti still knew Dahomey intimately.

Once again, it was Herskovits who posthumously documented the significance of the Fon and what could have been an open cultural relationship between them and their New World descendants. Herskovits, along with James G. Leyburn, linked the religion of the Fon to Hayti's unofficial religion, Vodoun, and other cultural manifestations, in *Life in a Haitian Valley* and *The Haitian People*, respectively.[7] Ironically, the physical distance between the Haytian Pavilion and the Dahomey Village, less than a mile and a half away, was exceeded by an ideological chasm created by the Haytian elite that was light years away in time as well as cultural orientation.

Hayti's presence in Chicago further revealed the chasm between the desires of its European-oriented elite and the apprehensions of its traditionally African-rooted peasantry. President Hippolite sought western capital to promote the economy, pleasing one sector, but in doing so raised fears that peaceful financial penetration would inevitably lead to foreign invasion and subsequent domination. The observations on the state of the island's economy at the time of the service of its first African American minister, the Hon. John Mercer Langston (1877-1885), are especially revealing. Interpreted one way, there appeared to be an underlying peasant realization about the threat of a recurrence of dreaded foreign domination of the pre-independence type. To the peasantry, an economically backward Hayti, one which resisted the market economy, stood a greater chance of remaining an emancipated Hayti. This position was counterbalanced by the elite's preference for maintaining an administrative and political hegemony while yielding commercial control to outsiders.[8]

Beyond the aforementioned feature of Haytian sociology, the pavilion itself became a favorite place for American whites as well as blacks who sought an audience with Frederick Douglass. As Ida B. Wells depicted the setting, "in it Mr. Douglass held high court. The peculiar thing about this arrangement was that nearly all day long it was crowded with white Americans who came to pay their respects to this black man whom his country had refused to honor. Needless to say, the Haitian building was the chosen spot, for representative Negroes of the country who visited the fair were to be found along with Haitians and citizens of other foreign countries."[9] Caucasians recognized also Hayti's significance in the history of Europe and the West Indies, which lay in the fact that Columbus, the Admiral of the Ocean Sea, had named Hayti Hispaniola because of its natural beauty and abundance. Moreover, the Admiral faced imprisonment there before he was returned to Spain in chains, and its waters harvested an anchor from the *Santa Maria*, which sank on December 14, 1493. That relic of Western achievement now appeared on display at the fair and drew the historically inquisitive.

The personnel administering the pavilion's operations included, in addition to Douglass, with his conversation and counsel, his counterpart, Mr. Charles A. Preston[10] (son of the former secretary of the Haytian legation to the U.S.). Emerging poet Paul Lawrence Dunbar found employment under Douglass's tutelage and from his personal funds at this structure. At the end of spring, Ida B. Wells had returned from Great Britain and found the pavilion to be an excellent distribution point for the pamphlet, *The Reason Why the*

Colored American Is Not in the World's Columbian Exposition. Will Marion
Cook met Douglass in this structure to confer with him about his plans for the
festivities on Colored American Day.

The first official use of the pavilion as an extension of Haytian sovereignty
came on January 2, 1893, as the Caribbean nation celebrated the eighty-ninth
anniversary of its self-liberation from foreign domination. Frederick Douglass,
as its commissioner to the World's Columbian Exposition, spoke militantly of
its past glory and promising future. Douglass, who had served as U.S. Consul
to the island nation between 1889 and 1891, represented the best that Hayti
could ever imagine in a spokesman. The Haytian elite perceived Douglass's
role in 1891 as a protector, so they diplomatically resisted American expansionist attempts to establish a permanent naval base at Mole St. Nicholas with
U.S. veto power over Hayti's relations with other nations. For his action, or, as
he claimed, inaction through his non-interference, Douglass faced vilifica-
tion in U.S. diplomatic circles as well as in the New York press as an obstruc-
tionist.[11] Yet his problems upon entering the realm of diplomacy preceded
this triumph for Hayti which was achieved at the expense of an expansionist
America. In the estimation of the Anglo-Saxon establishment, Douglass, the
mulatto in America, was too dark for white American commercial and naval
interests to support. The former minister placed himself in his father's people's
place and explained the scenario through their eyes:

> It was that I was not the right color for the place, although I matched well with
> the color of Haiti. It was held that the office should be given to a white man, both on
> the ground of fitness and on the ground of efficiency—on the ground of fitness be-
> cause it was alleged that Haiti would rather have in her capital a white Minister
> resident and Consul General than a colored one, and on the ground of efficiency
> because a white minister by reason of being white, and therefore superior, could
> obtain from Haiti concessions which a colored minister could not.[12]

No doubt with Douglass's perceived or real assistance to the integrity of the
Haytian nation in mind, President Louis Florvil Hippolite chose Douglass to
represent the republic at the World's Columbian Exposition in 1893. It was
a matter, the former minister wrote, of receiving an "unsought appointment
. . . to represent Haiti among all the civilized nations of the globe."[13]

The existence of Hayti and its celebrated anniversary appeared to persons
of African descent as a highly visible, internationally recognized manifesta-
tion of racial advancement. For the myopic among his race, Frederick Douglass reminded all assembled that afternoon on the fairgrounds and later that
evening at the Quinn Chapel A.M.E. Church of what Hayti represented—
the eternal military triumph of the African over the European, thereby giving
the black world a shining example of its highest source of agency. Douglass
further praised Hayti for its courage in seizing its own independence, thanked
the fair for the opportunity to show the world Hayti's advancement since its
monumental rise to independence, and welcomed visitors to the fair.

According to Douglass, the nemesis of the diasporan-continental link, "it

40. A newspaper sketch of the Reception Parlor in the Haytian Building. Courtesy of the Chicago Public Library.

remained for the Republic of Hayti, to make possible the representation that kept our race from entirely losing its identity at the exposition."[14] Because of the short duration between the completion of construction and the opening daytime ceremonies, the audience was small. Several fair officials appeared, with apologies for the small turnout. Also, several members of Chicago's African American civic leadership were there: merchant-tailor Lloyd G. Wheeler; Dr. A. M. Curtis; and the pastor of historic Quinn Chapel A.M.E., the Rev. John T. Jenifer. This small crowd did not deter Douglass from launching into some of his most effective oratory. Of Hayti, he boasted that "no act of hers is

41. Frederick Douglass and guests at the reception on Haytian Day, August 16, 1893, as that island nation entertained the world. Courtesy of the Chicago Public Library.

more creditable than her presence here. She has never flinched when called by her right name. She has never been ashamed of her cause or of her color. Honored by an invitation from the government of the United States to take her place here, and be represented among the foremost civilized nations of the earth, she did not quail or hesitate. Her presence here to-day is a proof that she has the courage and ability to stand up and be counted in the great procession of our nineteenth century's civilization" [*Applause*]. His speech also praised President Hippolite and his supporters for daring to buck opposition at home. "The theory that the world was made out of nothing does not apply here. Material itself, it has required material aid to bring it into existence and to give it the character and completeness it possesses. It could not have been begun or finished without having behind it, the motive power of money, as well as the influence of an enlightened mind and a liberal spirit."[15]

Douglass was just as quick to remind white Americans that it was Hayti that saved the day for its fellows of African descent when its decision to fund a building and choose him as its spokesman placed the African American on an elevated footing which matched all other groups. "Although there are eight millions of men of African descent in this country, not one of them seems worthy of a place on the platform of these inaugural ceremonies . . . it would have been a marked and grateful recognition of our national evolution from the barbarism of slavery and of our enlargement of the borders of American liberty . . . if some typical representative of Americans of African descent had been seen honorably participating in the glories of this Four Hundredth Anniversary of the Discovery of America."[16]

The Haytian Pavilion demonstrated yet another example illustrative of its contradictory presence during the celebratory activities on Haytian Day, August 16, 1893. The program avoided speeches but instead featured "music, merriment, and good cheer and that excellent musical organization, the Iowa State band, [which] opened the program with Rossini's overture to 'Semiramide.'" The Rossini was followed by Weber, Offenbach, and a selection from *The Bohemian Girl* by Balfe. Vocals by "gifted colored singers" and a "marimba" played by a Guatemalan wood quartet rounded out the amusements.[17]

Two omissions appear to be noteworthy. No mention of the pulsating, spirit-penetrating drumming associated with the Haytian peasantry and an integral part of their Fon heritage was reported, indicating that its absence was through deliberate planning. Further, not one word was uttered at the pavilion about Hayti's son and Chicago's founder, Jean Baptiste Pointe Du Sable. In 1885, city historian A. T. Andreas documented Du Sable's contribution to Chicago in what became a standard historical reference, and even newspapers infrequently mentioned him.[18] Except for a single reference to his accomplishment in one of a score of souvenir books and guidebooks to the fair, the matter appears to have been completely overlooked despite its relevance.[19]

10

DIASPORAN AND CONTINENTAL AFRICA MEET: THE CONGRESS ON AFRICA

The Chicago Congress was not a huge and prolonged missionary meeting. It was not a political or a religious or a scientific gathering. It was not a Negro-congress. It was not a summer university for African study. It was each and all. It was more. It was a parliament of man taking counsel for humanity's ward.

—Frederick Perry Noble, 1893

Probably the largest assemblage of African American participants in a world's fair event came as part of the Congress on Africa, or, as it was sometimes referred to, the Congress on African Ethnology, or the Congress on the Negro, which extended from Monday morning, August 14, 1893, to Monday evening, August 21, 1893. It included a citywide Sunday session that entered the sanctuaries of scores of churches, where hundreds of interested congregants listened to information on the status of the global African population. In this aspect, it was the antithesis of the Colored American Day festivities held the next week on the fairgrounds. Identified fully as anything other than a cultural conclave, the Congress on Africa combined the intellectual with the ideological, religious, philosophical, and scientific to formulate an agenda facilitating, in effect, a dualistic African American public policy on the status of continental and diasporan Africans.

Moreover, this conclave represented something beyond its original formulation as it passed into the hands of diasporans, for it was not a successor to the Congresses of Berlin and Brussels as envisioned by whites, but more a precursor of the first Pan-African Congress of 1900, in that diasporans such as Douglass, Crummell, Langston, Fortune, and Turner discussed the future of

Africa with a smattering of continental Africans in attendance. For the American nation, this congress brought about a recreation of the liberal arrangement between the races that originated in the abolitionist era. And, in its aftermath, it represented a first dialogue in substantive interracial cooperation. Accordingly, well-educated blacks as well as elite and middle class whites presented invited papers. Africans from the continent and from the Diaspora filled the black ranks, many being the most notable persons in their fields of endeavor—intellectually endowed, well-known, and respected by members of both races. With enthusiasm, Caucasians from Europe, Africa, and America collaborated in problem-solving based on African strengths rather than hand-wringing over African deficiencies.

The outgrowth of an idea developed by Frederick Perry Noble, the Congress on Africa aimed from its onset to be reflective of "democracy and Christianity."[1] Noble, the son of a Congregational pastor of a congregation on the racially diverse west side of Chicago, took pride in his denomination's causes. As a coreligionist, he described how "Congregationism, by its freedom from any taint of complicity with human bondage and its work since 1839, has done more for the American Negro than any other church." He continued, "Congregationists alone since 1861 spent over $12,000,000 for the freedmen, and the American Missionary Association has accomplished more in evangelizing and educating them than has any other society."[2] So, this conference was the culmination of the hopes and dreams of a panoply of white liberals and abolitionists,[3] along with Social Gospel advocates, as well as self-perceived humanistic imperialists, perhaps anti-imperialists,[4] who wished to continue the tradition of bringing Africa into the orbit of industrial, Christianizing Western Europe as established at the Congresses of Berlin and Brussels (held respectively during the winter of 1884-1885 and 1889-1890).

However, as humane as the Congregationalists and other Protestants thought they were, the most compelling question before the conference had a familiar ring, given the context of the times. It involved the possibility of transforming the African, whether diasporan or continental, into a new person—into an Afro-Saxon who conformed more readily in temperament, disposition, and level of civilization to Anglo-Saxon standards. Even when attendees to the conference heard the voices of past and present nationalism in the persons of Bishop Henry McNeal Turner, Rev. Alexander Crummell, and a certain Professor Henderson of Straight University of New Orleans, theirs, too, were the voices of transformation, of making the continental African in his home a new and better African, but constructed in the mold of Anglo-Saxonism.[5] Figuratively, in the distance on the streets of the Midway, the drumming of the Fon had to be heard, signifying their resistance and that of others on the continent to externally induced change, whether French, British, Belgian, or American.

Furthermore, the Congress served, because it was conducted under liberal white Protestant and abolitionist auspices, as an international forum for the discussion of whether or not America could or would adapt itself to treating its diasporan population fairly. In a strangely familiar sense, it revived the old visceral arguments from the emigration conventions held four to six decades previously. In the minds of its conveners, the measuring stick of the Congress, therefore, revolved around how well and how soon the so-called "Negro Problem" in America and the so-called "African Problem" involving continentals could be debated fully, and importantly, how soon they could ultimately be solved. One additional feature made this a unique gathering, and it originated in a sense of publicly acknowledged guilt for wrongs committed against Africa's children, diasporan and continental. The conference's chair, the Reverend Joseph E. Roy, a Congregationalist, stated: "All races have had a hand in making Africa, the 'pariah of continents.' But the Hand Divine is moving in this matter. Africans are to add new dimensions to civilization. It is ours to help her advance, and pay part of the debt 'Caucasians' owe Africa."[6]

At the culmination of eighteen months of planning, the limits of past conferences still haunted Noble. In 1884-1885, the delegations of fourteen countries, including the United States, and with the exclusion of any indigenous African polity, participated in the Berlin Conference. Called at the behest of Europeans, they sought collectively to clarify their imperialist aims to reduce conflict between superpowers. "Indeed, the concerns of the Conference were largely European concerns," concluded African historian Robert W. July, who added that "the subject of Africa on the agenda was largely adventitious . . . what was really at stake was the delicate balance of power among European nations."[7] At the conference's end, the imperial designs of European states were brought into conformance and a workable protocol reached. Theoretically, a new world order was established. Indigenous Africans, such as the Fon, although oblivious to the machinations that took place in Berlin, probably would have reacted to the pronouncements had they known of them as European territorial encroachments.[8] A follow-up conference assembled in Brussels in the winter of 1889-1890, adding Persia and Zanzibar to its ranks as discussions centered on the abolition of the Arab slave trade in central and east Africa. Once again, indigenous Africans were excluded.

In light of these apparent successes for European imperialists, the *Inter Ocean* reported that the conveners of the 1893 conclave attempted to "continue the best and most salient features of the Berlin and Brussels conferences and make this the most adequate and representative council upon humanity's ward the world has ever held." Because of its purpose and hopes, "it command[ed] the approval and interest of the statesmen, prelates, missionaries, explorers, educators, scholars, scientists, and philanthropists."[9] At the time of the fair, Prof. James M. McPherson maintained that there were "abolitionists who expressed an opinion about European colonialism[,] approv[ing] of it, applauding especially the British effort to abolish the Arab trade in Negro slaves. Overlooking the exploitation and brutality of colonial conquest, they saw it as a civilizing force bringing Christianity and Western culture to Africa."[10]

Because the Congress was being held in the United States, its scope was broadened to devote an immense amount of time to the status of the African American as subsumed under the rubric, "The Negro Problem." The latter was a saving point to many whites, because it allowed them the opportunity to work out a problem close to home. Of course, Frederick Douglass assessed the problem of America as a moral crisis involving inhumane treatment and requiring courageous action on the part of whites.

THE PROGRAM EXAMINED

Significantly, what originated as an endeavor conceived by white American humanitarians, intellectuals, and foreign policy advocates to examine, validate, and perpetuate the most humane features of Great Power hegemony over the African continent, along with finding ways of eliminating the worst features of American racism, was to a great extent (and to their amazement) dominated rhetorically by the diasporan and continental Africans themselves. This marvel occurred partially because of the dynamism inherent in the invited African American participants. In their ranks were Bishop Henry McNeal Turner, Rev. Alexander Crummell, John Mercer Langston, Frederick Douglass, Bishop Benjamin J. Arnett, Henry Ossawa Tanner, Prof. William Crogman, Hallie Q. Brown, and an impressive young member of Vai royalty from Liberia, Prince Monolu Massapiou. In his outspokenness and honesty, the Prince guaranteed that the conference would have at least one active voice of integrity representing his continent. Once these diasporan and continental Africans exercised intellectual hegemony over the Congress, its tone seemed as defiant of paternalism as it was of racist imperialism.

This coup over control of the spoken word and racial images also was made possible because of the compliance of the white conveners who considered Africa and worldwide Africans as worthy of respect. Led by second-generation abolitionists, such as the Reverend Joseph E. Roy,[11] who chaired the committee running the Congress, civility and openness reigned. Marvelously, these attributes were in evidence every day. Included among the 160 delegates and presenters, from both sides of the Atlantic, were twenty-three persons of African descent. With invited white Southerners absenting themselves voluntarily,[12] and with the African Americans from Chicago and from among the visiting fairgoers attending the sessions in record numbers, accounting for almost one-half the attendees, the stage was set for a racial happening. Shaping the course of the sessions allowed African Americans to demonstrate to the world that they were ready to assume responsibility over their own destiny to the extent that their resources and energy allowed.

Depending on one's point of view and sentiments, the Congress opened either auspiciously or unpropitiously. The Hon. William Bonny, the president of the World's Columbian Exposition, declared in his remarks that "the object of this Congress is to make such a review and presentation of the history and condition of Africa as well as to unite the whole world in the great work for its civilization and regeneration. It will mark the transition from the old Africa of darkness to the new Africa of light, and will stand in history as opening a new era of human progress."[13] That seemed favorable enough to whites and African Americans who accepted the need to transform Africans from their present state, including the likes of Crummell, Turner, Langston, and Douglass, as well as other nationalists and other assimilationists.

Next, the Reverend Roy reminded the audience that of all of the congresses and parliaments in session and upcoming, this one was the only one devoted to a "great division of the globe [which was] given a place among the congresses." Protocol dictated that the Belgian minister plenipotentiary to the United States, the Hon. Alfred Le Gait, be given a special place of honor at this international conference, so he spoke next. He paid homage to his sovereign, King Leopold, and praised the work he was doing to rid his overseas estate, the Congo Free State, of slavery, rum, and ignorance.

Yet, all of this sounded quite disingenuous to Prince Massaqiou, as he no doubt recognized the arrogance implicit in scheduling another international conference intent on plotting the destiny of a distant continent with the inhabitants having virtually no input. Aware that this course of action was consistent with Social Darwinian thought on racial inferiority, he reminded the conferees throughout the meetings, both in public and private, that while tribes in Liberia and elsewhere who knew of the conference prayed for its success, they also looked with apprehension at the possibility of another territorial partition as well as any condescension toward the African way of life which accompanied the outsider's interest in Africa. In describing his background, he talked of the Vai worshiping the "true God for centuries past. [But still] ignorant and unsympathetic missionaries [have come to] 'convert the savages.' They talk the jargon of Presbyterianism, Methodism, or what not, rather than the simple religion of Scripture." He also warned that his people were not favorably disposed to "theological speculations or the finely drawn distinction of sects." He concluded that "no intelligent African will believe them."[14]

In the same vein, a Yoruba minister, Abayomi, pastoring in Sierre Leone, referred to the same annoying trait in European Christians. "God is moving on. He is the soul of the universe. As He moves He moves the hearts of men along," he stated. "The mental life of the Negro was never more active. He is a man to-day more than ever in his existence. Intellectual lethargy, cowardice, monkeyism and stupidity are no longer his characteristics. What the Negro needs is Christianity, not Anglicanism or Americanism."[15] While Roman Catholicism and Anglicanism of the imperialistic French and British separated them as much as their languages and culture, the continental Africans were too aware of the true benefits that derived from Christianity as a unifying force to let that divide them. When the African Americans of the A.M.E. Church attempted to evangelize in Africa, they adopted the unique approach in South Africa of embracing the indigenous way of life. In contrast, the experience of the A.M.E. Church in West Africa, specifically in Liberia and Sierre Leone, proved less than successful because of its external pressures to change indigenous ways.[16] African American women, particularly within the Baptist and A.M.E. churches, served as missionaries to Africa also. Their attitudes toward continental Africans were as condescending as those of the men.[17]

Abayomi's continental colleague from the Lagos [Nigeria] Legislature, the Hon. James Johnson, could not attend the Congress but did send a paper. Johnson made the point that that his fellow Africans had developed impressive economic skills: "These Africans, even from a European standpoint, might be correctly described as a great deal civilized. Their wants are few [in comparison to the insatiably acquisitive Anglo-Saxon] but they had found ways to support them all."[18] Days later at another session, the Rev. L. P. Mercer, after reading a paper prepared by Dr. J. A. Kasson, a member of the Berlin Conference of 1884-1885, on "The Congo State and the Redemption of Africa," felt compelled to comment in a similar light as Massapiou. Mercer asserted, to loud applause, that the rights of foreign colonists and foreign governments did not extend without regard to the rights of the natives in their own soil.[19]

As the opening formalities ended, and the presentations proceeded, it was left to the iconoclastic Bishop Turner to create a "sensation." Following the reading of the paper on continental progress prepared by Johnson of Nigeria, Turner rose to cover the same topic written on diasporan progress. While he explored the progress and contributions made by Africans of the Diaspora in manufacturing and the trades, as was to be expected, he also touted the genius and resourcefulness of his group despite the obstacles imposed on African progress by an outwardly racist South and a smug, latently racist North.

Then Turner launched into a peroration on the African origin of humankind, the subsequent debt owed Africa, and the need for a new understanding between the races based on the two previous gifts:

> Revolting as the theory may appear to some present, I believe that all humanity started black—that black was the original color of mankind. That all of these white people present descended from black ancestors, however remotely in antiquity they may have existed. If theoretical geology is entitled to any consideration whatever, the time was when the poles of the earth and the now icebound arctics were so warm that the fjords of the now tropic zones grew there luxuriantly, and the same animals that now live at the equator roamed abroad in that ancient forest. This has been verified by the bones which have been found there of the animals now restricted to the tropical regions. So as I see it, instead of black being an abnormal color, as execrated color, a color to be despised and made the badge of degradation and infamy to the extent that it involves the humanity of those who are black, if it is any color at all it is the primordial, most ancient and original color of mankind.

I have reached this conclusion after years of meditation with such lights as revelation affords to my understanding, aided by the stylus of geology and the archaeological collections found in the British Museum. Yet my interpretations may be greatly at fault and my conclusions wholly absurd, but scientific analyses undoubtedly makes black the base of all color and the black man is, therefore, a primitive man.

The drift of nature, whether interpreted speculatively or historically, would, therefore, appear to be whiteward. Primitive man who doubtless has existed for ages longer than our chronology fixes it, in my opinion was black and is the father of the white races of the earth; and, the same black, primitive man gave to the intermediate color or red Egyptian civilization learning, sciences, and philosophy; including skilled labor in its highest form, and this red race has transmitted to the white races letters, poetry, logic mechanism, and all the fundamentalities that the white races have embellished, refined, and improved upon, until it has reached the grandeur of this world-famed Chicago exposition.

Without the black man, Christianity itself would lack a purpose. For while the white man gives it system, logic and abstractions the black man is necessary to impart feeling, sanctified emotion, heart throbs and ecstasy. Thus God and nature need the black man for without him there would be an aching void in earth and heaven. The universe would be in want of a balance wheel, and the God of eternity would again give to light the forgers of creation and perform another day's work before the morning stars would sing together and the sons of God shout for joy.[20]

Chicago's newspapers faithfully carried portions of Turner's postulation under such lurid headings as "Black Adam in Eden," "Was Adam a Negro?," and "Negroes, Not Apes." Yet reaction to his utterances was respectful, with significant portions recalled without sinister or malicious comment. Moreover, he was described in daily newspapers as "one of the most learned and eloquent colored clergy in America."[21]

Across the racial divide, the response from the African Americans was enthusiastic and ecstatic. "His address [was] . . . something of a revelation to many of those present. . . . [and] he concluded amid loud applause," read one newspaper account.[22] At one point in the program, occurring shortly after an especially stirring rendition of one of the traditional "Sorrow Songs" by one of the original Fisk Jubilee Singers, the magisterial Bishop Anderson of South Carolina arose from his seat on the platform, raised his right hand and proclaimed, "Bishop Turner is right!"[23]

Turner's allusions to African genius from the days of antiquity struck a responsive chord among many African Americans. Their sense of specialness, rather than a loathing of their very being, was pervasively evident in the city, as well as throughout the nation. Recognition of a special quality inherent in blacks was found everywhere in African American society and at every stratum of society. For the refined, their belief in a specialness in African Americans manifested itself in their ability to compete and achieve in a hostile Anglo-Saxon world so rapidly after citizenship status was conferred. This constituted their *raison d'être* for demanding an equal footing in planning, executing, and participating in the world's fair. For the masses of African American peasants found in the South and domestic workers located in the North, and filling the ranks of the respectables, they believed as their ministers had told them of their messianic mission to redeem America through their past and current sufferings and deprivations. Even the lower stratum of the undesirables knew enough about Anglo-Saxon foibles, as the latter wallowed in vice and corruption along the Levee, to know that there was nothing morally or physically special about being cloaked in a white skin.

If Turner's ending was thought-provoking and "sensational" at a fair ostensibly committed to proving WASP supremacy worldwide, his expected presentation on the topic assigned was just as significant. He mentioned, to an enthusiastic audience, that it was Frederick Turner of Atlanta who had invented an air traction engine likely "to revolutionize" locomotion; that Stephen Smith of Philadelphia successfully turned a $15 start-up amount in the coal business into an endeavor capitalized at $350,000 at his death; that a Mr. Jackson in Bermuda had established the largest dry goods store on that island; and that William "Bill" Fisher of Columbia and Charleston, South Carolina, used his genius and skills to gain recognition as "the greatest architect in his day."

The program featured papers on such interrelated topics as "What the Africans Have Done to Develop Themselves," "Egyptian Folklore," "National Customs and Popular Life in Africa," African Men," "African Women," "The Influences of the Brussels Treaty of 1891 upon the African Slave Trade," "The Negro in Literature," "The Negro in Journalism," "The Principles of Colonization and the Difference between Slave Labor and Wages," and Henry Ossawa Tanner's "The Negro as Artist." One entire session was devoted to philology, with papers on "The Function of African Languages" and "The Future of European Languages in Africa." A paper on "Diseases and Medicine in Africa" was written by Dr. R. W. Falkin of the University of Edinburgh's School of Medicine, a former resident of Uganda. His presentation was followed by Chicago Provident Hospital's Dr. Daniel Hale Williams, who spoke on "American Negroes as Surgeons and Nurses." When Prof. Seward's paper on "American Negroes as Musicians" was read, it concluded with a statement by noted Bohemian composer Antonín Dvořák:

> I am now satisfied that the future music of the country must be founded upon what are called the Negro melodies. This must be the real foundation of any serious and original school of composition to be developed in the United States. When I first came here last year I was impressed with this idea and it has developed into a settled conviction. These beautiful and varied themes are the product of the soil. They are American. I would like to trace out the individual authorship of the Negro melodies, for it would throw a great deal of light upon the question. In the Negro melodies of America I discovered all that is needed for a great and noble school of music. They are pathetic, tender, passionate, melancholy, solemn, religious, bold, merry, gay, or what you will. It is music that suits itself to any mood or purpose. There is nothing in the whole range of composition that cannot be supplied with themes from this source.[24]

The highest expectations of African American intellectuals and their white abolitionist supporters were surely being met. A series of well-prepared papers on the most cogent topics readily proved that the African race was advancing. Both in their scholarship and depth, it was obvious that this was the quality of work that would inspire the formation of Crummell's American Negro Academy within two years. For their part, contemporary accounts repeatedly attested to the quality of the conclave.

By the time Frederick Douglass spoke on the fourth day, Thursday, August 17, 1893, the tone of the proceedings would have been enough to leave a Southerner or racist Northerner reeling. The assemblage had been melded into a coherent phalanx committed to racial advancement everywhere, no matter what the odds encountered. Douglass's topic was field work and the slave. He again denounced the existence of a "Negro Problem," and instead focused on an American problem—not having the moral courage to make good on its constitutional and religious commitments. Douglass had long ago accepted the reasonableness of Colored Americans accepting the culture of this nation and becoming Americans through and through, indistinguishable from other citizens except for pigmentation.

At this point, the eagerly awaited debate over African emigration began. To the white abolitionists and liberals of the 1890s, the mere mention of, let alone a debate on, emigrationism caused disappointment, embarrassment, and consternation. The voluntary departure of African Americans from the country would have clearly indicated that the nation had failed to live up to its avowed principles as embodied in the Declaration of Independence and the Constitution. Seeking to keep faith in the ability of their fellow Americans to respect both the spirit and the intent of the law in a nation of laws, they sought affirmation from interracial gatherings such as the Congress. As they interacted with diasporan Africans as fellow human beings, governed under the same rules under which they were, they aspired to convince them of white sincerity. During the fair, Frederick Douglass constantly appeared to remind them of their shortcomings.

When Professor Henderson of Straight University read his paper in defense of leaving the United States, Bishop Turner had more than adequately spread the gospel of emigration with enthusiasm wherever he went in the city. Turner was correctly described as "having no faith in the future of his race in the United States, as he believe[d] the ignoble status of the colored people in the South and their scullion employment in the North [were] sources of degradation and nothing but nationalization [would] work out the elevation of the race and he holds that Africa is the field for that."[25] Henderson began his address with a scenario familiar to students of this nation's history:

> Let there be formed a joint stock company such as those under which Virginia and
> Massachusetts were colonized, and let distinguished philanthropists without regard

to race be asked to assist. Let a commission of experts be selected and sent to Africa to find a place for settlement. . . . Let 10,000 . . . persons be selected, such as artisans, bricklayers, machinists, doctors, lawyers, preachers, and teachers, every trade and profession necessary for the establishment of a civilized society. I have no doubt such a plan would be feasible. Our race would respond to such an appeal.[26]

Attorney Ferdinand L. Barnett of Chicago ably presented his side in rebuttal as he read New Yorker T. Thomas Fortune's paper on why diasporan Africans should keep faith in the American Promise. Fortune's paper was entitled, "Should Negroes Colonize Africa?" Its strength lay in the recognized failure of recent emigrationist projects, one of which less than a year ago left hundreds of diasporan Africans on the way home stranded in New York. Fortune's basic challenge rested in this question: "Why did the Germans or Irish not go back to their native land? What advantages does Africa offer the Negro that are superior to those of the United States?" The *Inter Ocean*, a newspaper with a predilection to favor the anti-emigrationist, abolitionist position, reported, perhaps accurately, that "ringing applause . . . followed that left no mistake as to the answer."[27] However, it was Barnett's own personal comments, challenging the emigrationist position through ridicule, that supposedly neutralized it.[28]

Sunday activities included an afternoon session that featured Crummell and Douglass who addressed separate audiences in the Art Palace following and preceding church services throughout the city. At Columbus Hall, Crummell spoke on "The Relations of Africa to the Scriptures," a paean to ancient Africans whose contribution to world civilization is still being overlooked. African Americans' leading intellectual spoke on how the members of the Negro race were the descendants of Ham, the son of Noah, and he "traced in detail the connection between the early Egyptians, who were the founders of ancient civilization, and the Negro race today, and he said all that was great in the early civilization and art upon which the glory of Greek and Roman civilizations rested, was the work of the Hamites, the progenitors of the Negro race."[29] Based on the warm reception given these assertions earlier in the Congress, as well as nearly identical comments by Frederick Perry Noble, it can be assumed that these remarks were similarly found acceptable.[30]

ASSESSMENT

Whether hyperbolic or accurate, the white abolitionists and liberals evaluated the Congress as highly significant. Of all of the congresses held, and in deference to the highly successful Parliament of Religions, *The Independent* called the Congress on Africa "the most interesting and attractive of all the congresses," while Prof. William Scarborough declared in *Frank Leslie's Illustrated Weekly*, which kept an intense focus on the fair during its duration, that "among the many auxiliary congresses . . . none, perhaps, save one, has awakened such general interest and attracted such wide attention, as well as large attendance."[31] The Chicago press seemed to concur in these assessments, with the *Chicago Tribune* being especially complimentary. Moreover, all papers recognized this conference as a highly significant gathering, with some devoting daily coverage to this conclave, and unanimously reporting high attendance.[32]

At the end of the conference, white conveners rested, considering themselves successful in having placed before the assembled conferees as well as a sizable amount of the expanding American reading public a strong case for the elimination of most flagrant vestiges of American institutional racism as well as backward attempts to exploit Africa from afar. They also felt reassured that the emigrationist surge led by Bishop Turner had been repelled. Conference secretary Noble envisioned the event as triumph for American religious liberalism and described it thus: "The Chicago Congress was not a huge and prolonged missionary meeting. It was not a political or a religious or a scientific gathering. It was not a Negro-congress. It was not a summer university for African study. It was each and all. It was more. It was a parliament of man taking counsel for humanity's ward."[33]

African Americans left the Congress with a sense of accomplishment in having interacted commendably with their ideological opposites and supporters. Both Turner and Douglass could take satisfaction in the outcome on that count. The former could also rest assured that had there been more southern diasporans present from the ranks of the working class agrarians, his case might have received even broader support in debate. Perhaps most importantly, both leaders took home with them a greater sense of hope in the more salutary features of the different societies they admired as the best hopes for their race. For the Rev. John T. Jenifer, his hopes at the beginning of the conclave proved true at its conclusion. He had said, "We feel assured that such an assembly will by method, learning and influence give Africa a place in the world's interest and confidence that nothing else could. You bring the African-American into the best condition that nothing else could. You save American Negroes from an obscurity and mortification which the failure to award them place in the Exposition has caused them to feel keenly."[34]

For emigrationists, the Congress on Africa and the presence of continental Africans at the fair had stimulated both an increased interest in returning to Africa and a growing scholarship on African American and continental African thought and life. In addition to Bishop Turner's enthusiasm for emigration, southern regional interest remained high despite the stand-off the bishop encountered in Chicago. Emigrationist organizations proliferated in the South and on March 19, 1895, the small, 728-ton steamer S.S. *Horsa* departed her Savannah dock with two hundred African Americans on board.[35] This sailing was eventful and, no doubt, provided part of the inspiration for Booker T. Washington's "Cast Your Buckets" admonition to southern blacks later that year.

What the Congress also made obvious was the quality and volume of intellectual inquiry being completed on African American and continental African life. Bishop Henry McNeal Turner became so enthusiastic about what he heard in Chicago that he offered to buy a collection of the papers presented. Frederick Perry Noble exuberantly talked of an *Encyclopedia Britannica on Africa.*[36] Further, within two years of the Congress, Crummell's American Negro Academy was organized. Where emigration to Africa slacked off, migration to the North picked up, proving itself incessant.

EPILOGUE

When the gates of the World's Columbian Exposition permanently closed on October 30, 1893, the world had borne witness to anything but an unsubstantial African American presence at this event. No visitor to the fair could have overlooked the involvement of the African American and continental African as lecturer, observer, patron, worker, and performer. In the case of the congregation of the Quinn Chapel A.M.E. Church, they acted as buyers of the salable goods left on the fairgrounds. They purchased a beautiful German organ, one of the items of pride of that great nation's exhibit. Significantly, it is still in use to this date. Within the world's fair city, social change in its fullest dimensions accompanied the external phenomenon of migration from the South. Nationally, change was even more pervasive. Externally produced forces, most times totally unrelated to the exposition, such as economic depression, court-supported racism, debt peonage, and disfranchisement affected American life just as dramatically.

Participation at the fair in Chicago might have been limited, to be sure, but no more restricted than the African American's ability a century later to take a full role in all of America's endeavors. After a period of only twenty-eight years of freedom leading into a period of severe racial proscription, the era of Social Darwinism, the relevant question remained, how much progress had the race achieved despite the odds it faced? Whether the World's Columbian Exposition qualified as an epochal event in African American life the same way it did in America's is unclear. It was an important experience, but in the aftermath of the fair, other signal events took place and influences took rise, some in continuation of what was begun at the fair, some independent of the experience. A generational succession took place in 1895 as Frederick Douglass died and Booker T. Washington achieved prominence because of his address at Atlanta. Douglass's repeated attempts in 1893 to keep the focus on America's racial wrongs that continued uncorrected basically fell on deaf ears. Only the true believers of the old abolitionism such as Tourgée, Roy, Noble, and Couzins listened. Booker T. Washington's pronouncement of a racial rapprochement in the South pleased the ears of the nation, giving it what it wanted to hear. He even found many receptive ears among blacks at that moment in time.

With a view born not of pessimism but of realism, the latter derived from a combination of the experiential, the intellectual, and the possible, African Americans with this "New Negro" mentality of the 1890s sought only a "fair field" on which to devote their efforts. At the nearest opportunity, in 1895 at the Cotton States Exposition, a separate Negro exhibit housed in a separate building reflected the answer to many of the questions raised before Chicago. Most likely, the thinking of persons belonging to the generation that had endured slavery directly or had sympathized with loved ones in bondage from a distance, either social or physical, could not conceive of racial advancement in any terms other than that relating to opportunity. The social and intellectual milieu of the day extolled the virtues of both individual and group advancement that was able to persist despite obstacles. Those who proved themselves fit would simply survive, and ultimately, achieve their goals.

Yet, at the time of the Atlanta Exposition, ample evidence of deterioration in racial opportunities became so obvious that advocates of equal rights such as Tourgée's National Citizens Rights Association sounded an alarm.[37] Douglass had suspicions brought to his attention by Ida B. Wells,[38] but others, such as Du Bois, remained optimistic.[39] The next year, the U.S. Supreme Court decided in the landmark *Plessy v. Ferguson* case that a new racial code supporting caste was appropriate for the nation.

APPENDIX I. FREDERICK DOUGLASS'S SPEECH AT COLORED AMERICAN DAY (AUGUST 25, 1893)

Our presence here in such numbers is a vindication of our wisdom and of our good nature. I am glad that we have cheerfully embraced this occasion to show by our spirit, song, speech, and enthusiasm that we are neither ashamed of our cause nor of our company. It is known to many of you that there is a division of opinion among intelligent colored citizens as to the wisdom of accepting a "colored people day" at The Fair.

This division of opinion has been caused, in part, by the slender recognition we have received from the management of the exposition. Without expressing any satisfaction with this phase of that management, I think that we cannot wisely withhold our thanks to the World's Columbian Exposition for the opportunity now afforded us to define our position and set ourselves right before the world. It might perhaps have done more and better for us at its inception, but we should not forget that it might also have done less and worse for us.

The question will be asked and is asked by our transatlantic visitors, why we do not more fully share in the glory of the great World's Exposition. To answer that question and to protect ourselves from unfavorable inference and misrepresentation is, in part, the purpose for which we have assembled to-day.

Rejoicing in the liberty we have already secured and congratulating the nation upon the recognition given our rights in the fundamental law of the republic, we shall nevertheless fully expose and denounce the injustice, persecution, lawless violence and lynch law to which as a class we are still subjected. We wish especially to emphasize the fact that, owing to our two hundred years of slavery and the prejudices generated by that cruel system, all presumptions in law, government, and society in this republic are against us, so that it is only necessary to accuse one of our number of crime in order to secure his conviction and punishment. This state of affairs thus engendered, will in a measure explain to our transatlantic friends why we have a share so slender in this World's Columbian Exposition. I deny with scorn and indignation the allegation, by whomsoever made that our small participation in this World's Columbian Exposition is one either to our ignorance or to our want of public spirit.

That we are outside of the World's Fair is only consistent with the fact that we are excluded from every respectable calling, from workshops, manufactories and from the means of learning trades. It is consistent with the fact that we are outside of the church and largely outside of the state.

The people who held slaves are still the ruling class at the South. When you are told that the life of the Negro is held dog cheap in that section, the slave system tells you why it is so. Negro whipping, Negro cheating, Negro killing, is consistent with Southern ideas inherited from the system of slavery.

We hear nowadays of a frightful problem called a Negro problem. What is this problem? As usual, the North is humbugged. The Negro problem is a Southern device to mislead and deceive. There is, in fact, no such problem. The real problem has been given a false name. It is called Negro for a purpose. It has substituted Negro for Nation, because the one is despised and hated, and the other is loved and honored. The true problem is a National problem.

It has been affirmed on the one hand and denied on the other that the Negro since emancipation has made commendable progress. I affirm that no people emancipated under the same conditions could have made more commendable progress than has the Negro in the same length of time. Under the whole heavens there never was an enslaved people emancipated under more unfavorable circumstances, or started from a lower condition in life.

We fought for your country. We ask that we be treated as well as those who fought against your country. We love your country. We ask that you treat us as well as you do those who love but a part of it.

Men talk of the Negro problem. There is no Negro problem. The problem is whether the American people have honesty enough, loyalty enough, honor enough, patriotism enough to live up to their own Constitution.

A statesman has recently discovered that the only solution of this Negro problem is the removal of the Negro to Africa. I say to this man that we Negroes have made up our minds to stay just where we are. We intend that the American people shall learn the great lesson of the brotherhood of man and the fatherhood of God from our presence among them.

During the war we were eyes to your blind, legs to your lame, shelter to the shelterless among your sons. Have you forgotten that now?

Today we number 8,000,000 people. Today a desperate effort is being made to blacken the character of the Negro and to brand him as a moral monster. In fourteen States of this Union wild mobs have taken the place of law. They hang, shoot, burn men of my race without justice and without right. Today the Negro is barred out of almost every reputable and decent employment.

But stop. Look at the progress the Negro has made in thirty years! We have come up out of Dahomey unto this. Measure the Negro. But not by the standard of the splendid civilization of the Caucasian. Bend down and measure him—measure him from the depths out of which he has risen.

[N.B.: While the words above were spoken by Douglass, the paragraphs may not be the exact order as when the speech was delivered. It has been reconstructed from two newspaper accounts, and the only paragraph definitely in its proper order is the final one.]

APPENDIX II: *COLORED PEOPLE'S BLUE BOOK* (1906)

Introduction

Chicago, Ill. is a great city of 2,000,000 souls; more than twenty miles in length and about ten miles in width; having in its confines people of every shade and nationality known to civilization.

Great as Chicago is in its aggregate population, it is a colonized community. Every race known to Christendom is in a section only sparsely settled by other races. There are only a few of the race to the manor born. There are those in great numbers from every state of the union, the West Indies, the Barbadoes and other Foreign possessions.

At this age of the Nation's greatness every large city has its quota of prominent Negroes, eminent to a certain degree in every walk of life. Chicago is numerically blessed in this particular with prominent men and women in the church, at the bar, and in medicine. In each of the above professions the women are ably represented while there are a host of trained nurses and obstetricians.

There are photographers, grocers, storage-men, house-movers, furniture stores, dry goods and gents furnishing departments and one very large dry goods and department store that would do credit to the other races. Then there are the industries and the various trades represented by hundreds who are making the most of the opportunities that prevail in this great trade mart.

These great Negro forces augment race recognition in places of worth and prominence. The race contact with all that is great and progressive will so fit the aspiring men and women who have yet the most of their lives before them in matters of self help, race patronage and race protection as will astound those who see nothing in the race that is creditable. Thus the large city is acting upon us as large institutions of learning. Here we enlarge the scope of our vision. Here where opportunities are rife for us to develop all that is good and great in us, we get larger conceptions of life and all it means. We, in a word, come face to face too with the strongest proofs of well directed effort along all lines.

We are in the midst of so much which we as a race must put down, if it is to be put down, burdened in spite of our smiles, and yet happy in spite of our tears, not unmindful of some of the principles of life that the race is slowly imbibing and from this latter view take heart in our struggles and continue onward and upward, educate our youth and teach both by precept and example.

M. A. Majors, M.D.
Chicago, Ill.

APPENDIX III: COMMENTARIES FROM

MIDWAY TYPES

Four Amazons (Figure 36)

Hideous looking as they were, the Dahomeyan Amazons became objects of attraction and even admiration. This feeling could not have been caused by their beauty, but may have arisen from their fighting qualities and points in physique which every patron of the ring and turf is quick to discover and appreciate. The reputation of these black women is of the most sanguinary character, though happily, no proof of their fierce nature was displayed in Midway life. It is said that they are absolutely ignorant of fear; and they are credited with being educated to the use of war-like weapons and schooled in the tactics of their savage battles from childhood, so that when they fight it is to kill or be killed. The bodies of several of the women in the Dahomeyan Village were frightfully scarred, the results of contests in which they had been engaged. In several of the gala day processions through the Exposition grounds these people approached the frenzy that borders on bloodshedding, but were restrained from actual violence. Under the protectorate of the French over their territory it is believed a little of the mildness and virtues of civilization may be introduced.

A Group of Dahomeyans (Figure 27)

If you were on the Midway and heard wild thumping of a drum and harsh shouting, and a parting of the people right and left, you were sure to see a large white man borne on a palanquin by half-dressed Negroes, who went by on a sort of canter. These were a detachment from the Dahomeyan village, carrying their master. They were representatives from the colony from its home in South Africa [*sic* — West Africa]. Though they were not handsome, people flocked into the village and witnessed the rites and ceremonies of the villagers. Though they were representatives of Cannibal tribes they restrained their appetites for human flesh while at the Exposition. There were sixty men and forty women in the village.

In True Dahomeyan Style (Figure 31)

Here is a picture fit for a comedy. Behold an Amazon warrior, a belle of the village of duskiness, carried in state down the highway of nations. Great husky blacks are supporting the hammock hung to a long heavy pole, and so quickly were their motions caught by the sun that no time was given to let them plant their feet firmly on the ground. The beauty reposes in state. Her hands were raised to smooth down her frizzes, for woman's vanities are the inherent and universal peculiarities of her sex. This vanity seems to have extended to the Amazon's legs, which dangle carelessly over the edge of the hammock and display all the fine points of anatomy incident to those extremities. Cleopatra never journeyed in happier state than rode this dusky beauty on the bright summer day that gave to the Midway a procession combining African savagery with the civilization of the Exposition. If contrasts teach lessons, then such spectacles as the one depicted—and they were frequent—must have leavened the multitudes with a great many seeds of knowledge.

Black Continentals in Their Scarce Regimentals (Figure 34)

Now that the Dahomey Village is far away it may be remarked with safety that its inhabitants were just the sort of people the managers of the Exposition did not banquet or surfeit with receptions. The group pictured shows a regretful absence of tailor-made clothes, and a leaning toward a plethora of black skins. In the occasional parades these gentle reminders of Africa never allowed themselves to be overlooked. Their Amazons, feather-decked and sword girded, bearing the scars of hasty carvings, and savage as tigresses, were the belles of the occasion. None of them seemed to know the meaning of fear. Once when a fire broke out in the village a few of the people trampled upon the flames with their bare feet and others tore at the burning shingles with their teeth. There were sixty men and forty women in the village and they amused the public by giving war dances, songs and specimens of savage amusements that made our native Indian seem "a thing of beauty and a joy forever." The front of the village of these people was made of wood brought from Dahomeyan forests, and kept the inhabitants from ambushing stray Columbian guards.

APPENDIX IV: "JUDGE,"

BY A. T. WORDEN

Behold in this calm face
The modern Sphinx, with such a thoughtful mien
As bids us pause, when like a Frankenstein
A nation dares create another race.

No longer here the crude
And unformed features of a savage face;
But in those pleading eyes a kindred race
Asks for the highway out of servitude.

Like as the Amazon
With mighty currents marks the ocean's hue
Until her leagues of tide blend with the blue,
So do these patient millions still press on.

Such at the cradle-side
Have crooned as foster-mothers, sung and wept,
Across the chamber doors of pain have slept,
And for their sisters pale have gladly died.

Two hundred weary years
Of burden-bearing in a shadowed path,

And yet no hand is raised in cruel wrath,
And all their wrongs evoke as yet but tears

Study the problem well,
For in this Sphinx a message somewhere lies,
A nation's glory or its shame may rise
from out the reading what these features tell.

Poem and illustration reprinted from *The Bulletin of Atlanta University* (July 1893), p. 1.

NOTES

Preface

1. See Benjamin Quarles, *Frederick Douglass* (Washington, D.C.: Associated, 1948), pp. 345–347, and William S. McFeely, *Frederick Douglass* (New York: W. W. Norton, 1991), chapter 27. Major articles examining the difficulties of participation by African Americans at the fair are August Meier and Elliott Rudwick, "Black Man in the 'White City': Negroes and the Columbian Exposition, 1893," *Phylon* 26 (Winter 1965): 354–361; Frank A. Cassell, "A Confusion of Voices: Reform Movements and the World's Columbian Exposition of 1893," *Mid-America* 67 (October 1985): 59–75; and Thomas J. Schlereth, "Columbia, Columbus, and Columbianism," *Journal of American History* 79 (December 1992): 964.

2. Eugene Levy, *James Weldon Johnson: Black Leader, Black Voice* (Chicago: University of Chicago Press, 1973), pp. 37, 38.

3. Pertinent books and articles emphasizing the role of black feminism/womanism are: Bettina Aptheker, *Woman's Legacy: Essays on Race, Sex, and Class in American History* (Amherst: University of Massachusetts Press, 1982); Paula Giddings, *When and Where I Enter* (New York: William Morrow, 1984); Hazel V. Carby, *Reconstructing Womanhood: The Emergence of the Afro-American Woman Novelist* (New York: Oxford University Press, 1987); Ann Massa, "Black Women in the 'White City,'" *Journal of American Studies* 8 [Cambridge, U.K.] (December 1974): 319–337; and Anna R. Paddon and Sally Turner, "African Americans at the World's Columbian Exposition," *Illinois Historical Journal* 88 (Spring 1995): 19–36. The latter essay also creatively moves beyond protest to document what results the fair produced from positive human agency.

4. David F. Burg, *Chicago's White City of 1893* (Frankfort: University of Kentucky Press, 1976), pp. 216–219; Reid Badger, *The Great American Fair: The World's Columbian Exposition and American Culture* (Chicago: Nelson Hall, 1979); Robert W. Rydell, *All the World's a Fair: Views of Empire at American Expositions, 1876–1916* (Chicago: University of Chicago Press, 1984), pp. 40, 65, 66; and James Gilbert, *Perfect Cities: Chicago's Utopias of 1893* (Chicago: University of Chicago Press, 1991), pp. 82, 111, 115–117.

5. Curtis M. Hinsley, "The World as Marketplace: Commodification of the Exotic at the World's Columbian Exposition, Chicago, 1893," pp. 344–365 in Ivan Karp and Steven D. Lavine, eds., *Exhibiting Cultures: The Poetics and Politics of Museum Display* (Washington, D.C.: Smithsonian Institution Press, 1991).

6. See Arna Bontemps and Jack C. Conroy, *They Seek a City* [also known as *Anyplace but Here*] (New York: Doubleday, 1945), pp. 68–85, as well as Ida B. Wells's recollections in Alfreda Duster, ed., *Crusade for Justice: The Autobiography of Ida B. Wells* (Chicago: University of Chicago Press, 1970), pp. 115–120.

7. "Miss Ida B. Wells Informs Our Readers as to the Condition of the World's Fair Pamphlet Movement," *Cleveland Gazette*, July 22, 1893, p. 1.

8. Massa, "Black Women in the 'White City,'" pp. 336, 337.

9. *The Reason Why the Colored American Is Not in the World's Columbian Exposition: The Afro-American's Contribution to Columbian Literature* (Chicago: Ida B. Wells, et al., 1893), p. 9, in Archives, Chicago Historical Society.

10. "Miss Ida B. Wells Informs Our Readers as to the Condition of the World's Fair Pamphlet Movement," *Cleveland Gazette*, July 22, 1893, p. 1.

11. *The Reason Why the Colored American Is Not in the World's Columbian Exposition*, pp. 6, 12.

12. Ibid., p. 80.

13. H. F. Kletzing and W. H. Crogman, *Progress of a Race, Or, the Remarkable Advancement of the Afro-American* (Atlanta: J. L. Nichols, 1897; rpt. New York: Negro Universities Press, 1969), p. 168.

14. *The Reason Why the Colored American Is Not in the World's Columbian Exposition*, p. 10.

15. W. E. B. Du Bois, *The Souls of Black Folk* (Boston: Bedford Books, 1997), p. 38.

16. Ibid., p. 39.

17. Albert G. Barnett, "No Part in Chicago's Fair for Race in 1893: Facts Recently Discovered Prove How Strong Jim Crow Was Even Then," *Chicago Defender*, May 16, 1933, p. 16.

18. M. A. Majors, "What the Negro Contributed to the World's Fair in 1893," in Frederick H. H. Robb, comp., *The Negro in Chicago, 1779–1929* (Chicago: Washington Intercollegiate, 1929), p. 51.

19. The work of August Meier, in particular his classic *Negro Thought in America, 1880–1915: Racial Ideologies in the Age of Booker T. Washington* (Ann Arbor: University of Michigan Press, 1963), described and analyzed both conflicting and conforming patterns of thought during this period.

20. See Carby, *Reconstructing Womanhood*, p. 4. She wrote: "It appeared that the Columbian Exposition had provided the occasion for women in general and black women in particular to gain a space for themselves in which they could exert a political presence." What follows is a catalogue of misfortunes that beset African Americans as they sought representation in various forms but no specifics as to any instances of affirmation of success.

21. St. Clair Drake and Horace R. Cayton, *Black Metropolis: A Study of Negro Life in a Northern City* (New York: Harcourt, Brace, 1945), p. 53. Their abbreviated historical sketch of Chicago covering the period between the fair and the advent of World War I (1893–1914) reads differently and poses a source for confusion in this matter. Importantly, Drake, in his "Churches and Voluntary Associations among the Negroes of Chicago" (Chicago: WPA, mimeographed, 1940), p. 105, made no distinctions as to income and occupational differences, the only criterion for membership in the "refined class" being educational training and cultural attainments. Comparatively, W. E. B. Du Bois found New York City's black population to be similarly structured; see *The Negro in the North* (reprint, New York: Arno, 1969; orig., *New York Times*, 1901), p. 45. Boston, however, proved a different case altogether. See Adelaide M. Cromwell, *The Other Brahmins: Boston's Black Upper Class, 1750–1950* (Fayetteville: University of Arkansas Press, 1994), p. 58. Chapter 4 carries a description of Boston's elite which parallels the evolutionary process at work in Chicago. Servants and other workers were excluded from the upper tier of leadership.

22. Theodore Rosengarten, *All God's Dangers: The Life of Nate Shaw* (New York: Alfred A. Knopf, 1975).

23. Leon F. Litwack, *Trouble in Mind: Black Southerners in the Age of Jim Crow* (New York: Alfred A. Knopf, 1998), p. xvi.

24. Tunde Adeleke, *UnAfrican Americans: Nineteenth-Century Black Nationalists and the Civilizing Mission* (Lexington: University of Kentucky Press, 1998).

25. Du Bois, *The Souls of Black Folk*, p. 118.

Introduction

1. Contemporary accounts accepted the importance of the moment. Recent works covering the fair as an event of momentous importance as well as containing significant dimensions are: Burg, *Chicago's White City of 1893*; Badger, *The Great American Fair*, 1979; Rydell, *All the World's a Fair*, 1984; Hinsley, "The World as Marketplace," (1991); and Gilbert, *Perfect Cities*, 1991.

2. Duster, *Crusade for Justice*, p. 119.

3. Edwin S. Redkey, *Black Exodus: Black Nationalist and Back-to-Africa Movements, 1890–1910* (New Haven: Yale University Press, 1969), p. 1.

4. David Levering Lewis, *W. E. B. Du Bois: Biography of a Race, 1868–1919* (New York: Henry Holt, 1992), pp. 162, 248. Also see p. 152 for an example of Du Bois' infatuation with things both Victorian and British.

5. Teresa Dean, *White City Chips* (Chicago: Warren, 1895), pp. 193–196.

6. *Indianapolis Freeman*, April 9, 1892, p. 4.

7. "Days for Southrons," *Chicago Herald*, August 5, 1893, p. 9.

8. Jonathan Gilmer Speed, "The Midway Plaisance," *Harper's Weekly* (May 13, 1893), p. 442.

9. Julian Hawthorne, *Humors of the Fair* (Chicago: E. A. Weeks, 1893), pp. 35, 38, 77, 150; and Hawthorne, "Foreign Folk at the Fair," *Cosmopolitan* 15 (September 1893), p. 571.

10. Dean, *White City Chips*, p. 243.

11. Mrs. D. C. Taylor, *Halcyon Days in the Dream City* (No city; published by the author, 1894), p. 44, at the Chicago Historical Society.

12. Hinsley, "The World as Marketplace," pp. 358, 359.

13. Hezekiah Butterworth, *Zigzag Journeys in the White City with Visits to the Neighboring Metropolis* (Boston: Estes & Lauriat, 1894), pp. 137–146.

14. James B. Campbell, *Campbell's Illustrated History of the World's Columbian Exposition* (Chicago: N. Juul, 1894), p. 411. 15. F. Hopkinson Smith, "The Picturesque Side," *Scribner's Magazine* (May 1893): 611.

16. Franz Boas, "Human Faculty as Determined by Race," pp. 221–242 in George W. Stocking, ed., *The Shaping of American Anthropology, 1883–1911: A Franz Boas Reader* (New York: Basic Books, 1974). Both Stocking and Vernon J. Williams, Jr., *Rethinking Race: Franz Boas and His Contemporaries* (Frankfort: University of Kentucky Press, 1996) question whether Boas's commitment to a concept of racial egalitarianism in 1894 was total but agree that this paper nonetheless represented a major breakthrough in America's thinking on race as culture overtook biological inheritance as the determinant of hierarchical ranking.

17. Melville J. and Frances S. Herskovits studied under Boas at Columbia University between 1920 and 1927. For a glimpse of their relationship as seen through ongoing correspondence, see Franz Boas to WHOM IT MAY CONCERN, February 6, 1925; Boas to Melville J. Herskovits, May 12, 1930; Herskovits to Boas, May 22, 1930; Herskovits to Boas, April 10, 1933; and Boas to Herskovits, January 26, 1934, all in the correspondence files of the Papers of Melville J. Herskovits, University Archives, Northwestern University, Evanston, Illinois.

The most impressive consequence of this mentor-protégé relationship as it pertained to the Fon of Dahomey was Melville J. and Frances S. Herskovits, *Dahomean*

Narrative: A Cross-Cultural Analysis (Evanston: Northwestern University Press, 1958) [see p. vi], and Melville J. Herskovits's *Dahomey: An Ancient African Kingdom*, 2 vols. (Gluckstadt, Hamburg, and New York: J. J. Augustin, 1938; rpt. Evanston, Ill.: Northwestern University Press, 1967).

18. Sol Bloom, *Autobiography of Sol Bloom* (New York: G. P. Putnam's Sons, 1948), pp. 105–111; 116–142.

19. Carl S. Smith, "Insight and Irony: The Literary Heritage of the White City," p. 1 in *1992 World's Fair Forum Papers*, vol. 1: "Great American Fairs and American Cities: The Role of Chicago's Columbian Exposition" (Evanston, Ill.: Center for Urban Affairs and Policy Research, Northwestern University, April 1984).

20. James Weldon Johnson, "At the World's Fair," *Bulletin of Atlanta University*, May 1893, p. 3.

21. James M. McPherson, *The Abolitionist Legacy: From Reconstruction to the NAACP* (Princeton, N.J.: Princeton University Press, 1975). In a recent conversation with McPherson at the Chicago Civil War Roundtable on January 25, 1997, he maintained that the portrayal of individuals listed correctly conveyed their attitudes and showed their commitment to race egalitarianism as late as the World's Columbia Exposition of 1893 and beyond.

22. Hinsley, "The World as Marketplace," p. 357.

23. *Chicago Evening Post*, June 26, 1893, p. 2.

Part One. Around the Nation

1. Ferdinand L. Barnett, "The Reason Why," in *The Reason Why the Colored American Is Not in the World's Columbian Exposition*, p. 63.

1. Expectations

1. This figure was, of course, exaggerated. It served the purpose of creating the illusion that this was the world's most significant international conclave. Many visitors made multiple trips to the fairgrounds because of the sheer immensity of the undertaking.

2. *Indianapolis Freeman*, July 22, 1893, p. 9.

3. Memories of slavery remained deeply embedded in this older generation of African Americans to such an extent that Frederick Douglass's oratory throughout 1893 continually dwelled on the debt the nation owed its black citizens because of its centuries of inhumanity toward them. His speech on August 25, 1893, at Colored American Day and his contribution to *The Reason Why the Colored American Is Not in the World's Columbian Exposition*, p. 12, confirm this. See also Anna R. Paddon and Sally Turner, "Douglass's Triumphant Days at the World's Columbian Exposition," *Proteus* (Spring 1995): 43–47, and "Douglass' Truths," *Cleveland Gazette*, September 16, 1893, p. 3.

4. *Chicago Tribune*, August 26, 1893, p. 3.

5. John W. Blassingame and John R. McKivigan, eds., *The Frederick Douglass Papers, Series One: Speeches, Debates, and Interviews*. Vol. 3, 1881–95 (New Haven: Yale University Press, 1992), pp. 146, 147.

6. *Chicago Tribune*, May 28, 1893, p. 27.

7. Lawrence W. Levine, *Black Culture and Black Consciousness* (New York: Oxford University Press, 1977), p. 325.

8. Hollis R. Lynch, *Edward Wilmot Blyden: Pan-Negro Patriot, 1832–1912* (London: Oxford University Press, 1970), p. 111.

9. "Wonderful Place for Fun: What the Money Catchers Offer in Midway Plaisance," *New York Times*, June 9, 1893, p. 9.

10. "West African Folk," *Chicago Tribune*, May 4, 1893, p. 2.

11. *Portfolio of Photography of the World's Fair* (Chicago: Weiner, 1893), n.p. [caption under Zarofetta (A Soudanese Woman)].

12. Lewis, *W. E. B. Du Bois*, p. 162.

13. Wilson J. Moses, *Alexander Crummell: A Study of Civilization and Discontent* (New York: Oxford University Press, 1989), pp. 48, 49, 96, 148, 188.

14. [Letters], from Alex Crummell, *Southern Workman and Hampton School Record* (January 1894): 5.

15. Lewis, *W. E. B. Du Bois*, p. 170.

16. Meier, *Negro Thought in America*, p. 43.

17. Moses, *Alexander Crummell*, pp. 141, 228. Also, Lewis, *W. E. B. Du Bois*, p. 170.

18. Moses, *Alexander Crummell*, pp. 226, 227.

19. [Letters], p. 5.

20. *Chicago Legal News*, May 29, 1897, p. 333.

21. Roi Ottley, *The Lonely Warrior: The Life and Times of Robert S. Abbott* (Chicago: Henry Regnery, 1955), pp. 6, 7, 74.

22. *Southern Workman and Hampton School Record*, May 1893, p. 84.

23. See Alberry A. Whitman, "The Freedmen's Triumphant Song," and Caddie Whitman's "The Veteran" at the Schomburg Center for Research in Black Culture, New York Public Library.

24. James Weldon Johnson, "At the World's Fair," *Bulletin of Atlanta University*, May 1893, p. 6.

25. "Henry M. Turner's Speech, 1868" in Herbert Aptheker, *A Documentary History of the Negro People in the United States: From the Reconstruction Years to the Founding of the N.A.A.C.P. in 1919*, vol. 2 (New York: Citadel, 1951; 4th pbk. ed., 1968), pp. 569–571.

26. Redkey, *Black Exodus*, pp. 36, 37.

27. The best scholarly treatment of Washington is Louis R. Harlan's two-volume set, *Booker T. Washington: The Making of a Black Leader, 1856–1901* (New York: Oxford University Press, 1972), and *Booker T. Washington: The Wizard of Tuskegee, 1901–1915* (New York: Oxford University Press, 1983). Of his personality, which is touched on only slightly in this work but is of interest to most readers, the following is taken from p. viii of the former work:

> Those who try to understand Washington in ideological terms, as the realistic black philosopher of the age of Jim Crow, or as the intellectual opposite of W. E. B. Du Bois, miss the essential character of the man. He was not an intellectual, but a man of action. Ideas he cared little for. Power was his game, and he used ideas as instruments to gain power. Washington's mind as revealed in formal public utterance was a bag of cliches. His psyche as the directing force of his private actions, on the other hand, was a kaleidoscope of infinitely changing patterns. The complexity of Booker T. Washington's personality probably had its origin in his being black in white America. He was forced from childhood to deceive, to simulate, to wear the mask. With each subgroup of blacks or whites that he confronted, he learned to play a different role, wear a different mask. He was so skillful at this that it is no wonder his intimates called him the "wizard."

28. See Henry Demarest Lloyd to Booker T. Washington, February 16, 1893 and Washington to Lloyd, July 29, 1893, both in Louis R. Harlan, ed., *The Booker T. Washington Papers, vol. 3, 1889–95* (Urbana: University of Illinois Press, 1974).

29. Ibid., Washington to Robert C. Bedford, August 22, 1893.

30. See "A Negro Chautauqua," *The Independent* 45 (August 31, 1893), p. 1182;

National Baptist World, November 23, 1894, p. 1; Harlan, *Booker T. Washington: The Making of a Black Leader,* pp. 207, 208; and Booker T. Washington, *Up from Slavery* (1901; rpt. New York: Oxford University Press, 1995), p. 122.

31. See Benjamin Quarles's introduction to John Mercer Langston, *From the Virginia Plantation to the National Capital* (New York: Arno Press, 1969), n.p.

32. Wilson J. Moses, *The Wings of Ethiopia: Studies in African-American Life and Letters* (Ames: Iowa State University Press, 1990), p. 65.

33. Vernon Wharton, *The Negro in Mississippi, 1865–1890* (1947; rpt. New York: Harper Torchbooks, 1965), pp. 270–272. See also *Leading Afro-Americans of Vicksburg, Mississippi* (Vicksburg: Biographia, 1908), pp. 77, 78.

34. *Indianapolis Freeman,* March 26, 1892, p. 1. See also "To the Grand Officers and Members of the Fraternity," World's Fair Masonic Headquarters, Chicago, January 15, 1893 [Pamphlet], Schomburg Collection, New York Public Library.

35. [World's Columbian Exposition,] *Dedication Ceremonies Memorial* (Chicago: Metropolitan Art and Engraving, 1893), p. 132, and Hubert Howe Bancroft, *The Book of the Fair: An Historical and Descriptive Presentation on the World's Science, Arts and Industry, as Viewed through the Columbian Exposition at Chicago, 1893* (Chicago: Bancroft, 1893), p. 88.

36. *Chicago Tribune,* September 3, 1893, p. 3.

37. Thomas J. Bell, "The Chicago Fair," *Bulletin of Atlanta University,* July 1893, p. 3.

38. "Country's Richest Negro Arrives," *Chicago Tribune,* October 29, 1893, n.p. [clipping file].

39. The first era of the "New Negro" came forth in the 1890s. Its successor generation of the World War I period and the 1920s is, of course, better known. As for Binga's future, he was to become black Chicago's financial wizard *par excellence* in the first third of the twentieth century through successful real estate and banking activities. As such, he inspired the next generation of "New Negroes" in business.

40. Carl R. Osthaus, "The Rise and Fall of Jesse Binga, Black Financier," *Journal of Negro History* 58 (January 1973): 40, 41. Also, Abram L. Harris, *The Negro as Capitalist: A Study of Banking and Business among American Negroes* (1936; rpt. Gloucester, Mass.: Peter Smith, 1968), pp. 153, 154.

41. Mrs. [Gertrude] N. F. Mossell, *The Work of the Afro-American Woman* (1894; rpt. Freeport, N.Y.: Books for Libraries, 1971), p. 104. Mrs. Mossell writes that septuagenarian Charles Purvis of Philadelphia served as a commissioner for Pennsylvania, but no supporting evidence is available.

42. Ibid., pp. 112, 113. Parker assisted his father with his patents on the inventions and in its March 12, 1892, edition the *Indianapolis Freeman* (p. 5) reported another achievement for the father, the invention of a tobacco press.

43. *Indianapolis Freeman,* April 21, 1892, p. 1.

44. *Southern Workman and Hampton School Record,* July 1893: 122; August 1893: 134; and November 1893: 173.

45. Rackham Holt, *George Washington Carver: An American Biography* (Garden City, N.Y.: Doubleday, Duran, 1943), pp. 87, 88.

46. "Doings of the Race," *Cleveland Gazettte,* October 5, 1892, p. 2.

47. Fannie Barrier Williams, "A Northern Negro's Autobiography," *The Independent* 57 (July 14, 1904), p. 92. In 1895, when she was nominated for admission into the prestigious, all-white Chicago Woman's Club, a determined minority attempted to block her membership because of her race. In the end, she prevailed, but not before experiencing the anguish of initial rejection that destroyed the complete faith she previously had in a color-blind city (p. 94).

48. "Story of Old Settler Reads Like Fiction," *Chicago Defender,* May 3, 1930, p. 23.

49. Alma Herbst, *The Negro in the Slaughtering and Meat-Packing Industry in Chicago* (Boston: Houghton Mifflin, 1932; rpt. Arno Press, 1971), p. 17, n.2.

50. Rayford W. Logan, *The Betrayal of the Negro: From Rutherford B. Hayes to Woodrow Wilson* (New York: Collier Books, 1965; formerly *The Negro in American Life and Thought: The Nadir, 1877–1901* (1954), p. 285.

51. Ralph Nelson Davis, "The Negro Newspaper in Chicago" (Ph.D. diss., University of Chicago, 1939); Drake, "Churches and Voluntary Associations among the Negroes of Chicago," pp. 14, 78f.

52. "Story of Old Settler Reads Like Fiction," p. 23.

53. Virginia Cunningham, *Paul Lawrence Dunbar and His Song* (New York: Dodd, Mead, 1947), p. 92.

54. Minutes of the Meeting of the Council of Administration, April 18, 1893, pp. 14, 15, the World's Columbian Exposition Collection, Potter Palmer Papers, the Chicago Historical Society.

55. Roi Ottley and William Weatherby, eds., *The Negro in New York: An Informal Social History* (New York: New York City Library, 1967), p. 145. Also see Willard B. Gatewood, *Aristocrats of Color: The Black Elite, 1880–1920* (Bloomington: Indiana University Press, 1990), pp. 104–106.

56. *Report of the Board of General Managers of the Exhibit of the State of New York at the World's Columbian Exposition* (Albany: James B. Lyon, State Printer, 1894), p. 176.

57. Gatewood, *Aristocrats of Color*, p. 97.

58. Mossell, *The Work of the Afro-American Woman*, pp. 107–109.

59. James Weldon Johnson, *Black Manhattan* (1930; rpt. New York: Atheneum, 1968), p. 92.

60. Mossell, *The Work of the Afro-American Woman*, pp. 106, 107; Majors, "What the Negro Contributed to the World's Fair in 1893," p. 52.

61. Lewis, *W. E. B. Du Bois*, p. 127.

62. Letter to the *Herald*, *Fisk Herald* (September 1893): 5.

63. "Manuscript written on the celebration of his 25th birthday," in Aptheker, *A Documentary History of the Negro People*, p. 753.

64. Giddings, *When and Where I Enter*, p. 94.

65. "Miss Ida B. Wells Informs Our Readers as to the Condition of the World's Fair Pamphlet Movement," *Cleveland Gazette*, July 22, 1893, p. 1.

2. Participation and Protest

1. "A Distinguished Negro," *Chicago Inter Ocean*, May 7, 1891, p. 7.

2. Barnett, "The Reason Why," p. 65.

3. Maurine Christopher, *America's Black Congressmen* (New York: Thomas Y. Crowell, 1971), p. 158.

4. U.S., Senate, *Congressional Record*, 52nd. Cong., 1st sess., July 15, 1892, p. 6191; U.S., House, *Congressional Record*, 52nd Cong., 1st sess., July 16, 1892, p. 6313; and U.S., House, *Congressional Record*, 52nd Cong., 1st sess., August 5, 1892, p. 7129.

5. Cassell, "A Confusion of Voices," p. 69.

6. Giddings, *When and Where I Enter*, pp. 6–8. See Elsa Barkley Brown, "What Has Happened Here: The Politics of Difference in Women's History and Feminist Politics," p. 42 in *"We Specialize in the Wholly Impossible": A Reader in Black Women's History* (Brooklyn: Carlson, 1995), ed. Darlene Clark Hine, Wilma King, and Linda Reed.

7. Giddings, *When and Where I Enter*, p. 13, re-cited on p. 82. Also see Evelyn Brooks Higginbotham, "African-American Women's History and the Metalanguage of Race," p. 17 in *"We Specialize in the Wholly Impossible,"* ed. Hine, King, and Reed.

8. Giddings, *When and Where I Enter*, pp. 6, 7. In modern times, historian Elsa Barkley Brown called for recognition "not only of differences but also the relational nature of those differences." p. 42 in *"We Specialize in the Wholly Impossible,"* ed. Hine, King, and Reed.

9. Woman's Columbian Auxiliary Association, *Aim and Plan of Action, Constitution and By-Laws* (February 1891), Albion Tourgée Papers, Chautauqua County Historical Society, Westfield, N.Y.

10. Jeanne Madeline Weimann, *The Fair Women* (Chicago: Academy Press, 1981), p. 103.

11. Badger, *The Great American Fair*, p. 122.

12. Mary Frances Cordato, "Representing the Expansion of Women's Sphere: Women's Work and Culture at the World's Fairs of 1876, 1893, and 1904" (Ph.D. diss., New York University, 1989), p. 225.

13. Badger, *The Great American Fair*, p. 122.

14. Cordato, "Representing the Expansion of Women's Sphere," p. 220. Also see Massa, "Black Women in the 'White City,'" p. 327.

15. *Chicago Tribune*, July 22, 1893, p. 9.

16. Weimann, *The Fair Women*, p. 104.

17. Barnett, "The Reason Why," p. 67.

18. Massa, "Black Women in the 'White City,'" p. 322.

19. Woman's Columbian Auxiliary Association, *Aim and Plan of Action.*

20. See Thomas C. Holt, "The Lonely Warrior: Ida B. Wells-Barnett and the Struggle for Black Leadership," pp. 39–61, in *Black Leaders of the Twentieth Century*, ed. John Hope Franklin and August Meier (Urbana: University of Illinois Press, 1982), for one of the most accurate and incisive treatments of this racial stalwart.

21. Palmer to Trent, October 29, 1891, World's Columbian Exposition Papers, vol. 2, Chicago Historical Society. Trent did not reside at 4032 State Street, a commercial thoroughfare, but in the better Englewood section of the city. In the age of "conspicuous consumption," this perception could have impressed the Palmer cohort not at all.

22. Weimann, *The Fair Women*, pp. 105, 110, 111.

23. Massa, "Black Women in the 'White City,'" pp. 323–326. Also see Virginia Grant Dabney, "Women and World's Fairs: American International Expositions, 1876–1904" (Ph.D. diss., Emory University, 1982), p. 97.

24. Dabney, "Women and World's Fairs," p. 99.

25. *The Illustrated World's Fair*, (Chicago: Illustrated World's Fair Publishing Co., 1893), p. 209.

26. Hallie Q. Brown to Hon. Rutherford B. Hayes, October 12, 1891, Correspondence, the Hayes Presidential Center Library, Fremont, Ohio.

27. Weimann, *The Fair's Women*, p. 117.

28. *Chicago Tribune*, December 13, 1891, p. 9.

29. Weimann, *The Fair's Women*, p. 120.

30. *Chicago Inter Ocean*, January 1, 1893, p. 5.

31. Albion Winegar Tourgée's biographer, Otto H. Olsen, writes that Wells credited Tourgée with having inspired both the protest and the pamphlet. See *Carpetbagger's Crusade: The Life of Albion Winegar Tourgée* (Baltimore: Johns Hopkins University Press, 1965), p. 320 and n.16.

32. *Indianapolis Freeman*, May 6, 1893, p. 7.

33. Ibid., August 5, 1893, p. 4.

34. Ibid., July 29, 1893, p. 1.

35. *Chicago Inter Ocean*, March 4, 1893, p. 4.

36. Olsen, *Carpetbagger's Crusade*, pp. 306–311, 319–320.

37. *Chicago Inter Ocean*, August 22, 1893, p. 6.

38. Duster, *Crusade for Justice*, p. 118.

39. Barnett, "The Reason Why," p. 80.

40. "Emancipation Day Jubilee," *Indianapolis Freeman*, May 13, 1893, p. 2.

41. Barnett, "The Reason Why," p. 72.

42. *Chicago Inter Ocean*, November 28, 1890, p. 8.

43. Bancroft, *The Book of the Fair*, p. 88.

44. [World's Columbian Exposition,] *Dedication Ceremonies Memorial*, p. 132.

45. Ben C. Truman, *History of the Columbian World's Fair*, (Chicago: Mammoth Publishing, 1893), p. 93.

46. *Chicago Legal News*, May 29, 1897, p. 333.

47. [World's Columbian Exposition,] *Dedication Ceremonies Memorial*, p. 132, and Bancroft, *The Book of the Fair*, p. 88.

48. Campbell, *Campbell's Illustrated History of the World's Columbian Exposition*, p. 250.

49. [World's Columbian Exposition,] *Dedication Ceremonies Memorial*, p. 89.

50. McFeely, *Frederick Douglass*, p. 366.

3. Race, Class, and Gender

1. Quoted from the *Ladies Pictorial* (London), May 1893, in Duster, *Crusade for Justice*, p. 108.

2. Nell Irvin Painter, *Exodusters: Black Migration to Kansas after Reconstruction* (Lawrence: University Press of Kansas, 1976), p. viii.

3. Cited in Charles V. Hamilton and Stokeley Carmichael, *Black Power: The Politics of Liberation in America* (New York: Random House, 1967), p. 36.

4. Moses, *The Wings of Ethiopia*, p. 97.

5. Robert Russa Moton, *What the Negro Thinks* (New York: Doubleday, Doran, 1929), pp. 8, 9. Moton wrote:

> Negroes feel that any person outside the race is simply deceiving himself when he professes to know them, for the reason that the very circumstances recited operate effectively to prevent such knowledge. The Negro does not pretend that there is anything mysterious about his people, but simply that the very attitude of the white man himself prevents his having that thorough knowledge not only of the circumstances of Negro life, but less so of his inner thoughts and feelings.

6. St. Clair Drake, *The Redemption of Africa and Black Religion* (Chicago: Third World Press, 1970), p. 19.

7. John Langston Gwaltney, *Drylongso: A Self-Portrait on Black America* (New York: Random House, 1980), pp. xxvi–xxvii.

8. Moton, *What the Negro Thinks*, pp. 30, 31.

9. p. xvi.

10. Frederick Douglass's insistence on building a race's future on the ruins of slavery and hope of interracial cooperation and fairness explained his repeated utterances at the fair to all who came to hear him. Sociologist E. Franklin Frazier reiterated the need to emphasize this point also in his 1962 essay, "The Failure of the Negro Intellectual," pp. 57–58, cited in *The Death of White Sociology* (New York: Random House; Vintage Book edition, 1973), ed. Joyce A. Ladner.

11. Rosengarten, *All God's Dangers*, p. 7.

12. Charles S. Johnson, *Shadow of the Plantation* (Chicago: University of Chicago Press, 1934), pp. 22, 23. See also the classic on remembrances of African cultural survivals: Georgia Writers Project, *Drums and Shadows* (1934).

13. See Ray Stannard Baker, *Along the Color Line* (New York: Scribner's, 1908), pp. 144, 145. The progressive journalist observed at the dawn of the new century that the result of a growing color consciousness among African Americans was a self-imposed color line, much to his disgust.

14. Bontemps and Conroy, *They Seek a City*, p. 52.

15. *Indianapolis Freeman*, March 26,1892, p. 1.

16. Lewis, *W. E. B. Du Bois*, pp. 281, 282.

17. Gwaltney, *Drylongso*, p. xxiii.

18. Higginbotham, "African-American Women's History and the Metalanguage of Race," p. 3 in *"We Specialize in the Wholly Impossible,"* ed. Hine, King, and Reed.

19. Ibid., p. 17.

20. Clarence Albert Bacote, "The Negro in Georgia Politics, 1880–1908" (Ph.D. diss., University of Chicago, 1955), p. 26.

21. Ibid., pp. 29–33.

22. Pete Daniel, *The Shadow of Slavery: Peonage in the South, 1901–1969* (New York: Oxford University Press, 1973). See p. 11: "Vestiges of the system [of debt peonage] had been visible since the Civil War, yet it was only in 1901 that any legal action was taken to combat the practice."

23. V[incent]. P. Franklin, *Black Self-Determination: A Cultural History of the Faith of the Fathers* (Westport, Conn.: Lawrence Hill, 1984), pp. ix–xi; 4–9. According to Franklin, "at the core of the racial consciousness that developed among Afro-Americans in the United States was the cultural objective of black self-determination, which operated in a dialectical relationship with white supremacy."

24. Rydell, *All the World's a Fair*, p. 52.

25. Clifton O. Dummett, *Charles Edwin Bentley: A Model for All Times* (St. Paul: North Central, 1982), pp. 22, 23.

26. Ibid., p. 21. Given the small size of the elite, the question arises as to just who among their ranks constituted the *many*, beyond attorneys Edward Morris and John G. "Indignation" Jones. See Williams's biographer for the dynamics of the dialogue: Helen Buckler, *Doctor Dan: The Life of Daniel Hale Williams, Pioneer Negro Surgeon* (Boston: Little, Brown, 1954; 2nd ed., New York: Pitman, 1968), pp. 68–72.

27. See "Colored Belles to Come: Chicago's African '400' Agog over Prospective Visit," *Chicago Daily News*, May 4, 1896, p. 4.

The more adventurous, younger, wealthy white men seeking to satisfy their vices were informed that they should view the African American area south of the Loop known as "Cheyenne" with caution, because there dwelled, along with male cutthroats, the dreaded "Amazons," whom even policemen feared. These women were so anti-feminine as to be almost masculine. "Most [police] officers would rather engage in a grapple with half a dozen male desperados than with one of those formidable Negresses. They are Amazonians in physique," wrote Harold Richard Vynne in his *Chicago by Day and Night: The Pleasure Seeker's Guide to the Paris of America* (Chicago: Lake City, 1892), pp. 154–157.

The contemporary references in the guidebooks to the women of Dahomey as ugly were unfortunately commonplace and reflect white abhorrence of their skin color as much as anything.

See also Gatewood, *Aristocrats of Color*, chapter 6, for the problem of the internal color line.

28. *Chicago Tribune*, October 29, 1893, p. 26.

29. Ibid., May 28, 1893, p. 27.

30. Gatewood, *Aristocrats of Color*, p. 219.

31. Reverdy Ransom, *Pilgrimage of Harriet Ransom's Son* (Nashville, Tenn.: Sunday School Union, 1947), pp. 91f.

32. *Chicago Broad Ax*, December 1904.

33. Williams, "A Northern Negro's Autobiography," p. 94.

34. Some of Williams's relatives evinced resentment over his physiognomy and seemingly white identification. See Buckler, *Dr. Dan*, pp. xi, xii.

35. *Illinois Record*, July 1898, p. 3. During the Spanish American War (1898), enlisted men serving under Marshall in Cuba accused the captain of being a "white man with a black head and heart" and "too near white." See Willard B. Gatewood, Jr., *"Smoked Yankees" and the Struggle for Empire: Letters from Negro Soldiers, 1898–1902* (Urbana: University of Illinois Press, 1971), pp. 204, 213.

36. Gatewood, *Aristocrats of Color*, p. 228.

37. See Bishop Daniel Payne's activities in behalf of eliminating emotive church activities throughout the A.M.E. church world in James T. Campbell, *Songs of Zion: The African Methodist Church in the United States and South Africa* (New York: Oxford University Press, 1995), pp. 39–43; 62.

38. Richard Harlan Thomas, "Jenkin Lloyd Jones: Lincoln's Soldier of Civic Righteousness" (Ph.D. diss., Rutgers University, 1967), pp. 6, 198.

39. See W. E. B. Du Bois' paean to his fallen comrade in protest advocacy over the first quarter of the twentieth century in his editorial "Postscript," *Crisis* (December 1929): 423, and Clifton O. Dummett's biography, *Charles Edwin Bentley: A Model for All Times*. It was in the early twentieth century that Bentley made his mark in organizational activities as a leader *par excellence*. See also Christopher Robert Reed, *The Chicago NAACP and the Rise of Black Professional Leadership, 1910–1966* (Bloomington: Indiana University Press, 1997).

40. Moses, *The Wings of Ethiopia*, p. 65.

41. Harlan, *Booker T. Washington: The Making of a Black Leader, 1856–1901*, pp. 208–211.

42. Barnett, "The Reason Why," pp. 73, 80.

43. *Chicago Inter Ocean*, August 19, 1893, p. 9.

44. See Meier, *Negro Thought in America*, pp. ix, x. The thoughts of the rank and file, more likely than not, were revealed through institutional activities.

45. Recognition of Harris's directory as a major historical tool used to validate the significance of the African American presence in late nineteenth century Chicago is seen in Bessie Louise Pierce, *A History of Chicago, vol. 3: The Rise of a Modern City, 1871–1893* (Chicago: University of Chicago Press, 1957), pp. 48, 237.

46. Meier, *Negro Thought in America*, chapter 3.

47. Isaac C. Harris, *Colored Men's Directory*, n.p.

48. *Indianapolis Freeman*, April 29, 1893, p. 3.

49. "Color at the Fair," *Chicago Inter Ocean*, December 19, 1892, p. 13 [Hale G. Parker to the Editor].

50. Eric J. Sundquist, ed., *The Oxford W. E. B. Du Bois Reader* (New York: Oxford University Press, 1996), pp. 42, 43.

51. See the *Indianapolis Freeman* of March 19, 1892, p. 4; March 26, 1892, p. 3; April 2, 1892, pp. 1, 2; June 17, 1893, p. 4; July 8, 1893, p. 6; August 5, 1893, p. 2.

52. Lynch, *Edward Wilmot Blyden*, p. 110.

53. Ibid., pp. 110, 111; Redkey, *Black Exodus*, pp. 48–50; and Drake, "Churches and Voluntary Associations among the Negroes of Chicago," p. 36.

54. Rosengarten, *All God's Dangers*, p. 300.

55. Ibid.

56. Ida B. Wells, "Afro-Americans and Africa," *A.M.E. Church Review*, July 1892, pp. 40–45.

Part Two. In Host City Chicago

1. Drake, "Churches and Voluntary Associations among the Negroes of Chicago," p. 87, and Drake and Cayton, *Black Metropolis*, pp. 51–57, 266–270.

2. Lorenzo R. Greene and Carter G. Woodson, *The Negro Wage Earner* (Washington, D.C.: Association for the Study of Negro Life and History, 1930), p. 77.

4. The Domain of Work

1. [Preface], *The Reason Why the Colored American Is Not in the World's Columbian Exposition*, n.p.

2. Cited opposite the frontispiece in Willam H. Harris, *The Harder We Run: Black Workers since the Civil War* (New York: Oxford University Press, 1982).

3. H. C. Brunner, "The Making of the White City," *Scribner's Magazine* 12 (October 1892): 399. See also Robert Anderson, *Across the Atlantic* (London: Roxburghe Press, 1893), p. 90.

4. Cunningham, *Paul Lawrence Dunbar and His Song*, p. 93.

5. James Weldon Johnson, "Atlanta University Boys at the World's Fair," *Bulletin of Atlanta University*, April 1893, p. 6.

6. Barnett, "The Reason Why," p. 80.

7. Harris, *The Harder We Run*, pp. 52, 53.

8. W. E. B. Du Bois, *The Philadelphia Negro: A Social Study* (Philadelphia: University of Pennsylvania Press, 1899; rpt. New York: Schocken Books, 1967), p. 129.

9. Ibid., p. xxxvii, and asterisked note on pp. 129–131.

10. *Report of Conferences between the Board of Directors of the World's Columbian Exposition and Representatives of the Labor Organizations of Chicago, Relative to the Employment of Labor, 1891* (Chicago: Wm. C. Hollister & Bro., Printers, 1891).

11. Sterling D. Spero and Abram L. Harris, *The Black Worker: The Negro in the Labor Movement* (New York: Columbia University Press, 1931; rpt. New York: Atheneum, 1969), pp. x, xi; 41–45.

12. "Opinion of the Chicago Colored Women's Club," *Chicago Inter Ocean*, March 13, 1894 [unlocatable], cited in Philip S. Foner and Ronald L. Lewis, eds., *The Black Worker: A Documentary History from Colonial Times to the Present, Vol. 3, The Black Worker during the Era of the Knights of Labor* (Philadelphia: Temple University Press, 1978), p. 282.

13. Harris, *The Harder We Run*, pp. 20, 21. Also see Cassell, "A Confusion of Voices," p. 66.

14. Drake, "Churches and Voluntary Associations among the Negroes of Chicago," p. 106.

15. Joseph Kirkland, "Among the Poor of Chicago," *Scribner's Magazine* 12 (July 1892): 5.

16.

Year	Total Population	Black Workers	Sources
1885	9,481	— — —	Harris *Directory*
1890	14,271	8,562	Eleventh U.S. Census
1896	22,742	13,645	Work's "Crime" essay
1900	30,150	17,986	Twelfth U.S. Census

17. Monroe Nathan Work, "Crime among the Negroes of Chicago," *American Journal of Sociology* (1900): 206.

18. Williams, "A Northern Negro's Autobiography," pp. 92–94.

19. Drake, "Churches and Voluntary Associations among the Negroes of Chicago," p. 87.

20. H. C. Bunner, "The Making of the White City," *Scribner's Magazine*, 12 (October 1892): 417.

21. "Story of Old Settler Reads Like Fiction," p. 23.

22. Greene and Woodson, *The Negro Wage Earner*, p. 36.

23. Perry R. Duis, "'Commodores of the Dining Room': Race and Restaurant Waiters, 1850–1900," unpublished manuscript, University of Illinois at Chicago, undated, pp. 26–48.

24. Isaac C. Harris, *The Colored Men's Directory*, p. 36. Harris fixed the number of workers in hotels and restaurants at between 1,800 and 2,000 in 1885. Subtracting the porters, janitors, and other non-waitstaff, the estimate here is 1,500.

25. Benefits and attitudes are cited in *Indianapolis Freeman*, May 6, 1893, p. 7, and May 20, 1893, p. 5.

26. Sharon Harley, "When Your Work Is Not Who You Are: The Development of a Working-Class Consciousness among Afro-American Women," pp. 25, 26 in *"We Specialize in the Wholly Impossible,"* ed. Hine, King, and Reed.

27. Interview with May Anna Madison, in Gwaltney, *Drylongso*, pp. 172–174.

28. For twentieth century southern variations and continuities on how African Americans molded the sphere of work as much as it shaped their thinking, behavior, and lives, see Robin D. G. Kelley, "'We Are Not What We Seem': Rethinking Black Working Class Opposition in the Jim Crow South," *Journal of American History* 80 (June 1993): 75–112.

29. David W. Kellum, "Model Railroad Man Retires after 51 Years . . . ," *Chicago Defender*, December 3, 1932, p. 9.

30. See "Laughing at the Man," pp. 300–320, in Levine, *Black Culture and Black Consciousness*.

31. Allan H. Spear, *Black Chicago: The Making of a Negro Ghetto, 1890–1920* (Chicago: University of Chicago Press, 1967), pp. 65, 66.

32. Cunningham, *Paul Lawrence Dunbar and His Song*, p. 93.

33. E. Franklin Frazier, "The Negro Family in Chicago" (Ph.D. diss., University of Chicago, 1931), p. 106.

34. Cunningham, *Paul Lawrence Dunbar and His Song*, pp. 93, 94.

35. David M. Katzman, *Before the Ghetto: Black Detroit in the Nineteenth Century* (Urbana: University of Illinois Press, 1973), pp. 111, 112, 115.

36. Richard R. Wright, Jr., "The Industrial Condition of Negroes in Chicago" (B.D. thesis, University of Chicago, 1901), pt. II, p. 21.

37. *Chicago Tribune*, May 11, 1893, p. 6.

38. Bancroft, *The Book of the Fair*, p. 80.

39. Mrs. Mark Stevens, *Six Months at the World's Fair* (Detroit: Detroit Free Press, 1895), pp. 141, 142.

40. For the depth of his feelings see Hobart C. Chatfield-Taylor, *Chicago* (Chicago: 1917), pp. 41, 50–51, 70.

41. Harris, *The Harder We Run*, p. 20.

42. Spero and Harris, *The Black Worker*, p. 430.

43. Frederick Perry Noble, "Chicago Congress on Africa" (no city: no publisher, 1893), p. 292. Schomburg Center for Research in Black Culture, New York Public Library. Florence Pullman, the magnate's daughter, had won praise in 1891 for her financial support of the newly founded Provident Hospital. See Buckley, *Daniel Hale Williams*, p. 73.

44. Wright, "The Industrial Condition of Negroes in Chicago," p. 22.

45. For an example of what image the Pullman porter represented to African Americans as the century turned, see the prototype in action in J. A. Rogers, *From "Superman to Man* (New York: J. A. Rogers, 1917). During a cross-country rail journey, a southern racist "superman" is challenged intellectually by Dixon, a porter, who is more than his match cerebrally, thereby affecting a transformation in the thinking of the former by the time the trip concludes.

46. Patricia and Frederick McKissick, *A Long Hard Journey: The Story of the Pullman Porter* (New York: Walker, 1989), pp. 30, 31. While written for a youth audience and devoid of documentation, this work is extremely useful in understanding the circumstances under which the Pullman porters emerged as a working unit along with the character of their performance during the late nineteenth century.

47. Frazier, "The Negro Family in Chicago," pp. 125. See also E. Franklin Frazier, *The Negro Family in Chicago* (Chicago: University of Chicago Press, 1932).

48. *Illinois Record*, July 2, 1898, p. 1.

49. Data on the first generation of Pullman porters are elusive to unavailable. However, see Rogers, *From "Superman" to Man*; McKissick, *A Long Hard Journey*; and David D. Perata, *Those Pullman Blues: An Oral History of the African American Railroad Attendant* (New York: Twayne, 1996) for insight into the continuous struggles of these railroad workers for decent pay and dignity.

50. Franklin, *Black Self-Determination: A Cultural History of the Faith of the Fathers*, pp. 149–151; 153–155.

51. See Rogers's *From "Superman" to Man* in its entirety.

52. Hawthorne, *Humors of the Fair*, pp. 9, 10.

53. See the biographical sketch along with the correspondence between Fritsch and Pullman, summer 1893, in the George M. Pullman Papers at the Chicago Historical Society.

54. Cunningham, *Paul Lawrence Dunbar and His Song*, pp. 106, 107.

55. *The Presto*, June 29, 1893, p. 11. See also "The Negro Music of the South," *Southern Workman*, November 1893, p. 174.

56. Ibid., July 13, 1893, p. 13.

57. "City Gives 'Jazz' to Musical World," *Chicago Defender*, October 29, 1932, p. 7. Also see Edward A. Berlin, *King of Ragtime: Scott Joplin and His Era* (New York: Oxford University Press, 1994), pp. 11, 12. Berlin pinpointed ragtime's emergence from this event and at this time: "The fair was also a signal event in ragtime history, for, according to numerous accounts during the next two decades, it was here that ragtime surfaced from its incipient stages in black communities and became known to the wider American public."

58. Monroe Nathan Work, "The Origin of 'Ragtime Music,'" *Negro Year Book: An Annual Encyclopedia of the Negro, 1925–1926* (Nashville: A.M.E. Sunday School Union, 1926), p. 343.

59. *Chicago Legal News*, May 29, 1897, p. 333.

60. "Colored Folks' Day," *Chicago Herald*, August 25, 1893, p. 9.

61. "Report of [the] Janitor's Department," October 31, 1893, Appendix 5, *Official Report of the Columbian Guard*, pp. 3, 4, Chicago Historical Society.

62. Ibid., p. 1.

63. Ibid., p. 4.

64. Cunningham, *Paul Lawrence Dunbar and His Song*, pp. 94, 95.

65. Majors, "What the Negro Contributed to the World's Fair in 1893," p. 52.

66. James Weldon Johnson, "At the World's Fair," *Bulletin of Atlanta University*, May 1893, p. 6.

67. J. A. Mitchell, "Types and People at the Fair," *Scribner's Magazine* 12 (August 1893): 191.

68. "Raiding the 'Levee,'" *Chicago Inter Ocean*, July 16, 1892, p. 3.

69. "See "Great Game of Craps," *Chicago Inter Ocean*, July 15, 1892, p. 8, and "Raiding the 'Levee,'" *Chicago Inter Ocean*, July 16, 1892, p. 3.

70. Work, "Crime among the Negroes of Chicago," pp. 206, 208–222.

71. Du Bois, *The Philadelphia Negro*, pp. 312, 313.

72. "Robbed of $50 by Colored Women," *Chicago Tribune*, September 20, 1893, p. 6.

73. Dennis B. Downey, "Rite of Passage: The World's Columbian Exposition and American Life" (Ph.D. diss., Marquette University, September 1981), p. 182.

74. William T. Stead, *If Christ Came to Chicago* (Chicago: Laird & Lee, 1894), p. 247.

75. Du Bois, *The Philadelphia Negro*, p. 313.

76. Stead, *If Christ Came to Chicago*, pp. 247, 251.

77. Ibid., pp. 248, 250.

5. The Social Order

1. Drake and Cayton, *Black Metropolis*, p. 543.

2. Drake, "Churches and Voluntary Associations among the Negroes of Chicago," p. 87.

3. Wright, "The Industrial Condition of Negroes in Chicago," pt. 2, p. 7. See Du Bois, *The Philadelphia Negro*, pp. 309–311. Du Bois called for a recognition of differences among African Americans, but he wrote they "are not, to be sure, so great or so patent as those among the whites of to-day."

4. Hylan Lewis, *Blackways of Kent* (Chapel Hill: University of North Carolina Press, 1955), pp. 223, 224.

5. Jackson Turner Main, *The Antifederalists: Critics of the Constitution, 1781–1788* (Chicago: Quadrangle Books, 1961), p. 1.

6. Robert H. Wiebe, *The Search for Order, 1877–1920* (New York: Hill and Wang, 1967), p. 112.

7. "Colored Belles to Come," *Chicago Daily News*, May 4, 1896, p. 4.

8. Frazier, "The Negro Family in Chicago," p. 121.

9. "Colored Belles to Come," *Chicago Daily News*, May 4, 1896, p. 4.

10. Edward H. Wilson, "The Line of Equality among Negroes Is Almost Imperceptible," *Chicago Broad Ax*, December 25, 1909, p. 1.

11. Darlene Clark Hine, *Speak Truth to Power* (Brooklyn: Carlson, 1996), pp. 174, 188.

12. Buckler, *Daniel Hale Williams*, p. 23.

13. Kletzing and Crogman, *Progress of a Race*, p. 450.

14. Ibid., p. 448.

15. Jessie Carney Smith, "Fannie B. Williams" in *Notable Black American Women* (Detroit: Gale Research, 1992), ed. Jessie Carney Smith, pp. 1251–1254; Rayford W. Logan and Michael R. Winston, eds., *Dictionary of American Negro Biography* (New York: W. W. Norton, 1982), p. 656; Massa, "Black Women in the 'White City,'" p. 330.

16. Harlan, *Booker T. Washington: The Making of a Black Leader*, p. 357.

17. Davis, "The Negro Newspaper in Chicago," p. 26.

18. Ibid., p. 17.

19. Painter, *Exodusters*, pp. 49, 50.

20. Davis, "The Negro Newspaper in Chicago," p. 17.

21. Kletzing and Crogman, *Progress of a Race*, p. 534.

22. Richard R. Wright, Jr., "The Negro in Chicago," *Southern Workman* 35 (October 1906): 564.

23. African American church information is found in Drake, "Churches and Voluntary Associations among the Negroes of Chicago," pp. 104–106, and Wright, "The Industrial Condition of Negroes in Chicago," pp. 12, 13.

24. Gatewood, *Aristocrats of Color*, pp. 119–124. See also Cunningham, *Paul Lawrence Dunbar and His Song*, pp. 96–97.

25. Duster, *Crusade for Justice*, p. 120.

26. *Indianapolis Freeman*, February 13, 1893, p. 6.

27. Ibid., May 20, 1893, p. 5.

28. Wright, "The Industrial Condition of Negroes in Chicago," p. 12.

29. Mary J. Herrick, *The Chicago Schools: A Social and Political History* (Beverly Hills, Calif.: Sage Publications, 1971), pp. 74, 81, 82.

30. Interview with Mrs. Lorraine Cherry Heflin on March 17, 1997, in Chicago. See also *Black's Blue Book* (Chicago: Celerity Press, 1906), p. 54.

31. Work, "Crime among the Negroes of Chicago," pp. 206–208.

32. Vynne, *Chicago by Day and Night*, p. 153.

33. Ibid., p. 157.

34. Work, "Crime among the Negroes of Chicago," pp. 204–206; 212f.

35. Vynne, *Chicago by Day and Night*, pp. 155, 156.

36. Spear, *Black Chicago*, p. 54.

37. Ibid., pp. 51, 52.

38. Ibid., p. 56.

39. Floyd Hunter, *Community Power Structure: A Study of Decision Makers* (Chapel Hill: University of North Carolina Press, 1953; rev., 1968), pp. 24, 37.

40. Spear, *Black Chicago*, chapter 3.

41. Fannie Barrier Williams, "Social Bonds in the 'Black Belt' of Chicago," *Charities* (October 15, 1904), p. 42.

42. Meier, *Negro Thought in America*, pp. 139, 146, 149.

43. Du Bois, *The Philadelphia Negro*, pp. 7, 316.

44. McFeely, *Frederick Douglass*, p. 366. See also Cunningham, *Paul Lawrence Dunbar and His Song*, pp. 96–97.

45. Frazier, "The Negro Family in Chicago," p. 102.

46. Ibid., pp. 102–104.

47. "Colored Aristocracy: Their Ward McAllisters Reign in All Our Cities," *Atchison [Kansas] Blade*, October 7, 1893, p. 3.

48. Drake and Cayton, *Black Metropolis*, p. 515.

49. Dummett, *Charles Edwin Bentley*, p. 167. As a social arbiter among socially minded blacks, Avendorph's rise is marked as 1893 in the *Illinois Record*, July 2, 1893, p. 1, while the social arbiter already in "office" was Lloyd Wheeler, according to the *Atchison [Kansas] Blade*, October 7, 1893, p. 3.

50. Buckler, *Daniel Hale Williams*, pp. 66–82.

51. See Christopher Robert Reed, *The Chicago NAACP and the Rise of Black Professional Leadership* (Bloomington: Indiana University Press, 1997).

52. Hunter, *Community Power Structure: A Study of Decision Makers*, p. 114.

53. Ransom, *Pilgrimage of Harriet Ransom's Son*, pp. 83, 84.

54. Duster, *Crusade for Justice*, pp. 249, 250.

Part Three. At the Fair

1. Drake, "Churches and Voluntary Associations among the Negroes of Chicago," p. 106.

6. "They Met at the Fair"

1. This chapter bears the same title as the influential essay on the fair in Bontemps and Conroy, *They Seek a City*.

2. For the effect of Nancy Green's popularity, along with that of the free pancakes, see *Chicago Evening Journal*, August 19, 1893, p. 4. As to the image Green projected, clothed in head wrap and other plantation apparel, it represented a model southern African American wife, mother, or sister. A sketch in *The Bulletin of Atlanta University*, July 1893, page 1 (see Appendix IV), bears a striking resemblance to Aunt Jemima at the fair and later on boxes of pancake mix. The accompanying poem serves as a paean to this indomitable worker and producer of families, nations, and

wealth. See Polk's photograph entitled "The Boss" in Chester Higgins, Jr., "P. H. Polk and Me," *Crisis* 105 (December 1998): 39. Other current literature takes the image to task as racially degrading and manipulative, e.g., Donald Bogle, *Toms, Coons, Mulattos, Mammies, and Bucks* (New York: Continuum, 1989) and Sarah P. Morris, "Aunt Jemima," pp. 53–54 in *Black Women in America: An Historical Encyclopedia*, vol. 1, ed. Darlene Clark Hine (Brooklyn: Carlson, 1993).

3. Arthur F. Marquette, *Brands, Trademarks and Goodwill: The Story of the Quaker Oats Company* (New York: McGraw-Hill, 1967), pp. 137–139.

4. Bontemps and Conroy, *They Seek a City*, p. 103.

5. Kletzing and Crogman, *Progress of a Race*, p. 592.

6. Logan, *The Betrayal of the Negro*, p. 356. John Graziano believes that "their collaborative efforts were limited to about two or three years." Letter, Graziano to Reed, October 17, 1997, in the author's possession.

7. Badger, *The Great American Fair*, p. 120. Badger wrote, but without documentation, that "while Paderewski performed Chopin for swooning audiences in the Court of Honor's Music Hall, Scott Joplin played ragtime for the pleasure throngs along the Midway." If Joplin played a forerunner of ragtime, it would have occurred outside the fair complex and not on the Midway, where space equaled revenue for the registered vendors.

8. "City Gives 'Jazz' to Musical World," *Chicago Defender*, October 29, 1932, p. 7.

9. "Heard Way-Down South Music," *Chicago Herald*, July 19, 1893 n.p., in the Moses P. Handy Papers, Newspaper Clippings File—"Music," William L. Clements Library, University of Michigan.

10. Levy, *James Weldon Johnson*, p. 41.

11. Kletzing and Crogman, *Progress of a Race*, pp. 571–573.

12. Most Worshipful Grand Lodge and Appendant Orders, State of Illinois Jurisdiction, January 15, 1893, n.p., Schomburg Research Center, New York Public Library.

13. Ibid., n.p.

14. *Chicago Inter Ocean*, August 22, 1893, p. 5.

15. For examples, see the *Indianapolis Freeman* issues of August 19, 1893, p. 1, and August 26, 1893, p. 1.

16. Drake, "Churches and Voluntary Associations among the Negroes of Chicago," p. 108.

17. Church and mission locations in proximity to the expanding south side black community in 1893, located between the south Loop and 35th street (*** = in the central core community; Sources: Drake, "Churches and Voluntary Associations among the Negroes of Chicago," *Bloom's Directory*; *Chicago Inter Ocean*):

***   Quinn Chapel A.M.E. Church, Wabash Avenue near 22nd Street (moving to Wabash and 24th Street)

        Olivet Baptist Church, Harmon Court and Holden Place [Loop], (moving to 27th and Dearborn)

        Providence Baptist Church, 26 North Irving Place (West Side)

        St. Stephen A.M.E. Church, 682 Austin Avenue (West Side)

***   Bethel A.M.E. Church, Dearborn and 30th

***   Grace Presbyterian Church, Dearborn, near 30th

***   St Monica's Roman Catholic Church, 2251 Indiana Avenue

***   St. Thomas Episcopal Church, Dearborn, near 30th

        Bethesda Baptist Church, Forty-fourth and Butterfield (Hyde Park area)

***   Zion A.M.E. Church Mission, Dearborn, near 29th

        Allen A.M.E. Church Mission, Avondale (South Side)

***   Christian Church Mission, 2719 Dearborn

Shiloh Baptist Church Mission, 430 Sixty-third (Englewood, Far South Side)
Hermon Baptist Church, (North Side)

18. July 22, 1893, p. 1.

19. Within a generation, the "New Negroes" of the World War I era established the famous Black Metropolis, an attempt at *imperium in imperio*—a self-contained racial enclave or city within a city. Political, economic, cultural, and social hegemony were the hallmarks of the 1920s and 1930s. See Drake and Cayton, *Black Metropolis.*

20. Nathan D. Young, "A Negro Chautauqua," *The Independent* 45 (August 31, 1893), p. 1182.

21. Bell, "The Chicago Fair," *Bulletin of Atlanta University*, July 1893, pp. 3, 4.

22. *Report of the Board of General Managers of the Exhibit of the State of New York at the World's Columbian Exposition,* p. 176.

23. Work of Colored Women: Some Excellent Exhibits Made by Them at the World's Fair," *New York Times*, June 10, 1893, p. 5.

24. *Report of the Board of General Managers of the Exhibit of the State of New York at the World's Columbian Exposition,* p. 164. See also Massa, "Black Women in the 'White City,'" p. 335, for a reference that essentially gives this impressive effort short shrift.

25. Mossell, *The Work of the Afro-American Woman,* p. 106, and Majors, "What the Negro Contributed to the World's Fair in 1893," p. 52.

26. *Cleveland Gazette,* May 6, 1893, p. 2.

27. World's Columbian Exposition, Exhibit Records, Mississippi, #216, Chicago Historical Society.

28. Cora M. Folsom, "Columbian Fair Notes," *Southern Workman and Hampton School Record,* July 1893, p. 122.

29. C. H. Stokes, "World's Fair Notes," *Southern Workman and Hampton School Record,* November 1893, p. 173.

30. Folsom, "Columbian Fair Notes," *Southern Workman and Hampton School Record,* July 1893, p. 122.

31. "Wilberforce's Exhibit," *Cleveland Gazette,* May 20, 1893, p. 2.

32. Bell, "The Chicago Fair," *Bulletin of Atlanta University*, p. 3.

33. *Indianapolis Freeman,* May 27, 1893, p. 5.

34. Carl Bowen Johnson, "World's Fair Letter," *The Independent* 45 (July 20, 1893), p. 977.

35. *A Portfolio of Photographic Views of the World's Columbian Exposition* (1894), n.p.

36. "Captured by Zulus: Dusky Warriors Take Possession of an Illinois Central Train," *Chicago Evening Post*, April 25, 1898, p. 1. This newspaper account of an altercation on a fair-bound train reported that 200 Zulu warriors were on board.

37. "Attacked by Zulus," *Chicago Tribune*, June 4, 1893, p. 6.

38. "Africa at the Fair," *Chicago Post*, September 8, 1893, n.p., in Handy Papers, William L. Clement Library, University of Michigan.

39. Ibid., and "Captured by Zulus: Dusky Warriors Take Possession of an Illinois Central Train," *Chicago Evening Post*, April 25, 1898, p. 1.

40. John Hope Franklin and Alfred A. Moss, Jr., *From Slavery to Freedom: A History of African Americans* (New York: McGraw-Hill, 1998, 7th ed.), p. 298.

41. Philip G. Wright, *The Cuban Situation and Our Treaty Relations* (Washington, D.C.: Brookings Institution, 1931), pp. 11, 12; Jose M. Hernandez, *Cuba and the United States: Intervention and Militarism, 1868–1933* (Austin: University of Texas Press, 1993), pp. 16–24.

42. J. L. Nichols and W. H. Crogman, *The New Progress of a Race, Or, the Remarkable Advancement of the American Negro* (Naperville, Ill.: J. L. Nichols, 1925),

pp. 131–134. While an earlier edition of this work in 1897 does not mention these Cuban heroes, it is reasonable to assume that their inclusion following the involvement of large numbers of African American troops in the Spanish American War of 1898 spurred this inclusion in 1925 based on previous knowledge (see Kletzing and Crogman, *Progress of a Race*, p. 168).

43. Jules R. Benjamin, *The United States and the Origins of the Cuban Revolution* (Princeton: Princeton University Press, 1990), p. 25.

44. Franklin and Moss, *From Slavery to Freedom*, p. 297.

45. Campbell, *Campbell's Illustrated History of the World's Columbian Exposition*, vol. 2, p. 588.

46. Wilson, *Black Involvement in Previous World's Fairs*, p. 6.

47. "To the Grand Officers and Members of the Fraternity, M. W. Grand Lodge and Appendant Orders, State of Illinois, January 15, 1893," Schomburg Research Collection, New York Public Library.

48. *Chicago Inter Ocean*, August 19, 1893, p. 12.

49. *Indianapolis Freeman*, August 12, 1893, p. 1.

50. Meier and Rudwick, "Black Man in the 'White City,'" p. 357. One egregious Jim Crow episode in the downtown section occurred at the intersection of Michigan and Madison. African Americans were relegated to a balcony in the Grotto amusement center and charged seventy-five cents for admission. Whites paid a twenty-five-cent general admission. See *Chicago Inter Ocean*, August 18, 1893, p. 1, and August 19, 1893, p. 12.

51. Duster, *Crusade for Justice*, p. 120.

52. Paddon and Turner, "African Americans at the World's Columbian Exposition," pp. 34–36.

7. The Scope of Involvement

1. Carby, *Reconstructing Womanhood*, p. 3. See also pp. 1, 69.

2. May Wright Sewall, ed., *The World's Congress of Representative Women* (Chicago: Rand, McNally, 1894), p. 704.

3. Ibid., p. 710.

4. Ibid., p. 706.

5. Ibid., p. 697.

6. Ibid., p. 708.

7. Ibid., p. 716.

8. Ibid., p. 706.

9. Ibid., pp. 717, 718.

10. Criticism of Williams's lecture and presence is found in Massa, "Black Women in the 'White City,'" p. 334, and McFeely, *Frederick Douglass*, p. 367. If Wells had criticized Williams for contacting Tourgée, this is inconsistent with the relationship Wells and Tourgée enjoyed. Tourgée held the same esteem as a white among many blacks in the 1890s that Garrison and Brown did in the antebellum period. In fact, a Tourgée Club existed along the Dearborn Street corridor in the 2900 block. See *Crusade for Justice*, pp. 120–122.

11. Sewall, *World's Congress of Representative Women*, p. 714.

12. Ibid., p. 711.

13. Ibid., p. 435.

14. Ibid., p. 434.

15. Carby (*Reconstructing Womanhood*, p. 107) mentions that Wells did not appear at the Women's Congress but was active at the Haytian Pavilion in behalf of marketing *The Reason Why the Colored American Is Not in the World's Columbian Exposition*, implying that this was the totality of Wells's fair experiences, which paled in comparison to Anna Julia Cooper's feminist contributions. Wells was on her way from England when the fair opened.

16. *Chicago Inter Ocean,* June 27, 1893, p. 1.

17. Ibid.

18. *Chicago Evening Post,* June 26, 1893, p. 2.

19. Ibid.

20. For a full list of participants, including members of the Chicago elite, see Majors, "What the Negro Contributed to the World's Fair in 1893," p. 53, and *Indianapolis Freeman,* August 5, 1893, p. 1.

21. Remarks of Anna J. Cooper in Sewall, *World's Congress of Representative Women,* p. 713.

22. *Chicago Evening Journal,* September 2, 1893, p. 1.

23. Ibid. and *Chicago Inter Ocean,* September 3, 1893, p. 1.

24. Washington's reliance on personal will power for success seemed appropriate for these times. Marcus Garvey arrived in America seeking Washington's counsel partially because of this attribute. Needless to say, Garvey's famous challenge to oppressed African Americans and continentals, "Up You Mighty Race, You Can Accomplish What You Will!," aimed at the same group to which Washington appealed.

25. Majors, "What the Negro Contributed to the World's Fair in 1893," p. 52.

26. *Chicago Tribune,* September 9, 1893, p. 9.

27. John Henry Barrows, ed., *The World's Parliament of Religions* (Chicago: Parliament, 1893), pp. 1114, 1115.

28. *Chicago Inter Ocean,* August 22, 1893, p. 6.

29. Johnson, *Black Manhattan,* p. 93.

30. "No Cake Walks," *Chicago Inter Ocean,* March 14, 1892, p. 1. Jenifer explained the cakewalk thus: "In former times, for the sake of raising money for charitable purposes the prize of a cake was offered for the most graceful walker. Sometimes the cake contained a ring to enhance the interest in the affair. In time these events were carried to the extreme; they became outlandish. The best people began to hold the affairs in disrepute." Physically, it involved "parading with [a] dusky partner with gigantic and graceful stride, the buck and wing dancing, the buzzard lope, etc."

31. *Indianapolis Freeman,* August 19 and 26, 1892, p. 1.

32. Telephone interview with Prof. John Graziano, Department of Music, City University of New York, August 14, 1997, in New York City.

33. Johnson, *Black Manhattan,* p. 100.

34. *Chicago Tribune,* August 26, 1893, p. 3.

35. *Chicago Inter Ocean,* August 26, 1893, p. 2.

36. *Chicago Tribune,* August 26, 1893, p. 3, and *Indianapolis Freeman,* September 2, 1893, p. 1.

37. Letter from Prof. John Graziano, Department of Music, City University of New York, October 15, 1997. See also *Cleveland Gazette,* October 21, 1893, p. 1.

38. *Chicago Tribune,* August 26, 1893, p. 3.

39. *Chicago Herald,* August 25, 1893, p. 9; *Chicago Tribune,* August 26, 1893, p. 3; and *Chicago Inter Ocean,* August 26, 1893, p. 1.

40. Marva Griffin Carter, "The Life and Music of Will Marion Cook" (Ph.D. diss., University of Illinois at Urbana, 1988), p. 31, n.2.

Part Four. "All the World Is Here!"

1. *Oriental and Occidental Northern and Southern Portrait Types of the Midway Plaisance: A Collection of Photography of Individual Types of Various Nations from All Parts of the World Who Represent, in the Department of Ethnography, the Manners, Customs, Dress, Regions, Music and Other Distinctive Traits and Peculiarities of Their Race* (St. Louis: N. D. Thompson, 1894), n.p., with an introduction by Frederick Ward Putnam. Compared to the especially racist *Midway Types: A Book of Illustrated Lessons about the People of the Midway Plaisance,* World's Fair, 1893, the former is a model of objectivity.

2. Noble, "The Chicago Congress on Africa," pp. 316–317.

3. *Chicago Herald*, August 16, 1893, p. 9.

8. Continental Africa at the Fair

1. For a brief historical description of the Fon, see J. F. A. Ajayi and Michael Crowder, *History of West Africa*, vol. 1 (London: Longman, 1971), p. 24. For an anthropological exploration of Fon life at the time of the world's fair, the work that has assumed definitive status on the Fon is Herskovits, *Dahomey*. The origin of the group's name is described by Herskovits in vol. 1, p. 15, n.3.

2. *Frank Leslie's Illustrated Weekly*, June 25, 1893, p. 25.

3. Bancroft, *The Book of the Fair*, p. 967.

4. Consultation with Nancy Buenger, Textile Conservator at the Chicago Historical Society, on September 17, 1997. See "Representing America" [970], *The Chicago Times Portfolio of the Midway Types*, n.p., in which this comment is made: "Foreigners generally comment on the slimness and willowiness of American women and regard them as too delicate for good wives and mothers."

5. *Midway Types: A Book of Illustrated Lessons about the People of the Midway Plaisance World's Fair*, 1893, n.p.

6. Campbell, *Campbell's Illustrated History of the World's Columbian Exposition*, p. 411.

7. The Fair as Educator," *Harper's Weekly*, 37 (June 10, 1893), p. 543.

8. *Chicago Tribune*, August 16, 1893, p. 1, *Chicago Herald*, August 19, 1893, p. 2, and *Chicago Tribune*, May 4, 1893, p. 1.

9. Dean, *White City Chips*, p. 52.

10. "Dahomey Village Opened: Amazons and Their Escorts Dance to the Tom-tom Music," *Chicago Inter Ocean*, May 30, 1893, p. 7.

11. Julian Hawthorne, *Humors of the Fair*, pp. 35, 38, 77, 150.

12. Dean, *White City Chips*, p. 244. For a similar continental reaction to Caucasians by the Fon of Dahomey, see p. 52.

13. Stevens, *Six Months at the World's Fair*, pp. 110, 111.

14. Max Kozloff, *Photography and Fascination* (Danbury, N.H.: Addison House, 1978), p. 13.

15. Ibid., p. 23.

16. See Rydell, *All the World's a Fair*, pp. 40, 65, 66; Gilbert, *Perfect Cities*, pp. 82, 111, 115–117; Burg, *Chicago's White City of 1893*, pp. 96, 111, 219; and Levy, *James Weldon Johnson*, p. 39. Bancroft attested to their ability to draw crowds, relating that their journey to San Francisco to the California Midwinter International Exposition was one of "a few of the most attractive features in the Midway Plaisance." See *The Book of the Fair*, pp. 975, 990.

17. *The Reason Why the Colored American Is Not in the World's Columbian Exposition*, p. 9. Douglass explained thus: "[America] has brought to her shores and given welcome to a greater variety of mankind than were ever assembled in one place since the day of Pentecost. Japanese, Javanese, Soudanese, Chinese . . . and if to shame the Negro, the Dahomians are also here to exhibit the Negro as a repulsive savage." In his mind, denial of guilt by whites improved with every example affirming black inferiority.

18. References to this phenomenon abound: *Chicago Tribune*, May 4, 1893, p. 1; some examples from *The Chicago Times Portfolio of the Midway Types*: in "A Pretty Brazilian [#781]," "She certainly was not bad looking. . . . And her brown skin only increased her attractiveness"; "Boushareens [981]," "Once in a while a type of the African is presented to the white race and is counted as handsome: The Boushareens were generally so regarded"; and "A Star from the Nile [#1 68]," "It must not be taken for granted that Egypt and her people are as black as they are painted."

19. Kozloff, *Photography and Fascination*, p. 24.

20. "Dahomey Village Opened: Amazons and Their Escorts Dance to the Tomtom Music," *Chicago Inter Ocean*, May 30, 1893, p. 7.

21. *Chicago Evening Post*, September 16, 1893, p. 5, and John J. Flinn, *The Best Things to Be Seen at the World's Fair* (Chicago: Columbian Guide, 1893), pp. 168, 169.

22. John Durham Peters, "Beauty's Veils: The Ambivalent Iconoclasm of Kirkegaard and Benjamin," in *The Image in Dispute: Art and Cinema in the Age of Photography*, ed. Dudley Andrew (Austin: University of Texas Press, 1997), p. 25.

23. Paul L. Anderson, *The Fine Art of Photography* (New York: J. B. Lippincott, 1919; rpt. New York: Arno Press, 1973), p. 155.

24. Kozloff, *Photography and Fascination*, p. 35.

25. Francis Bruguiere, "Creative Photography," in *Photographers on Photography: A Critical Anthology*, ed. Nathan Lyons (Englewood Cliffs, N.J.: Prentice-Hall, 1966), p. 34.

26. Edward Weston, "Seeing Photographically," ibid., pp. 159, 160.

27. Dean, *White City Chips*, p. 52. See also "West African Folk," *Chicago Tribune*, May 4, 1893, p. 1.

28. Bancroft, *The Book of the Fair*, p. 878.

29. For a conveyance similar to that shown in figure 31, see Herskovits, *Dahomey*, vol. 2, Plate 52b opposite p. 16.

30. Herskovits, *Dahomey*, vol. 1, p. 29.

31. W. J. Argyle, *The Fon of Dahomey: A History and Ethnography of the Old Kingdom* (Oxford, U.K.: Clarendon Press, 1966), p. 1.

32. *Chicago Evening Post*, May 28, 1893, p. 11.

33. Dov Ronen, *Dahomey: Between Tradition and Modernity* (Ithaca: Cornell University Press, 1975), p. 45.

34. Herskovits, *Dahomey*, vol. 1, Preface, n.p. [unpaginated p. 1], and p. 25. Dahomey "represents a West African civilization that has been almost less affected than any other by the circumstance of European control." And, "Life in Dahomey goes on today little different from the way it was lived before contact with Europeans."

35. Rydell, *All the World's a Fair*, p. 52, and "A Charming Vista," [#1481] *The Chicago Times Portfolio of the Midway Types*, n.p.

36. Gilbert, *Perfect Cities*, p. 119. As mentioned before, whites of all classes were also the butts of jokes, ridicule, and caricatures throughout the fair. See "Wonderful Place for Fun," *New York Times*, June 19, 1893, p. 9. However, historian Rydell saw more than that, writing: "The Chicago's Worlds Fair, generally recognized for its contributions to urban planning, *beaux arts* architecture, and institutions of the arts and sciences, just as importantly introduced millions of fair goers to evolutionary ideas about race — ideas presented in a utopian context and often conveyed by exhibits that were ostensibly wrong," in *All the World's a Fair*, pp. 40, 41.

37. *Chicago Daily News*, August 25, 1893, p. 3.

38. Herskovits, *Dahomey*, vol. 1, p. 209.

39. "Wonderful Place for Fun," *New York Times*, June 19, 1893, p. 9.

40. Treseder, "A Visitor's Trip to Chicago in 1893," p. 24. This visitor also found fault with a white choir at Rev. Frank Gunsaulas's church: "The choir consisted of five who sat in a sort of gallery above the minister's pulpit. To well-educated people I suppose it was exquisite harmony but to me it simply grated on my nerves" (pp. 29, 30).

41. "Coon Songs and the Classics," *The Presto*, September 1, 1898, p. 7.

42. "Wonderful Place for Fun," *New York Times*, June 19, 1893, p. 9. Putnam, in his Introduction to *Portrait Types of the Midway Plaisance*, wrote: "What is a dance, is a question one was forced to ask after a trip through the Midway. Every nation had its

form. With some it was a rhythmic movement of the hands and arms; with others of the feet and legs; and with others of the body; some were ceremonial, others for amusement, according to the national tradition and custom" (p. vii).

43. *Chicago Daily Herald*, September 10, 1893, p. 3.

44. See Carole De Vale, Foreword, in *The Federal Cylinder Project*, vol. 8, ed. Dorothy Sara Lee (Washington, D.C.: Library of Congress, 1984), p. vii.

45. "Opening of the Dahoman Village: After Amazons Fight and Dance, Fred Douglass Makes a Speech," *Chicago Tribune*, May 30, 1893, p. 2.

46. *Chicago Daily Herald*, July 9, 1893, p. 25.

47. Herskovits, *Dahomey*, vol. 2, p. 317.

48. Bancroft, *The Book of the Fair*, p. 878.

49. Ibid., p. 932.

50. Henry Edward Krehbiel, *Afro-American Folksongs* (1913; rpt. New York: Frederick Ungar, 1967), pp. 60, 64–65.

51. Carter, "The Life and Music of Will Marion Cook," p. 65. Cook's early career included study with Antonín Dvořák, who was at the fair to present Slavonic music as well as to learn about the music of the Africans.

52. Johnson, *Black Manhattan*, p. 106.

53. *Chicago Inter Ocean*, May 30, 1893, p. 7.

54. Herskovits, *Dahomey*, vol. 2, pp. 354f.

55. *Frank Leslie's Illustrated Weekly*, May 26, 1893, p. 25. Also, *Chicago Daily Herald*, July 9, 1893, p. 25.

56. Herskovits, *Dahomey*, vol. 1, chapter 11.

57. William Dean Howells, *Letters of an Altrurian Traveller, 1893–1894* (1894; rpt. Gainesville, Fla.: Scholars' Facsimile & Reprints, 1967), p. 25.

58. Bancroft, *The Book of the Fair*, p. 868. See also *The Chicago Times Portfolio of the Midway Types*, n.p., "From Africa — Soudanese Warrior [#1871]:" "The Soudanese were not pets, but curiosities, because of their fighting qualities. They were the types of a black race that has proved the danger of their enmity, by opposition to the role of the white man, and a cruel, relentless opposition at that. The African fights with the rudest, most inefficient of weapons, against the finished war goods of the ingenious nations; and has, so far, remained unconquered."

59. William Ingleheart, A *"Fair" Comparison* (Chicago: Poole Bros., 1893), p. 6.

60. Even the contemporary souvenir book promoters knew enough about Dahomey to include information about the military commitment and contributions of the women, all performed in service to the king and state. See Flinn, *The Best Things to Be Seen at the World's Fair*, pp. 168, 169.

61. Ibid., p. 169.

62. See Herskovits, *Dahomey*, vol. 2, pp. 84–90, for a scholarly evaluation of the role of female warriors in this society.

63. *Chicago Sunday Post*, May 28, 1893, p. 11.

64. Flinn, *The Best Things to Be Seen at the World's Fair*, p. 169. See also "West African Folk," *Chicago Tribune*, May 4, 1893, p. 1.

65. "Wonderful Place for Fun," *New York Times*, June 19, 1893, p. 9. See also "West African Folk," *Chicago Tribune*, May 4, 1893, p. 1.

66. *Chicago Daily Herald*, August 19, 1893, p. 2; *Chicago Sunday Post*, May 28, 1893, p. 11; also, *Midway Types*, n.p. See Herskovits, *Dahomey*, vol. 1, chapter 15, for a comprehensive explanation of scarification.

67. *Chicago Evening Post*, May 28, 1893, p. 11, and September 16, 1893, p. 5.

68. *Chicago Tribune*, May 4, 1893, p. 2; see Herskovits, *Dahomey*, vol. 1, chapters 19, 20, and 21 on Fon funerary practices, and especially plates 47 and 48 after p. 384.

69. *Chicago Inter Ocean*, August 17, 1893, p. 6.

70. Herskovits, *Dahomey*, vol. 2, p. 54.

71. "West African Folk," *Chicago Tribune*, May 4, 1893, p. 1.

72. Bancroft, *The Book of the Fair*, p. 968.

73. *Chicago Tribune*, August 16, 1893, p. 1, and *Chicago Daily Herald*, August 19, 1893, p. 2.

74. "West African Folk," *Chicago Tribune*, May 14, 1893, p. 1.

75. Herskovits, *Dahomey*, vol. 2, pp. 103, 127, 292.

76. Ibid., p. 296.

77. Ibid., p. 293.

78. Herskovits and Herskovits, *Dahomean Narrative*, p. v. The authors wrote further: "The student of the spoken arts of nonliterate peoples is confronted with many problems that need never concern those who deal with written literature. The critics who work with written forms from historic cultures control in good measure the essential clues to social connotation, and the referents of idiom, analogy, and allusion. Yet, even within our own tradition, we need only recall the discussions that followed on the publication of James Joyce's *Finnegans Wake* to see how many questions can be posed by improvisation on established usage. And we need but mention *Ulysses* to bring to mind the questions that the restructuring of traditional categories can similarly raise—raise, that is, before the reader can grasp the clues that lay bare the expressive superstructure" (p. 3).

79. *Chicago Herald*, July 9, 1893, p. 25.

80. Gatewood, *Aristocrats of Color*, part 3, "Color, Culture and Behavior."

81. Commentary below "Zaroteffa. Soudanese Woman," *Portrait Types of the Midway Plaisance*, n.p. Also see "Wonderful Place for Fun," *New York Times*, June 19, 1893, p. 9, for racial disparagement by diasporan Africans of continental Africans with a Caucasian having the last say.

82. Moses, *Alexander Crummell*, p. 225; also pp. 148, 149, 152, 189, and 253.

83. Herskovits, *Dahomey*, Preface, n.p. [unpaginated p. ii].

84. James Alston, "A Visit to the World's Fair," *A.M.E. Church Review* 12 (July 1894): 496.

85. Campbell, *Songs of Zion*, p. 83.

86. Rosengarten, *All God's Dangers*, p. 300.

87. Meier, *Negro Thought in America*, p. ix; Levine, *Black Culture and Black Consciousness*, pp. ix–xi; and Redkey, *Black Exodus*, p. 309.

88. Campbell, *Songs of Zion*, p. ix.

9. On the Fairgrounds

1. Duster, *Crusade for Justice*, p. 116.

2. McClure, *The World's Columbian Exposition*, p. 343, and Flinn, *The Best Things to Be Seen at the World's Fair*, p. 143.

3. Blassingame and McKivigan, eds., *Frederick Douglass Papers*, p. 502.

4. Frederick Douglass, "Haiti among the Foremost Civilized Nations of the Earth: An Address Delivered in Chicago, Illinois on 2 January 1893," in ibid., p. 505. The *Chicago Inter Ocean*, August 17, 1893, p. 7, however, reported that champagne flowed on Hayti Day.

5. *The Illustrated World's Fair*, p. 415.

6. Langston, *From the Virginia Plantation to the National Capital*, p. 370. For a contrasting view, see Carter, "The Life and Music of Will Marion Cook," p. 19. Cook, whose middle name was originally Mercer in honor of the distinguished Virginia political leader, changed it in disgust after hearing of a disparaging remark attributed to the latter about his African heritage.

7. See Melville J. Herskovits, *Life in a Haitian Valley* (New York: Alfred A. Knopf, 1927), pp. 24–31, and James G. Leyburn, *The Haitian People* (New Haven: Yale University Press, 1941), pp. 135–141, 146–148, 167, 179, 200–201.

8. Langston, *From the Virginia Plantation to the National Capital*, pp. 367–369. See also Frederick Douglass, "Haiti among the Foremost Civilized Nations of the Earth," in *The Frederick Douglass Papers*, p. 503. Douglass makes reference to the opposition within Hayti to an American exhibit.

9. Duster, *Crusade for Justice*, p. 116.

10. McFeely, *Frederick Douglass*, p. 333. This author lists Preston as the son of the former Haytian ambassador to the United States. Other sources differ.

11. Frederick Douglass, *Life and Times of Frederick Douglass*, (1892; rpt. New York: Bonanza Books, 1962), pp. 600–619. For a more recent and analytical treatment by a historian, see McFeely, *Frederick Douglass*, pp. 347–351, 355, 367.

12. Douglass, *Life and Times of Frederick Douglass*, pp. 596, 597.

13. Ibid., p. 620.

14. Ibid. In addition, in the diasporan psyche, it produced a truer racial identity and place in the world. John Mercer Langston claimed that "he was impressed that in all respects . . . he would find in this Negro country, with its Black Republic, a condition of life, which, while it realized, would justify the dream of his youth with respect to an actual Negro nationality" (Langston, *From the Virginia Plantation to the National Capital*, p. 356). In 1855, he named his first-born son Arthur Dessalines Langston (p. 157).

15. Langston, *From the Virginia Plantation to the National Capital*.

16. Frederick Douglass, "Inauguration of the World's Columbian Exposition," in Campbell, *Campbell's Illustrated History of the World's Columbian Exposition*, p. 250.

17. *Chicago Inter Ocean*, October 17, 1893, p. 7.

18. A. T. Andreas, *A History of Chicago* (Chicago: A. T. Andreas, 1884, 1885), pp. 70–72. See also *Chicago Inter Ocean*, August 14, 1892, p. 17, and *Chicago Herald*, issues of June 28, 1893, p. 12, and September 8, 1893, p. 12.

19. Bancroft, *The Book of the Fair*, p. 30.

10. Diasporan and Continental Africa Meet

1. Noble, "The Chicago Congress on Africa," p. 315.

2. Ibid., p. 311.

3. The tradition of abolitionism did not die with the end of Reconstruction, but continued as abolitionists and their progeny branched into areas other than Negro rights. See McPherson, *The Abolitionist Legacy*, p. 5.

4. Richard Hofstadter, *Social Darwinism*, chapter 9, "Racism and Imperialism."

5. Moses, *Alexander Crummell*, p. 188.

6. Noble, "The Chicago Congress on Africa," p. 282.

7. Robert W. July, *A History of the African People* (New York: Charles Scribner's Sons, 1970), p. 313.

8. Ibid., p. 315.

9. *Chicago Inter Ocean*, August 16, 1893, p. 8.

10. McPherson, *The Abolitionist Legacy*, p. 324. See also p. 318.

11. Ibid., Appendix A.

12. "Negro Congress," *The Independent*, August 24, 1893, p. 11.

13. *Chicago Herald*, August 15, 1893, p. 9.

14. *Chicago Evening Journal*, August 21, 1893, p. 4.

15. Frederic[k] Perry Noble, "Africa at the Columbian Exposition," rpt. from *Our Day*, November 1892, pp. 12–13, Chicago Historical Society.

16. For the A.M.E. experience in West Africa, see Campbell, *Songs of Zion*, pp. 88–99, in Book One; for South Africa, see Books Two and Three.

17. Sylvia M. Jacobs, "'Say Africa When You Pray': The Activities of Early Black Baptist Women Missionaries among Liberian Women and Children," *Sage* 3 (Fall 1986): 16–21, rpt. in *Black Women in United States History*, ed. Darlene Clark Hine,

(Brooklyn: Carlson, 1990), pp. 711–725. See also "Afro-American Women Confront the African Way of Life," pp. 121–132, originally in *Women in Africa and the African Diaspora*, ed. Rosalyn Terborg-Penn et al. (Washington, D.C.: Howard University Press, 1988), now in *Black Women in United States History*, pp. 727–738.

18. *Chicago Herald*, August 16, 1893, p. 9.

19. *Chicago Inter Ocean*, August 16, 1893, p. 8.

20. *Chicago Inter Ocean*, August 16, 1893, p. 8, and *Chicago Times*, August 16, 1893, p. 4. In his assertions about a black origin of humanity, Turner was saying too much different from those things white scholars were. See the comments of Congress secretary Noble in "Negro Problem," *Frank Leslie's Illustrated Weekly*, September 28, 1893, p. 206.

21. First reference, *Chicago Herald*, August 16, 1893, p. 9; second, *Chicago Record*, August 16, 1893, p. 5.

22. *Chicago Inter Ocean*, August 16, 1893, p. 8.

23. *Chicago Times*, August 16, 1893, p. 4.

24. *Chicago Inter Ocean*, August 16, 1893, p. 8.

25. Ibid., August 15, 1893, p. 8.

26. Ibid., August 19, 1893, p. 9.

27. Ibid.

28. Ironically, the firebrand of protest advocacy at the fair, Ida B. Wells, with whom Barnett and Douglass had collaborated on *The Reason Why the Colored American Is Not in the World's Columbian Exposition*, had just written a ringing defense of free debate because of the poignancy and substance of the emigrationist argument. See "Afro-Americans and Africa" [originally published in the *A.M.E. Church Review*, July 1892, pp. 40–45], rpt in Hine, ed., *Black Women in American History*, pp. 165–169. Also see *Indianapolis Freeman*, June 17, 1893, p. 4.

29. *Chicago Inter Ocean*, August 19, 1893, p. 9.

30. See Scarborough quote of Noble in "The Negro Congress," *Frank Leslie's Illustrated Weekly*, September 1893, p. 20.

31. "The Negro Congress at Chicago," *The Independent*, August 24, 1893, p. 10, and "The Negro Problem," *Frank Leslie's Illustrated Weekly*, September 28, 1893, p. 206.

32. *Chicago Inter Ocean*, August 15, 1893, p. 8, and August 16, 1893, p. 8; *Chicago Evening Post*, August 15, 1893, p. 7.

33. Noble, "The Chicago Congress on Africa," p. 315.

34. Ibid., p. 282.

35. Redkey, *Black Exodus*, chapters 8 and 9.

36. Noble, "The Chicago Congress on Africa," p. 316.

37. Olsen, *Carpetbagger's Crusade*, p. 312.

38. McFeely, *Frederick Douglass*, pp. 377–380.

39. Lewis, *W. E. B. Du Bois*, p. 175.

INDEX

Christopher Robert Reed is director of PROJECT: FIRST CENTURY, a Chicago-focused research effort aimed at recovering the history of black Chicago between 1833 and 1933, and is a member of the history faculty at Roosevelt University. He is author of *The Chicago NAACP and the Rise of Black Professional Leadership, 1910–1966.*